SCIENCE AND CULTURAL THEORY

A Series Edited by Barbara Herrnstein Smith and E. Roy Weintraub

COMPLEXITIES

Social Studies of Knowledge Practices

JOHN LAW AND ANNEMARIE MOL, EDITORS

Duke University Press   Durham and London 2002

© 2002 Duke University Press   All rights reserved
Printed in the United States of America on acid-free paper ∞
Designed by Rebecca M. Giménez   Typeset in Adobe
Minion with Meta display by Keystone Typesetting, Inc.
Library of Congress Cataloging-in-Publication Data
appear on the last printed page of this book.

CONTENTS

ANNEMARIE MOL AND JOHN LAW

Complexities: An Introduction

Much recent work in the sociology of science, history of technology, anthropology of medicine, cultural studies, feminism, and political philosophy has been a revolt against simplification. The argument has been that the world is complex and that it shouldn't be tamed too much—and certainly not to the point where simplification becomes an impediment to understanding. But what *is* complexity? One way of starting is with a simple definition. There is complexity if things relate but don't add up, if events occur but not within the processes of linear time, and if phenomena share a space but cannot be mapped in terms of a single set of three-dimensional coordinates.

No one would deny that the world is complex, that it escapes simplicities. But what is complexity, and how might it be attended to? How might complexities be handled in knowledge practices, nonreductively, but without at the same time generating ever more complexities until we submerge in chaos? And then again, is the contrast between simplicity and complexity itself too simple a dichotomy? These are the questions explored in this book.

I

The arguments against reducing complexity by simplification have been well rehearsed. In *Modernity and the Holocaust* Zygmunt Bauman offers an elaborate (and by now classic) articulation of some of the most important of these arguments.[1] Bauman rejects the self-satisfied way of writing European history that treats this reductionism as if it were the revelation of a process of continuous improvement. "What is untenable is the concept of our—European—history as the rise of humanity over the animal in man, and as the triumph of rational organization over the cruelty of life that is nasty, brutish and short. What is also untenable is the concept of modern society as an unambiguously moralizing force, of its institutions as civilizing powers, of its coercive controls as a dam defending brittle humanity against the torrents of animal passions" (212–13). After all, as Bauman notes, the much-vaunted institutions of modern European societies did not prevent the Holocaust. On the contrary, they precisely proved to be perfectly adapted to the organized murder of millions of people and the pursuit of genocide.

The lesson that Bauman asks us to draw is that the rationality of the Enlightenment is an ambivalent endowment. If it is a blessing at all (and there are no doubt many achievements to which it might also point), then it is a thoroughly mixed blessing. His argument is that rational schemes are reductive because they order, divide, simplify, and exclude. To use one of Bauman's most haunting metaphors, they make weeds as well as flowers,[2] and they cut out the many shades of gray that lie between black and white. They are dangerous because they seem to be able to tell good from evil and to discern who is to blame and who is not. On occasions they simplify to death as they create the means of materializing their verdicts, means that include bureaucracy together with science and technology—and the very medicine that was designed to cure also turns out to invent tools for torturing and killing.

These arguments are well known, and indeed there are good reasons for worrying about simplification both in intellectual and political history. The list of Bauman's concerns has been extended within science and technology studies. To take one example, the process of scaling up poses many problems. Large-scale technologies usually grow out of laboratory experiments, but the process of translation is tricky because laboratory experiments are simplificatory devices: they seek to tame the many erratically changing variables that exist in the wild world, keeping some stable and simply excluding others from the argument. This often works well in the laboratory: if one does an experiment in a test tube, it is not unreasonable to assume that the air in the lab will absorb any heat that is produced. Calculation is greatly simplified by choosing to neglect a variable such as "heat." However, it works less well when what was confined to a test tube is scaled up to become a power plant. What happens now to

2   Annemarie Mol and John Law

all the excess heat? Where does it go? And where do radioactive waste products go?[3]

So there is scaling, and then there are unpredictabilities, erratic forms of behavior. These do not fit the schemes of most sciences very well either because the latter prefer to treat with only a few variables, not too many. The problem is that what was not predictable tends to occur anyway. So how should this be handled?

The answer—one answer—is that such chaotic events are tamed by theories of chance. In being reduced to a probability and framed as a risk they are turned into something that, however erratic, is also calculable. The risk of an explosion in the factory on the edge of your town (an explosion that will take your town with it) is, say, 0.000000003 percent per annum. Now go and calculate whether this is a good enough reason to be anxious!

The modern world is full of technical and scientific simplifications like this, and they are used as a basis for action. For instance, in medicine the value of different forms of treatment is assessed in clinical trials. These are mostly carried out on populations of adult patients who are no older than sixty-five and who have only the disease in question. This is a simplification that generates methodologically sound results, but these results are not very useful when decisions are needed about patients who are older than sixty-five and have two, three, or four diseases.

The texts that carry academic stories tend to organize phenomena bewildering in their layered complexity into clean overviews. They make smooth schemes that are more or less linear, with a demonstrative or an argumentative logic in which each event follows the one that came before. What may originally have been surprising is explained and is therefore no longer surprising or disturbing. Academic texts may talk about strange things, but their tone is almost always calm.

This, then, is the first step. It is to say that simplifications that reduce a complex reality to whatever it is that fits into a simple scheme tend to "forget" about the complex, which may mean that the latter is surprising and disturbing when it reappears later on and, in extreme cases, is simply repressed.

To talk in this way is to denounce simplification. However, although it is important to be suspicious of simplification in the modern world (in the sciences, in technology, in medicine, in markets, in governing, or, as we call them here, in knowledge practices), it is equally important to be suspicious of the standard ways of reacting to these simplifications, the denunciations of simplicity. These denunciations tend to have a common intellectual shape. The trope that turns up in most of the criticisms of reductive simplification says that single orders are shaped to tame complex realities but that as they do so, they exert violence. Then the argument is that this is doubly wrong, for violence is bad in itself, but it also fails to capture the intricacies of the way the world really is.

One of the places where this trope first emerged was psychoanalysis, as it articulates the workings of the consciousness of the modern subject. This consciousness is seen as ordered, whereas unwelcome and disturbing events, thoughts, and feelings are repressed and delegated to the unconscious, where complexities gather, at the margins of the person. From there they may emerge, disruptively or otherwise, in the form of dreams or parapraxes.

The trope of repression and the productive ways it relates to what may be told have become a commonplace in much poststructuralist writing.[4] This trope is also found in endless other theories of society, economy, culture, and science.

In the work of Thomas Kuhn a scientific paradigm is a way of understanding, depicting, and handling scientific objects that presses these into a quite specific shape which holds despite the existence of anomalies that do not fit.[5] Kuhn describes the way such anomalies are displaced—often for many years. Sometimes they are simply not noticed, whereas on other occasions they are pushed to the margins, to a location that is the scientific analogy of the unconscious. From there they may emerge after a scientific revolution not as dreams but in the form of another paradigm, the next simplifying device, with its novel understandings and techniques.

Michel Foucault uses much the same trope.[6] He treats "rationality" and "madness" as a single historical invention. The one is a purification that was only made possible by designating and expelling the other. Marginalizing madness, then, is not a form of repression. Instead it is productive, creating a social order cleansed of those designated as special, abnormal, or unruly. Foucault tries to avoid romanticizing this too much, yet even so the hetero-topic and the marginalized somehow figure as holding promise, the possible kernel of a social and cultural revolution.

In Bruno Latour's Irreductions *objects of knowledge are presented as always too complex for the sciences to catch and order. They never really fit within the schemes that are made for them, schemes that are inevitably simplifications.*

Things-in-themselves? But they're fine, thank you very much. And how are you? You complain about things that have not been honored by your vision? You feel that these things are lacking the illumination of your consciousness? But if you missed the galloping freedom of the zebras in the savannah this morning, then so much the worse for you; the zebras will not be sorry that you were not there, and in any case you would have tamed them, killed, photographed, or studied them. Things in themselves lack nothing, just as Africa did not lack whites before their arrival. (Interlude IV, *Irreductions*, 193)

None of these traditions simply denounces the simplifications that occur in knowledge practices. Each sees these as productive, but so, too, is whatever escapes the paradigm, the episteme, consciousness. On the one hand there is an order that simplifies, and on the other there is an elusive and chaotic complexity expelled, produced, or suppressed by it. And this is what many of the debates concerning complexity are about: does order expel, produce, or suppress the complex, and if so how? Or is the chaotic forever elusive, however elaborate the attempts we make to catch and tame it?

III

Given the power of reductionism in the modern world, the complex is surely in need of some defenders. Yet celebrating complexity is not what we are out to do here. For we fear, ironically, that by now another critique of simplification is just too simple. The critique of simplification is so well established that it has become a morally comfortable place to be. Denouncing violence is no doubt appropriate, but it is also disturbingly agreeable and self-satisfying, too simple. So our position—and that of the contributors to this book—is that the endless mobilization of this single trope, in which simplification figures as a reduction of complexity, leaves a great deal to discover and articulate. We need other ways of relating to complexity, other ways for complexity to be accepted, produced, or performed.

As you read this, where are you? Are you sitting at a desk or on a sofa, in an aircraft, perhaps, or on a train? Or perhaps you are lying in the bath? Another question: how many versions did this text go through? What was added and deleted along the way?

The answers to these questions are among the many complexities that don't concern us here. We leave them out not because they are irrelevant to intellectual work in general; no doubt they are relevant in various ways, but a single text cannot be everywhere at once. It cannot do everything all at the same time nor tell all.

The question is how a text might be where it is, while also acknowledging that it is not everywhere. How might a text make room within for whatever it also necessarily leaves out, for what is not there, not made explicit? How might a simple text respect complexities? These are questions about texts, but they might just as well be addressed to policies, to therapies, to technologies, to methods of representation, to objects, or to scientific formalisms.

What happens to complexity when simplifications are made? Answering this question requires a theoretical, but also an empirical and a methodological, inquiry. Thus the stories told by the contributors of this book are not narratives that use complexity theory. Instead they are stories about what happens to complexity in practice.[7] Or, to multiply, they are stories about what happens to complexi*ties* in practi*ces*.

IV

If complexity and simplicity are not necessarily opposites, then what are their relations? It is tempting to try to present an overview of how *simple*

Annemarie Mol and John Law

and *complex* might relate in ways that do not turn them into interdependent opposites, dualisms related by difference. This is a temptation reflected in one of the classic tasks of an introduction: to survey the contents of the book that follows. However, if we say that we *have* no overview and we cannot catch it all, this should not be misread as a confession of professional incompetence. Rather, it expresses a refusal to make an order, a single—simple—order that expels complexity. Instead, in what follows we offer a list.

Lists are not overviews. We will explore this more fully below, but the brief version of the argument is that they assemble elements that do not necessarily fit together into some larger scheme. In addition, they make no claims to inclusiveness. So the short list that follows does not claim to catch everything. Instead it is intended to suggest some ways of traveling through the chapters and the arguments that make up the book. It offers a key for thinking about the various dealings with complexity explored by the contributors. Our list does not present a history of the literatures, the field, or the problem, but instead it is spatial in character. It reflects a desire to make a space, define outlines, sketch contours—and then to walk through what has been laid out.

The list comes in three parts. These don't stand in a hierarchical relation to one another. Imagine, then, not a grid drawn in ever more detail, with ever more subdivisions; imagine, instead, turning the pages of a sketchbook. Imagine looking at different pictures, one after the other. Each orders and simplifies some part of the world, in one way or another, but what is drawn is always provisional and waits for the next picture, which draws things differently.

Multiplicities

The trope of the single order that reduces complexity (or that is bound to fail in its attempts to do so) starts to lose its power when *order* is multiplied, when *order* turns into *orders*. This is the first entry on our list: *multiplicity.* When investigators start to discover a variety of orders— modes of ordering, logics, frames, styles, repertoires, discourses—then the dichotomy between simple and complex starts to dissolve. This is because various "orderings" of similar objects, topics, fields, do not always reinforce the same simplicities or impose the same silences. Instead they may work—and relate—in different ways. This raises theoretical and practical questions. In particular, the discovery of multiplicity suggests that we are no longer living in the modern world, located within a single *epistème*. Instead, we discover that we are living in different worlds. These are not worlds—that great trope of modernity—that belong on the one hand to the past and on the other to the present. Instead, we discover that we are living in two or more neighboring worlds, worlds that overlap and coexist.

Multiplicity is thus about coexistences at a single moment. To make sense of multiplicity, we need to think and write in topological ways, discovering methods for laying out a space, for laying out spaces, and for defining paths to walk through these.

One of the central concerns of political philosophy is the nature of the good. The most common approach to exploring this concern is indirect: it is to create procedures, which hang together coherently, for exploring what the good might be. Indeed the title of one of the most famous books written in this mode expresses this aspiration in an exemplary manner: A Theory of Justice. *In this classic study John Rawls presents a single theory that produces a single version of how justice might be reached, a single justice.[8] The book attempts to tame complexity and, indeed, pushes it to the margins of what can be rationally handled.*

This, then, is a singular solution, but there is another way of working. Spheres of Justice *is the title of another crucial contribution to political philosophy. Written by Michael Walzer, it argues against the singularity of an encompassing theory of justice.[9] First, it shifts the activity of theorizing "justice" out of departments of philosophy and into a plethora of ordinary sites and situations. Second, it catalogues these sites and situations into a number of different* social *spheres. These are domains within society that each have their own way of separating good from bad, right from wrong, just from unjust, so that what is appropriate to the sphere of the market differs from what is appropriate to the sphere of education or health care or government.*

There are other ways of multiplying "the just." For instance in Les Économies de la Grandeur *Laurent Thévenot and Luc Boltanski distinguish among* styles *rather than spheres.[10] At first these styles seem to map onto social institutions (the "industrial" style sounds as if it fits with production, whereas the "domestic" style sounds as if it has to do with the way families* are run, and so on). But in their empirical investigations Thévenot, Boltanski, and their colleagues show that in every specific situation two, three, or even more styles are likely to be mobilized to justify actions.

Walzer uses his "spheres of justice" in a normative manner: once we have found how "the just" is established in each specific sphere, we are encouraged to stick with that mode of justification. Indeed crucial to his argument is the idea that it is a pollution to use arguments that belong elsewhere. By contrast Boltanski and Thévenot are more persistently empirical: they investigate the kinds of justifications that happen to be convincing for various people in a variety of specific situations. They are concerned with the mix as it occurs.

The differences between the two approaches are instructive and important, but we'll stop here, for the point is made. Instead of a single order separating the just from the unjust in a clear-cut way, both approaches suggest that there may be different orders and with those orders different gradients—gradients of right and wrong that establish different versions of the good.

Analogous moves have been made in other disciplines, fields, and traditions. For instance in *organization studies* the questions have often been asked: what *is* an organization? what is it to organize?

In his Images of Organization *Gareth Morgan multiplied the picture of the single organization by elaborating on a variety of metaphors that are used in everyday and professional talk to frame and phrase the character of organizations. Organizations are talked about and handled as if they were machines, organisms, brains, cultures, political systems, psychic prisons, fluxes in transformation, or instruments of domination. Morgan argues that all these images are present, foregrounded here, backgrounded there, and he says that all catch something of organizational reality.*[11]

John Law has made a similar argument.[12] *He went to a single organization to investigate how different modes of ordering structure what goes on there. Organizing, he suggested, depends partly on ordering things—words, but also materials, desks, paperwork, computer systems—in an entrepreneurial manner, but vision or charisma are equally important, as is vocation and even administration. These various modes of ordering include, exclude, depend on, and combat one another.*

There are ways out of singularity that generate a pluralism in which different parts of the world coexist within their own insulated spheres, but different modes of ordering or different styles of justification or different discourses may also overlap and interfere with one another. Attending to multiplicity, then, brings with it the need for new conceptualizations of what it might be to hold together.

Where various styles of justification each have their own way of differentiating the just from the unjust, the just becomes a complex phenomenon, more than one. But does this mean that there are many?

A question such as this has been explored by the other author of this introduction, Annemarie Mol, in relation to the body and its diseases. Various medical disciplines, with their different techniques—cutting here, questioning a patient there, observing X-ray images a little further along—have different knowledges. How do these relate? The traditional idea was that each of them reveals an aspect of a single, coherent body. On the other hand, it can also be argued that the different knowledges (clashing at some points, ignoring each other at others) all know their own "body." If this is the case, then it becomes important to understand how these different bodies hold together in hospital practice. It appears that this requires a lot of coordination work: files that go from one floor of the building to another, routines, conversations, memos, case conferences, operations. In practice, if a body hangs together, this is not because its coherence precedes the knowledge generated about it but because the various coordination strategies involved succeed in reassembling multiple versions of reality.

If this is right, then we are not dealing with a single body, but neither are there many different and unrelated bodies; for the various modes of ordering, logics, styles, practices, and the realities they perform do not exist in isolation from one another, as if in some ideal-typical liberal state of laissez-faire. They are not islands unto themselves, closed cultures, self-contained paradigms, or bubbles. Instead, as Donna Haraway would say, they *interfere* with one another and reveal what Marilyn Strathern would call *partial connections*.[13] They meet—different ways of ordering the world, different worlds—just as (in Tzvetan Todorov's story about this) the Spaniards met with Malinche, who became Cortez's mistress as well as his translator. Malinche had been handed over as a present from some men to some other men, and she betrayed those who had betrayed her, which is why the Spaniards were able to conquer Mexico. Thus she, woman between worlds, *mixture*, mestiza, came before any of the illusions that in meeting each party might stay pure.[14] Sensitivity to multiplicity suggests a number of questions about similarity and difference, about the embeddedness of orders in language and materiality, and about what it is to be neither one nor fragmented into many individuals. We need to think about what it is to be more than one and less than many.

Multiplicity, Point 1. *If there are different modes of ordering that coexist, what is reduced or effaced in one may be crucial in another so that the question no longer is, Do we simplify or do we accept complexity? It becomes instead a matter of determining which simplification or simplifications we will attend to and create and, as we do this, of attending to what they foreground and draw our attention to, as well as what they relegate to the background.*

Multiplicity, Point 2. *Often it is not so much a matter of living in a single mode of ordering or of "choosing" between them. Rather it is that we find ourselves at places where these modes join together. Somewhere in the interferences something crucial happens, for although a single simplification reduces* complexity, *at the places where different simplifications meet, complexity is created, emerging where various modes of ordering (styles, logics) come together and add up comfortably or in tension, or both.*

Flowing and Churning
Order, the single order, isn't simply reductionist because it occupies so much of the available space, pushing potentially disturbing chaos to the margins. Its pretensions and its apparent size also grow out of the linear history in which most "orders" are presented.

From the very beginning sociology sought to take social order out of timelessness and to insert it into time. Society, it argued, has a history; its current configurations came into being one way or another, and they may—or will— fade away, collapse, or be overthrown. Questions about the creation and stability of social orders, about revolutions, upheavals, and qualitative changes, all these figure prominently in the concerns of the discipline. Things could have been otherwise, and in due course they will change, but right here and now they are overdetermined and cannot be wished away.

This, then, is also the time frame that was used when, in the social studies of science and technology, science and technology were drawn into "the social." They were redescribed as underdetermined by "nature" so that many other factors and actors were involved.[15] Without a microscope there are no slides. Without staining techniques there is no differentiation between cells. Without the discipline of pathology in the hospital there would have been no oncology, or it would have come out differently. Without clinical work there would have been no laboratory. Sciences and technology are not simply reflecting their object or doing what is most efficient, but at some point in the past they could have taken another course: things could have turned out differently.

A good image for this passage through time is the game of Go.[16] At first the stones on the board can be positioned anywhere, and no single pattern is privileged. However, every early move fixes the possibilities for later moves, so once there is a pattern, what follows comes to be inevitable.

So insofar as orders are put into time, the time that is mobilized is linear. It flows in one way only: on and on. It doesn't churn or slop from low to high tide and back again.

Fredric Jameson describes a house designed by architect Frank Gehry in Santa Monica.[17] This house juxtaposes two modes of building: a conventional, box-like, suburban, tract house and a "wrapper," composed of more or less junk materials (wire netting, corrugated metal) wrapped around the tract house to make all sorts of crazy shapes and volumes, inside and out. According to Jameson the tract house represents the affluent North, the wrapper the impoverished South, and—crucial this—the whole structure represents the contradictory unity of global capitalism, which (says Jameson) cannot be represented in two dimensions.

We might have presented this house as an example of multiplicity, of the interference, indeed, between two modes of building—but time also enters the story. The two-buildings-in-one, Jameson says, do not fit onto the two dimensions of a plan or photograph, which would show either one or the other, never both—for snapshots freeze time. By contrast, a visitor who walks through the house slides from wrapper into tract house and from tract house back into wrapper. The appreciation of each depends on the presence (and absence) of the other. Neither is complete when one is there. Each waits for the necessary move back to the other. Back and forth, not linear time but tidal time.

Once we start to attend to times that come and go, what is reduced at one moment may resurface the next. Elements that come to the foreground now shift to the background a little later. In this way the possibility of recomplexification is included in what is momentarily simple—and the nouns, simple and complex, give way to verbs, to talking of simplifying and complexifying.

Charis Cussins tells a story in which she makes time dance: a choreography.[18] Along the itinerary of women with problems of infertility, hope comes. This turns into success or disappointment—but then, later on, if they try again, the hope may come back again. The reality of infertility treatment doesn't stay the same. Now you assert your subjectivity while a little later you lie on your back, objectified, with your legs spread and some instrument inserted into your body, to come out proud and pregnant—or not.

What is said, what is allowed as an element in order, always depends on what is not said, on what is displaced and marginalized—this is the general trope. But in this time-sensitive version the expelled other has not gone away because while it is absent it is still present, too. It is deferred but will come back again, leaving traces, which is what Derrida calls différance.[19]

Time flies, but it flies like a swallow, up, down, off quickly and then coming slowly back again. Attending to such a time brings complexity into play, for simple orders may be made visible by snapshots of frozen moments. But they *are* only snapshots. What is visible in them may be hidden on the next image—and then become visible again a little later—and even snapshots may show traces of what is but also isn't there, of complexities that surface earlier, later, at and in some other time.

Lists, Cases, and Walks
Orders do not simply expel the complex and chaotic. In addition, they insist that what belongs to them is drawn together and properly assembled. No element may hold back, and what is inside must be named,

accorded a place. A proper order comes with the illusion that all relations can be specified and that it is possible to gain an all-inclusive overview. There are various ways of doing this.

One is a mode of representation that presupposes a single and conformable world. This is the *classificatory system,* which makes cages, big cages that are then subdivided into smaller ones, like the system that covers the animal kingdom: individuals go into species, species into families, and families come together into the genus. The system is materialized in classical museums: in this wing of the building you find the mammals, and the reptiles are over there. Rodents come with rodents. Walk around the corner, and you find the apes.

But this is not the only possibility. For instance, as we noted above, there is the list, which is not to say that there are no classificatory lists but that a list doesn't have to be classificatory. That lists may be other than classificatory is strikingly illustrated by the celebrated heteronomous list of animals Foucault borrows from Borges in the preface to The Order of Things, *a list derived from "a certain Chinese encyclopaedia." "Animals," Borges wrote, are divided into "(a) belonging to the Emperor, (b) embalmed, (c) tame, (d) sucking pigs, (e) sirens, (f) fabulous, (g) stray dogs, (h) included in the present classification, (i) frenzied, (j) innumerable, (k) drawn with a very fine camelhair brush, (l)* et cetera, *(m) having just broken the water pitcher, (n) that from a long way off look like flies." This list, says Foucault, "shattered . . . all the familiar landmarks of my thought . . . breaking up all the ordered surfaces and all the planes with which we are accustomed to tame the wild profusion of existing things."[20] Not classifying, at least not in any way the reader was able to recognize, the list abstains from taming. It groups together, but it doesn't tame.*

A list doesn't have to impose a single mode of ordering on what is included in it. Items in the list aren't necessarily responses to the same questions but may hang together in other ways, for instance socially, because a list may be the result of the work of different people who have each added something to it. Yet it remains open, for a list differs from a classification in that it recognizes its incompleteness. It doesn't even need to seek completeness. If someone comes along with something to add to the list, something that emerges as important, this may indeed be added to it.

A second way of representing that makes closed orders is to present examples as if they were representative of some larger law or point, as, for instance, in a physics textbook—or even more so in a school experiment in physics—in which some specificity, let us say an inclined plane, comes to exemplify or illustrate something larger, for instance Newton's laws of motion. Something similar happens in the social sciences when an event witnessed is presented as "the empirical instance" that is used to illustrate something general, larger, which may then be called "the theory." In situations like this there may be insistence on specificity, but if so, then this specificity is presented as a *detail* that illustrates and serves a larger whole.

There are other ways of mobilizing specificities that do not have to do with detail. One is to present cases as not being representative of something larger—into which they neatly fit. It is to take all cases as phenomena in their own right, each differing slightly in some (unexpected) way from all the others. Thus a case may still be instructive beyond its specific site and situation, and this tends to be why it is studied, but the lessons it holds always come with the condition that, elsewhere, in other cases, what is similar and different is not to be taken for granted. It remains to be seen, to be experienced, to be investigated.

Because they are not, so to speak, representative of something larger (a "theory"), cases are able to do all kinds of other work. For instance, they may sensitize the reader to events and situations elsewhere that have not been recognized so far and that may well be improbable. They may seduce the reader into continuing to read, to ask what is going to come next. They may suggest ways of thinking about and tackling other specificities, not because they are "generally applicable" but because they may be transferable, translatable. They may condense—anthropologists might want to say "symbolize"—a range of experiences, relations of a variety of different kinds. They may act as an irritant, destabilizing expectations. For instance, they may destabilize scale relations—undermining precisely the idea that details (or, better, specificities) are part of a larger whole. Or they may work allegorically, which means that they may tell not just about what they are manifestly telling but also about something else, something that may be hard to tell directly.

In contrast with the overview of the classificatory system, we suggest that *lists* are nonsystematic, alert, sensitizing but open to surprise. In contrast with the illustration that represents a larger theory, we suggest to treat *cases* as, again, sensitizing but also unique—as incitement to ask questions about difference and similarity, about what alters in moving from one place to another. A third way of making overviews we want to mention here is mapping. Maps draw surfaces that contain details (a set of sites or attributes of what is contained within these sites) that are related in an accountable manner. The accountancy involves measurable distance and proximity; it involves increase and decrease. Maps suggest transitive relations between entities that exceed or are subordinate to, but surely exclude, each other.

Imagine, as a contrast, walking through the little lanes that make up the inner city of Venice or walking through a jungle. In such places a map is unlikely to be the best tool for getting around. In Venice a local inhabitant who knows the place and can give directions is much better, and so are signposts that point in the right direction. In the jungle you might need something else to make your path a little simpler: a guide, for sure, but also a sharp machete and the skill to use it.

Here is the point: walking, as Michel de Certeau has noted, is a mode of covering space that gives no overview.[21] It immerses the walker in a landscape or a townscape. As we walk, we may encounter a variety of comforting—or stunning—sights and situations, and then we can bring these together instead or leave them separate, as they would be on a map, removed from one another. We may juxtapose them in the way we sometimes do after a journey, by telling stories or showing pictures. The picture of a large landscape is printed so that it has the same size as that of a plate filled with food, and the story about driving through the landscape is no bigger or smaller than the story about eating the meal. Other differences abound.

There are, then, modes of relating that allow the simple to coexist with the complex, of aligning elements without necessarily turning them into a comprehensive system or a complete overview. These are some of the ways of describing the world while keeping it open, ways of paying tribute to complexities, which are always there, somewhere, elsewhere, untamed: to list rather than classify; to tell about cases rather than present illustrative representatives; to walk and tell stories about this rather than seek to make maps. Of course—this is the nature of our list, of any list—there are other possibilities too, told elsewhere or waiting to be discovered.

v

The chapters in this book examine highly diverse knowledge practices: markets, therapeutic interventions, the governing of supranational states, aerospace mathematics, ecology, road building, photography, the complex sciences, and dealings with childhood trauma. Their narratives come from Kenya, Belgium, Britain, Papua New Guinea, the Netherlands, France, and that nonnational state, the republic of science. They are written by anthropologists, economists, philosophers, psychologists, sociologists, and students of science, technology, and society. And they treat complexity as if it were more than one but less than many—as a set of possibilities, strategies that are partially connected.

This means that they also interfere with one another. Those interferences are complex, and if what we have said about overviews and orders is right, we cannot hope to catch these different versions and treatments of complexity in a classification or a map. We can, however, go for another walk, make another list, or turn the pages of a sketchbook and outline a set of partial connections.

For instance, it is obvious that many of the authors write about multiplicity. The chapter by Laurent Thévenot considers the compromises between a series of different regimes for connecting the good with the real—and therefore the world of normativities with material objects in the environment. Thus he writes about a road that is both a set of different roads when it is located within different pragmatic regimes (the market, industry) and in some sense "the same" road, at least if it is actually built. More than one and less than many, it embodies a series of compromises. Complexity, then, emerges where the multiple "road/s" that Thévenot writes about interfere with one another.

Multiplicity also appears in John Law's chapter on an aerodynamic formalism. Different elements—for instance the behavior of airfoils in air, the sickness of pilots, strategic considerations, and the supposed capacity of the Russians—all appear within this formalism. Or, more accurately, and this is his point, they both appear and do not appear in what might be imagined as an endless oscillation between absence and presence. This, then, is Law's particular sense of complexity. Inferences between multiple configurations occur not in a linear sequence but as an oscillation between presence and deferral.

Oscillation is also important in the chapter by Nick Lee and Steve Brown, about the disposal of fear in childhood. These authors suggest that children are both beings and becomings, culturally located on a trajectory of normal development and the normalization that this trajectory implies. Viewed in this way there is a troubled relation—an oscillation—between the codependent cultural artifacts of the general (what children do as they develop "in general") and the particular (the actions of this particular child, in this case a three-year-old frightened by the characters in a dramatization of Barrie's *Peter Pan*). Complexity thus indexes a troubled and oscillatory relationship between general and particular, where generalized knowledges help to "dispose" fear onto the child, forcing him to bear the burden of disposing the general (childhood) and the specific (this child).

Marilyn Strathern, writing about the interpretation of pictures in anthropology, notes that anthropologists seek to describe events or pictures on the one hand and their preconditions on the other. We hear further echoes there, then, of the complexity of the link between general and particular touched on by Lee and Brown. Strathern introduces figure-ground reversals, the oscillation between appropriate and inappropriate interpretations and that between self-evidence (when what is depicted "speaks for itself") and the "excessive" interpretations of intertextuality. In her analysis complexity emerges as an oscillation, or at least mutual implication, between place (the particular) and space (its context, the general, understood as a set of coordinates). The general, Strathern suggests, is not beyond but already contained within the (particular) picture.

Complexity as tension between general and particular also appears in Michel Callon's essay, although he also mobilizes a further metaphor for imagining the relation among multiples, that of mediation. He describes service companies' methods for shaping their services, as well as the demands of customers. What methods do these companies use? The answer is that they deploy writing devices that both reflect and produce supply and demand and that mediate not only between the company and its consumers but also between the customer in general and this particular customer, between the "macrosocial" and the "microsocial." Callon argues that the writing device is a material and performative mediator that produces objects or classes of objects that are usually held apart.

Performativity, then, is another crucial complexity-relevant trope. The argument is that knowing, the words of knowing, and texts do not describe a preexisting world. They are rather part of a practice of handling, intervening in, the world and thereby of enacting one of its versions—up to bringing it into being. This understanding informs most of the chapters. Callon explores it for the case of marketing, and the known world is central to his analysis. It is crucial, too, to Andrew Barry's essay, which considers how rhetorics of complexity are deployed in the European Union (EU). But the term *rhetoric* is less than satisfactory. For the words and the practices of complexity and nonreduction (Barry mentions process, network, actor-network, and nonlinear scale) are mobilized by the European Commission precisely in order to perform the EU into being in a way that will elude the attention (and so the resistance) of the sovereign states that make up Europe's most visible and entrenched political units.

In Annemarie Mol's essay various entities that have to do with atherosclerosis of the leg vessels are followed while they are being performed—variably. Mol examines the specificities of the problems of the patients concerned, as well as the outline of two therapies, the actors who engage in treatment, as well as the treatment's aims. If all these, and more, configurations are locally performed, and variably delineated, how then to compare the improvements of "one" patient-condition that isn't one? How to compare two divergingly delineated interventions? In Mol's contribution complexities emerge as a result of a particular interference: that of comparison.

In Charis Thompson's essay comparison is equally crucial. Thomas describes a meeting where two modes of dealing with elephants in a Kenyan wildlife park were discussed. These modes appear to differ not just on a single point. Instead, they come with an entirely different framing of a list of things: what it is to engage in science, how elephants relate to humans and what is important about them, and even how to compare and engage in interaction. For this is important to the story: that differentiating incommensurabilities may help to clarify a discussion but where tensions need to be handled in practice, it may be wiser to seek interferences, to increase complexity.

Multiplicity, oscillation, mediation, material heterogeneity, performativity, interference—and the list of metaphors for making and handling complexity in ways that escape the dualism between order and chaos could be extended further. Thus most of the authors are concerned with unfinished process: for there is no resting place in a multiple and partially connected world. Some refer to the necessary tensions in knowing and in being. Some—Strathern and Lee and Brown most clearly—make explicit the essential reflexivity of the performativity of multiplicity and the production of knowing and known, for when subjects and objects are made together, there is no external resting place for those engaged in knowing and in writing.

There is not even a resting place for the one author in this book whose essay surveys models of complexity in the natural sciences: Chunglin Kwa. His description of the shift in models of complexity in ecology and meteorology is framed in terms of a distinction between romantic and baroque. Romanticism discovers complexity in emergent structures, whereas the baroque—a long-standing but recently popular understanding of the world that owes much to Leibniz—discovers complexity as a set of monads that know the world without being mechanically related to one another in the form of a system or an organism, that know the world, are conscious of it, but precisely resist being summed up. You may analyze to what extent his own writing has romantic or baroque characteristics.

There is room for many pictures on the pages of the sketchbook. And that is what this volume is: a book of sketches about complexities in knowledge practices; a book of sketches that seeks to imagine alternatives to the simplicity of the overview and its other, the forces of chaos; a book of sketches that, as this introduction suggests, makes any definition of complexity difficult if not self-defeating. For, recall, we started with a definition. We said if things relate but don't add up, then they are complex; if events occur but not within the processes of linear time, then they are complex; and if phenomena share a space but cannot be mapped in terms of a single set of three-dimensional coordinates, then they too are complex. This is not exactly wrong, but it is—too simple. It is too simple because it works with binaries. Addition, or not. Linearity, or not. A single space, or not. But in a complex world there are no simple binaries.

Things add up *and* they don't. They flow in linear time *and* they don't. And they exist within a single space *and* escape from it. That which is complex cannot be pinned down. To pin it down is to lose it.

NOTES

1. See Bauman (1989).

2. See Bauman (1987).

3. Radder (1988).

4. See, for instance, the distinction between "figure" and "discours" in the writing of Jean-François Lyotard (1984, 1985).

5. See Kuhn (1970).

6. See Foucault (1971).

7. The body of complexity theory that has emerged in the last twenty years is not explored in this volume, except in passing in the essay by Chunglin Kwa. The aim of this volume is not to contribute to a new theory of complexity but to ask how complexities, particularly elements that cannot be easily reduced to one another, are actually handled in instrumental, political, textual, medical, and economic practice.

8. See Rawls (1973).

9. See Walzer (1983).

10. See Boltanski and Thévenot (1987).

11. See Morgan (1986).

12. See Law (1994).

13. See Haraway (1991a, 1991b) and Strathern (1991).

14. Purity, Latour argues, is one of the great tropes of modernity. See Latour (1993).

15. See Bloor (1976) and Barnes (1997).

16. See Latour and Woolgar (1979).

17. For discussion see Jameson (1991, 97, 108–17).

18. See Cussins (1998).

19. See Derrida (1976).

20. Quoted from Foucault (1970, xv).

21. See de Certeau (1984).

REFERENCES

Barnes, B. 1977. *Interests and the Growth of Knowledge.* London: Routledge and Kegan Paul.

Bauman, Z. 1987. *Legislators and Interpreters: On Modernity, Postmodernity, and Intellectuals.* Cambridge: Polity Press.

———. 1989. *Modernity and the Holocaust.* Cambridge: Polity Press.

Bloor, D. 1976. *Knowledge and Social Imagery.* London: Routledge and Kegan Paul.

Boltanski, L., and L. Thévenot. 1987. *Les Économies de la Grandeur.* Cahiers du Centre d'Études de l'Emploi, vol. 32. Paris: Presses Universitaires de France.

Cussins, C. 1998. "Ontological Choreography: Agency for Women Patients in an Infertility Clinic." In M. Berg and A. Mol, eds., *Differences in Medicine: Unraveling Practices, Techniques, and Bodies,* 166–201. Durham, N.C.: Duke University Press.

de Certeau, M. 1984. *The Practice of Everyday Life.* Trans. S. F. Rendall. Berkeley: University of California Press.

Derrida, J. 1976. *Of Grammatology.* Baltimore: Johns Hopkins University Press.

Foucault, M. 1970. *The Order of Things: An Archaeology of the Human Sciences.* London: Tavistock.

———. 1971. *Madness and Civilization: A History of Insanity in the Age of Reason.* London: Tavistock.

Haraway, D. 1991a. "A Cyborg Manifesto: Science, Technology, and Socialist Feminism in the Late Twentieth Century." In *Simians, Cyborgs, and Women: The Reinvention of Nature,* 149–81. London: Free Association Books.

———. 1991b. "Situated Knowledges: The Science Question in Feminism and the Privilege of Partial Perspective." In *Simians, Cyborgs, and Women: The Reinvention of Nature,* 183–201. London: Free Association Books.

Jameson, F. 1991. *Postmodernism, or, the Cultural Logic of Late Capitalism.* London: Verso.

Kuhn, T. S. 1970. *The Structure of Scientific Revolutions.* Chicago: University of Chicago Press.

Latour, B. 1988. *Irreductions.* In *The Pasteurization of France.* Cambridge, Mass.: Harvard University Press.

———. 1993. *We Have Never Been Modern.* Brighton: Harvester Wheatsheaf.

Latour, B., and S. Woolgar. 1979. *Laboratory Life: The Social Construction of Scientific Facts.* Beverly Hills: Sage.

Law, J. 1994. *Organizing Modernity.* Oxford: Blackwell.

Lyotard, J.-F. 1984. "The Connivances of Desire with the Figural." In R. McKeon, ed., *Driftworks.* New York: Semiotext(e).

———. 1985. *Discours, Figure.* Paris: Editions Klincksieck.

Morgan, G. 1986. *Images of Organization.* Beverly Hills: Sage.

Radder, H. 1988. *The Material Realization of Science.* Assen: Van Gorucum.

Rawls, J. 1973. *A Theory of Justice.* Oxford: Oxford University Press.

Strathern, M. 1991. *Partial Connections.* Savage, Md.: Rowman and Littlefield.

Walzer, M. 1983. *Spheres of Justice: A Defence of Pluralism and Equality.* Oxford: Blackwell.

CHUNGLIN KWA

Romantic and Baroque Conceptions
of Complex Wholes in the Sciences

In the 1990s *complexity* came to mean something different from what it predominantly meant in the 1950s. The newer complexity is not simply an extension of, or a development from, the old complexity. For complexity comes in kinds. In this essay I distinguish between "romantic" complexity and "baroque" complexity. They have, I will argue, quite different conceptions of the structure of reality.[1] I develop the argument in three stages. First, I characterize these two forms of complexity. Second, I explore the ways in which the term changed in the twentieth century by considering certain writings in meteorology and evolution and so-called chaos theory. And third, I return to the distinction between the romantic and the baroque and argue that both—together with other commitments, including those to reductionism—are long-standing metaphors, tropes, or indeed metaphysical positions within the natural sciences.

ROMANTIC AND BAROQUE

A Romantic Expectation

Models seek to bring conceptual unity to what otherwise would not easily be put together. And in a mathematical model several basic laws can be made to work together to "mimic" nature. The computer makes this possible. The enthusiasm inspired by the computer was nicely expressed by population dynamicist Crawford Holling in 1966: "If biology has told us anything, it is that complex systems are not just the sum of their parts. There is an emergent principle when fragments act and interact in a whole system. The speed and large memory of modern digital computers for the first time allows the ecologist, in principle, *to incorporate all the relevant actions and interactions* of the fragments of complex ecological systems in an integrated manner."[2] The ideal of integrating all the workings of nature into one whole is called holism. And, indeed, for many years there was a special relationship between holism and the computer. If the assumption of holism is fed into a computer model, the computer faithfully reproduces it. But Holling was hoping for too much in 1966.

Holism
In the early twentieth century, organicists such as J. S. Haldane, Jan Smuts, and Paul Weiss reinvigorated romantic conceptions of nature through the notion of the complex unity of systems, in particular living systems.[3] Jan Smuts gave wide currency to the notion of "holism." "The whole as a real character is writ large on the face of Nature," he wrote in his *Holism and Evolution.*[4] So what is holism? Smuts's answer came in two parts. First, it is the idea that there are hierarchically different levels of organization in the natural world, each of which unites heterogeneous items of a lower level of integration into a functional whole. Second, holism is the suggestion that new levels of integration, or new wholes, have emerged at various times during the course of evolution on earth. Smuts's rather unsurprising paradigmatic example of the emergence of wholes is the organism. More controversially, he talks of higher levels of holism, the mind, and personality—where the latter is virtually in command of the universe. Although the latter, somewhat mystical, levels found few adherents in the scientific community, the word *holism* has stuck.

For many decades romantic holism and complexity were synonymous. If one took "complexity" seriously as a subject for science, one was a holist. If one objected to holism—usually on the grounds that it rests on unwarranted speculation—one was a reductionist. However, recently the word *holism* has disappeared more or less completely from discourse about complexity—which is, perhaps, an index of a different kind of complexity.

The Romantic Tradition: The Unity of the Whole
Romantic complexity sees an underlying unity in a world of heterogeneous objects and phenomena—ever since Rousseau wrote in the sev-

enth promenade of his *Rêveries* that all individual objects escape a sensitive observer of the natural world and "il ne voit et ne sent rien que dans le tout" (he sees and feels nothing but the unity of things).[5] In the natural sciences Cuvier's discovery of the unity of plan of, for instance, the vertebrates is romantic, as is Ørsted's discovery that an electrical current produces a magnetic field, a discovery to which he was led by his *naturphilosophische* intuition that there was a basic unity between physical forces. For the last two hundred years the romantic view of nature has been a constant in the modern sciences, however much the more extreme versions have been challenged or tempered by parallel strategies, such as reductionistic mechanism in the second half of the nineteenth century.

The Romantic Tradition: The Whole Is Real

Relatively few scientists have been content with Kant's insistence that the creation of unity is an activity of the subject. Kant's Copernican Revolution was not swallowed whole. "I have arranged the facts, not successively in the order in which they have presented themselves, but according to the relations which they have between themselves," writes Alexander von Humboldt in his *Voyage de Humboldt et Bonpland.*[6] And in *Kosmos:* "The scattered images offered to the contemplation of the senses, notwithstanding their number and diversity, were gradually fused into a concrete whole; Terrestrial nature was conceived in its generality."[7] However, not everyone would be able to follow von Humboldt. To see what von Humboldt was able to see takes "a sensitive observer," for instance like Rousseau. This is the romantic scientist's moderate version of Kant's Copernican Revolution.

Romantic Holism Looks Up, Baroque Complexity Down

Romantic holism integrates individuals who appear to be a heterogeneous lot at the phenomenological level to a single entity at a higher level of organization. Baroque complexity is much less severe on this point. For example, a community of different species of plants seems to be less of a single whole when conceived of as "table companions," as it was by the Swiss plant sociologist Josias Braun-Blanquet in 1923, than it does when taken as a single "superorganism," as conceived by his American contemporary Frederic Clements. In the former view plant and animal species may be seen as "cooperating," whereas in the latter they are "functionally" integrated.

The romantics look up—some all the way up to the world of Platonic forms—and recognize collections of individuals as higher-order individuals. This is a process of abstraction, a search for higher-order laws and principles. The higher-order individual may have the abstract structure of an organism; it is not a real flesh-and-blood organism. By contrast, the baroque looks down and, like Leibniz, observes the mundane crawling and swarming of matter: "Chaque portion de la matière peut être conçüe comme une jardin plein de plantes; et comme un Etang plein de poissons. Mais chaque rameau de la plante, chaque membre de l'Animal, chaque goutte de ses humeurs est encore un tel jardin, ou un tel étang" (Every bit of matter can be conceived as a garden full of plants or a pond full of fish. But each branch of the plant, each drop of its bodily fluids, is also such a garden or such a pond).[8] To Leibniz the unity of his body is political in form, a free republic of monads. So it is the *direction* of looking that matters. Only then does the fundamental difference between the romantic conception of a society as an organism and the baroque conception of an organism as a society appear.

The Historic Baroque
It may seem unnecessary to use an overloaded word like *baroque,* especially because it is not immediately apparent that there is a historic continuity with the grand style of the seventeenth century. In the case of romanticism it is much easier to argue for an uninterrupted lineage. Yet several important characteristics of the historic baroque make the term *baroque* attractive to use for later periods, including the present. First the historic baroque insists on a strong phenomenological realness, a sensuous materiality.[9] Second, this materiality is not confined to, or locked within, a simple individual but flows out in many directions, blurring the distinction between individual and environment.[10] And third, there is also the baroque inventiveness, the ability to produce lots of novel combinations out of a rather limited set of elements, for instance as in baroque music.[11] Similarly, action in early baroque theater is not based on the logical development of a plot but rather on a sequence of monologues, debates, and allegories. The great masters of baroque painting,

such as Caravaggio and Rembrandt, made stunning innovations with well-known iconographic commonplaces.[12]

Leibniz's Baroque Monads

Leibniz was a strict nominalist. His monads participate in the cosmos in a fashion that is entirely different from that imagined in the concept of system in romanticism. In Leibniz's baroque philosophy individuals are not linked to form greater systems. Individuals—monads—are not linked at all; they do not even communicate. But they are connected in the sense that, in their material aspect, they affect each other. If one individual had not existed, the whole universe would have been different.[13]

Gilles Deleuze sketches a baroque building, an allegory of the monad.[14] Its lower part has windows on the world, but the upper floor is entirely closed. Here, each monad has its context represented inside itself, as if on an inner screen. Lesser monads just have their own local context represented; the more important the monad, the richer its world. But no monad could read its own inner screen in its entirety; its folds go to infinity. Leibniz said, "Mais une Ame ne peut lire en elle-même que ce qui y est representé distinctement, elle ne sauroit developper tout d'un coup tous ses replis, car ils vont a l'infini" (But a soul can read in itself only that which is represented distinctly there; it cannot pursue all at once all of its folds, because they extend to infinity).[15] All monads are *forces primitives* (primordial forces). All laws of nature can be conceived as forces that spring from monads. The concept of field in physics is Leibnizian in origin. It makes no sense to think of abstract laws of nature, in which the process of abstraction has been carried to a point where they would exist without the monads that give rise to them.

Metaphors of Romanticism

Organicism provides the metaphor of choice to romanticism, but *system* is its favorite word. Behind *system* an organism may hide itself. But machines and engines are also systems. In graphical representations systems are usually depicted by connecting lines between constituent elements. If one draws them in the right way, the larger entity appears from the graph. By contrast, baroque monads are not connected to other monads at all. Each individual monad is a world in itself; each has its context represented on its own inner screen.[16]

Systems and Objects

According to Alfred North Whitehead, "nature appears as a complex system, whose factors are dimly discerned by us."[17] The fact that the mind creates individual entities for itself is necessary as procedure, but it is not a metaphysical necessity. "The immediate fact for awareness is the whole occurrence of nature" (14). Whitehead defines objects as "elements in nature which do not pass" (143). They are the durable ingredients in events, the items of which we can say, "There it is again" (144). Objects may be systems, that is, a multiplicity of entities, but Whitehead says that an arbitrary halt to the dissociation of matter is necessary, and the resulting material entities need to be considered as units (23). More important are systems; ultimately, nature is a complex of related entities.

In 1926 Alfred Tansley makes a Whiteheadian inventory of systems: atoms of the chemical elements of low atomic numbers, the sugar molecule, a single organism, the solar system. They are all physical systems, and they can be ranked on a scale of stability. Longevity—Whitehead used the word *endurance*—is the measure of their stability. Tansley includes a peculiar object that explains the entire inventory: ecological systems in their "climax stage." Tansley is an ecologist. He borrows the concept of "climax" from Frederick Clements, who considers ecological systems (we would now say "ecosystems," a word coined by Tansley in 1935) as superorganisms. Just as organisms develop toward maturity, to adulthood, ecosystems develop toward the climax, a final stage in which their species composition no longer changes. According to Tansley, climax ecosystems sustain themselves for a thousand years or more—not quite as long as an atom but long enough to qualify as systems.

A Romantic Reading of Whitehead

Was Whitehead a holist? Historian of ecology Donald Worster thinks so, largely on the basis of the following passage, which is close to the end of *Concepts of Nature:* "In Nature the normal way trees flourish is by their association in a forest. Each tree may lose something of its individual perfection of growth, but they mutually assist each other in preserving the conditions for survival."[18] The forest would be the new individual holist entity.[19] But elsewhere, in the context of Darwinian evolution, Whitehead is more explicit in his imagery. He writes that organisms *creatively* transform their own environments. And because a single organism would be almost helpless to do so, this requires societies of cooperating organisms.[20]

Deleuze Reads Whitehead

But Deleuze reads Whitehead as a neobaroque philosopher, a neo-Leibnizian. Whitehead frees Leibniz's world of the stringent requirement of "compossibility." There is a strong conceptual link between the notion of compossibility and harmony in music. In a polyphonic musical piece we may hear different melodies at the same time, but together they sound right. Harmony, as it was practiced throughout the baroque era, is the art of counterpoint, bringing together independent voices.[21] Similarly, all the different and individual story lines that are found in the world together form the one world we know. Remove one historical event, and everything goes wrong. In our world Caesar could not have crossed the Rubicon. In Leibniz's mathematics this idea is expressed through convergent series. Even though divergent series were mathematically possible, he didn't envisage them. This is not the place to speculate on Leibniz's reasons for holding on so strongly to compossibility. At any rate Whitehead includes divergent series, and the result is the emancipation of dissonance, the possibility of a chaotic side-by-side existence of mutually exclusive realities.[22]

A Fragmented Nature?

According to Walter Benjamin, in the German baroque drama of Andreas Gryphius and Daniel Caspar von Lohenstein, nature appears as a ruin, a heap of highly significant fragments, rather than as a seamless web. We should be careful not to invest the concept of "fragment" with its current postmodern significance as the ruins of the holistic project that was modernity. Although Benjamin sees a connection between the baroque vision of the world and the atrocities of the Thirty Years' War, the term *fragments* does not refer to what once was a greater whole. Rather, fragments are independent individual things with a monadological structure. The link between them is not connection but reciprocal reference. Gershom Scholem talks of a web of references, which remain in their allegorical immanence. But each individual thing can be severed from that contextual network at all times.[23] Benjamin also applies this vision of nature to the idea world of the baroque. "The idea is a monad—that means briefly: every idea contains the image of the world."[24]

ROMANTIC AND BAROQUE IN THE SCIENCES OF THE COMPLEX

Since World War II many so-called systems theories have been developed, most of which attempt to explain the structure and behavior of complex objects. In this section I focus not on the theories themselves but on some of the sciences in which assumptions about "complexity" have been made and put to use. I try to read them either as expressions of romantic complexity, in which the higher-order individuality of the whole is affirmed, or, alternatively, as examples of baroque complexity in which more attention is usually paid to the lower-order individuality of the many items making up complexity at the higher level.

Table 1 on the next page is indicative. My claim is not that a man like Tansley is "romantic" but that the ideas of his that I consider here reflect romanticism. The categorization of Darwin may seem surprising. It is true that his intellectual genealogy and context is overwhelmingly romantic, as are parts of his evolutionary theory, such as the idea of the phylogenetic tree, which unifies all living beings. But evolutionary theory can also be used in a nonromantic way as we see in Table 2.1.

The Atmosphere as a Romantic System or as a Baroque Collection of Structures

The physicist Vilhelm Bjerknes was much committed to mechanicism in physics, particularly in the development of hydrodynamic analogies to a variety of physical processes. Around 1920 he began to visualize the atmosphere as three-dimensional air masses moving around the globe, differing in temperature, density, and humidity. Out of this the concept of the "polar front" was born. This is a line separating cold air masses from the north and warm air masses from the south, stretching across the entire Atlantic. Along the polar front extratropical cyclones, or low-pressure areas, are formed, which more or less predictably arrive on the coasts of Europe with rain and winds. Dynamic meteorology essentially sees moving air masses, and pictures these as propagating waves on a watery

Table 1. Categorization of Great Thinkers from the
Eighteenth, Nineteenth, and Twentieth Centuries

Romantic	Neobaroque
Rousseau	Darwin
von Humboldt	Whitehead
Spencer	Benjamin
Smuts	Weiss
Clements	Holling
Tansley	May
Odum and Odum	Prigogine after 1968
Patten	Lorenz
Early Prigogine	Deleuze
von Neumann	
General Circulation Models	

surface, and conceives of cyclones as the vortexes that also can be seen in fluids in motion.

However, in post–World War II meteorology the typical structural features of the atmosphere became almost invisible. Instead, meteorologists such as Jules Charney, together with mathematician John von Neumann, developed atmospheric computer models of the atmosphere. For the computer enabled Charney and von Neumann to pick up another idea that Bjerknes had entertained but could not put into practice. This was to reduce the full complexity of the atmosphere to a small number of physical laws. According to Bjerknes, the physical laws that describe how one atmospheric state develops into another are the hydrodynamic equations of motion, the equation of state (the ideal gas law), and the laws of thermodynamics. Together these are seven equations with which changes in seven atmospheric variables (including temperature, humidity, pressure, and wind velocity) can be calculated.[25] In Bjerknes's (1904) vision this would allow for a completely deterministic description of the atmosphere.[26] Von Neumann shared these ideas, and in 1946 he announced his intention "of developing a very high speed electronic computing machine and of applying it to the prediction of natural weather and of calculating the effects of human intervention in the natural processes of the atmosphere."[27]

Ten years later, in 1955, he initiated a research program on "long-range forecasting" of the weather.[28] The result of putting the physical laws in the foreground, and basing the mathematical models on them, is that the original "fronts" have moved to the background in computer-based meteorology. Edward N. Lorenz puts it so:

> In making a numerical forecast, one takes a set of numbers representing the initial wind, pressure, and temperature fields, and, regardless of what synoptic structures may be present in these fields, plugs the numbers into the same program, obtaining another set of numbers representing the forecast. Inevitably the attitude arose that fields rather than structures or phenomena, such as cyclones and fronts or cyclogenesis and frontogenesis, were the essence of the atmospheric state.[29]

Atmospheric structures still have a place in the practice of forecasting, although their proponents are on the defensive.[30] It is quite possible that their substantial disappearance is contributing to an impression, shared by many meteorologists, that the atmosphere is ultimately completely predictable. This impression makes sense because the models to which Lorenz refers take it as a given that the atmosphere is a single whole. In Lorenz's own view the atmosphere is an assembly of temporary structures, constituting a contingent and possibly divergent "whole."

Theories of Directionality: Darwin as Romantic

The romantics' weak proof of the existence of a higher-order entity would be to show that it influences events and, minimally, its own self-maintenance. The strong proof would be its directional development, as a whole, to some other state.

At one point Darwin came quite close to a theory of directionality, and he has been read this way by his romantic adherents. A famous line from the final pages of the *Origin of Species* reads, "It is interesting to contemplate an entangled bank, clothed with many plants of many kinds, with birds singing on the bushes, with various insects flitting about, and with worms crawling through the damp earth . . . , dependent on each other in so complex a manner."[31] Darwin continues to argue that from the war of nature "the production of higher animals directly follows" (459). It is the unifying force of the entangled bank that ensures that the wholly undirected evolutionary change on the level of the individual organisms does have a direction toward greater complexity in nature. Or are we reading too much of Spencer into Darwin's text?

Within the corpus of Darwin's writings, it might seem a bit of a problematic passage. Darwin's evolutionary theory rests on the ecological consideration that individual organisms engage in various interactions with each other. The necessary result is speciation. New species, as organisms, may be of greater complexity and thus "higher." But the picture of the entangled bank is not compelling Darwin to assume that at one point the sum total of ecological interactions would have reached such a high level of complexity that evolution would come to a halt. On the contrary, the process of speciation will go on forever.

Herbert Spencer: Romanticism and Neo-Lamarckianism

For Herbert Spencer evolution did go toward a goal, even if he had trouble admitting it.[32] Spencer, a sociologist among other things, was an evolutionary theorist in his own right. He supported neo-Lamarckianism, a variety of Darwinism that was to grow popular among biologists around the turn of the century. According to the neo-Lamarckians, organisms can pass on acquired character traits to their offspring. Spencer thought that not only was increasing complexity thus ensured faster than it would be otherwise, but also that organisms would become increasingly fit to cooperate and so become integrated in a stable ecological configuration or equilibrium. For Spencer evolution ended there. Only disruptions from outside could cause living nature to readjust to the new conditions, once more finding equilibrium.[33]

Spencer seems to anticipate ecological theories between 1950 and 1975, such as those of Eugene Odum and Bernard Patten (see below). As Peel has pointed out, Spencer contributed much to functional thinking in sociology. Quite similar functionalist theorizing underpins systems ecology.[34]

The Maintenance of Equilibrium

Le Châtelier's principle is Spencer's idea of goal directedness toward equilibrium translated into physical chemistry. Formulated in the 1880s, in a precise thermodynamic manner, it gained some popularity as a model of life's processes from around the turn of the century.[35] The principle, the *loi de stabilité de l'équilibre chimique*, states that any change (imposed from outside) that affects chemical equilibrium is counteracted by another factor so as to restore equilibrium. Tansley may have been thinking of Le Châtelier's principle as a metaphor for the maintenance of equilibrium by ecosystems when he wrote in 1926 that "it is really the whole of the living organisms together, plus the inorganic factors working on them, which make up, in a climax community, a 'system' in more or less stable equilibrium."[36]

The principle seems to fulfill the romantic expectation with regard to complex systems in a mechanistic way. Tansley wrote before Schrödinger presented his solution to the problem of the Second Law. Schrödinger showed that "equilibrium," chemical equilibrium for instance, is unfit as a metaphor of life. Life sustains itself far from equilibrium. Approaching equilibrium is equivalent to nearing death.

The Problem of the Second Law: The Reduction of Complexity
Since its discovery by William Thomson (Lord Kelvin) and Robert Clausius in the nineteenth century, the Second Law of Thermodynamics appeared to put the order of nature at risk. It seemed to counteract Darwinian evolution, and, as a rival theory of evolution, it has often been put on the same footing. In its original version the Second Law states simply that whenever energy is put to work, for instance in an engine, there is at least some waste because of friction. Generalized to other kinds of energy transformations and to the universe as a whole, this idea led to the concept of impending "heat death." The ultimate fate of the universe would be a uniform distribution of matter and energy through space, with no order, or "complexity," for that matter.

Given the Second Law, how do complex systems emerge in the first place? How, during the evolution of life on Earth, have ever more complex living systems come into being? Hyman Levy, a professor of mathematics and a popular science writer, wrote in 1939: "Side by side with the Second Law of Thermodynamics, in so far as it may be valid for large-scale systems—if it is so valid—there must exist a law for the evolution of novel forms of aggregated energy and the emergence of new qualities. A generalization of this nature has not yet been made but that a general rule of this type must exist is evident."[37]

Hyman did not speak specifically about life. The coming-into-being of the sun as a body of concentrated energy would also fall within the scope of this unknown law. Following an analysis by L. Brillouin of the debate on the Second Law around World War II, we could classify Hyman as belonging neither to those hard-boiled physicalists who held that the Second Law could explain everything nor to the vitalists, who held that living organisms were somehow not subject to it but rather to the camp that awaited new principles to supplement existing insights on the Second Law.[38]

. . . and the Solution by Schrödinger

In 1944 physicist Erwin Schrödinger published a small book on the emergence of living order. His solution became very influential. "It is by avoiding the rapid decay into the inert state of 'equilibrium' that an organism appears so enigmatic. . . . How does an organism avoid decay? . . . What an organism feeds upon is negative entropy."[39] Schrödinger thus regarded life as islands of low entropy in a sea of high entropy, complex locations in an ocean of decreasing complexity.

Lotka

Alfred J. Lotka, a physical chemist, considered the evolution of a chemical system as a model for the general evolution of systems.[40] The advantage of the analogy was that it focused on the system as a whole rather than on individual species. Furthermore, in both types of systems laws of evolution could be formulated in the form of minimum laws, that is, laws that predict the evolution of the system toward a state in which certain variables are at a minimum.[41] Lotka's writings on the subject, which appeared long before Schrödinger's publication, apparently went unnoticed in the debate on the Second Law. He predicted that when the Second Law would make itself felt, humankind would have to return to a parsimonious living and give up many of the luxuries of the recent industrial age.[42] Troublesome, but not quite a heat death.

Lotka permitted the use of Le Châtelier's principle, provided it was extended correctly to steady-state conditions and was not confined to equilibrium proper. In this way he anticipated somewhat Schrödinger and Prigogine (see below), but again, this part of his ideas apparently went unnoticed.[43]

Ecological Succession

If a "virgin" piece of land is left long enough on its own, the weeds and grasses that populate it first are replaced by shrubs and eventually by trees. Ecologists call the process by which short-lived plants are replaced by longer-lived ones "succession." Succession becomes specially significant when it is understood as directional. This would be the proof that the group of plants together form a higher-order entity. The best-known—indeed more or less the only—directional theory of succession for the first quarter of the twentieth century was that of Clements. Clements took communities of plants to be superorganisms. For each of these succession was a process of growth toward maturity, in which the community superorganism retained its individuality, even though at its supposedly end stage, or climax, not a single plant species of its youth phase was left. However, this superorganism concept was undermined in 1935 by Tansley, who claimed that Clements had associated it with the mystical parts of Jan Smuts's holistic philosophy.

When Eugene Odum and his brother Howard T. (Tom) Odum revived directional successional theory in the 1950s, they did not make use of the superorganism concept. But that succession was directional, and that "climax" existed, was beyond dispute. Here is Eugene Odum's formulation:

> [Ecological succession] is an orderly process of community development that is reasonably directional and, therefore, predictable. . . . It culminates in a stabilized ecosystem in which maximum biomass (or high information content) and symbiotic function between organisms are maintained per unit of available energy flow. . . . In a word, the "strategy" of succession as a short term process . . . is increased control of, or homeostasis with, the physical environment in the sense of achieving maximum protection from its perturbations.[44]

Tom Odum found the basic mechanism for this directionality in contemporary developments in thermodynamics. The work of Ilya Prigogine enabled Odum to abandon the superorganism concept for something better, while preserving its holistic tenets.

The Early Prigogine: Direction in the Evolution of Complexity
Ilya Prigogine's area of study was chemical reaction systems, particularly open systems that exchange matter, energy, and entropy with their environment. Following the argument of Schrödinger's *What Is Life?*, Prigogine distinguished between a system by itself and the system in relation

to the outside world. Outside equilibrium, the overall production of entropy (of the system in combination with its environment), should be positive, as required by the Second Law of Thermodynamics.[45] But if large enough, entropy could actually decrease in the system itself. A very simple example is the so-called Soret effect: if one applies a temperature gradient to a homogeneous chemical solution, a concentration gradient develops. Hence, an extremely simple form of order is created, of course at the expense of energy.[46]

Prigogine concluded that in the stationary state (outside equilibrium), the entropy of the matter entering the system is smaller than the entropy of the matter given off by the system to its environment. "From the thermodynamic point of view the open system 'degrades' the matter it receives and it is this degradation which maintains the stationary state."[47] Accordingly, there is a sharp distinction between equilibrium (as in Le Châtelier's principle) and the steady state. Prigogine supplied a metaphor for "life": an open chemical reaction system, such as in (but not only in) living organisms.

We know that closed systems eventually go to equilibrium, when entropy is at a maximum. The equilibrium state is the necessary end point to which closed systems must develop—the equilibrium acts as an attractor no matter what the initial state of a system. The terms *attractor* and *domain of attraction* are often used in the mathematical descriptions or depictions of the equilibrium state. But we have seen above that closed systems are not fit to describe the emergence of life or of complexity.

Open systems are necessarily outside equilibrium, and stationary states may be many in principle. Is there yet a necessary evolution to a particular state? Prigogine thought so. "Internal irreversible processes," he wrote, "always operate in such a way that their effect is to lower the value of entropy production."[48] And he added that once in the stationary state of minimum entropy production, the system cannot leave this state spontaneously. Hence, this state would be stable; the system would deviate only slightly from it and would return to it when disturbed by a fluctuation.

The fact that open systems also undergo a necessary evolution toward an end state was grist to the Odums' mill. Ecosystems are open systems. The climax can be thought of as the state of least entropy production.

Ecosystems and Biological Evolution

Can Darwinian evolution be brought nearer to ecological succession, now that the latter seems to go toward an end state? As we have seen, neo-Lamarckianism became discredited in the 1920s. But ideas similar to Spencer's were advanced much later. In 1975 ecologist Bernard Patten, a colleague of Eugene Odum, advanced an evolutionary theory with the controversial feature that evolution (biological, not physical) was directional. According to Patten, nature evolves in such a way that nonlinear processes are gradually replaced by linear dynamics through natural selection, and he writes that the ecosystem is a holistic unit of coevolution.[49] Equally striking is the assertion that *mathematical* traits exist and can be selected against. The terms *linear* and *nonlinear* designate whether the relationship between two variables, that is between cause and effect, is proportional. Patten readily conceded that "virtually all of modern biology demonstrates to be nonlinear." But in mature ecosystems, Patten reasoned, cataclysmic outbreaks, or mass starvations, are prevented by checks and balances operating in the system, as he argued that nature had an "exact analog in practical engineering. . . . The engineering experience indicates overwhelmingly that linear or linearized systems are reliable and *desirable* whereas systems which express nonlinear behavioral characteristics are not" (529, emphasis added). Patten was an ecosystem ecologist who was in the business of representing whole ecosystems by models. These models were mathematized and made fit for simulation on digital computers. The project of systems ecology in the 1960s and early 1970s would be to mimic ecological nature in its full complexity. Virtually no limit was set to the phenomenological details of ecological nature to become part of the models.

But below the surface of this immense complexity in the ecosystem models a rigorous functionalism is lurking. A romantic trope indeed. There is no superfluousness in nature. Every little plant and insect has its place as a cog in a giant machinery. Remove one of them, and the machine's performance goes down. As we have seen, Patten thinks of ecosystems as "natural control systems" that regulate their own primary production (that is, the amount of biomass produced by green plants). Even more than most of his colleagues, Patten identifies ecosystems as technical control devices, thus taking the metaphor of an automatic machine quite literally. And this is where Patten's argument in favor of the disappearance of nonlinearity in natural ecosystems crucially rests on the idea that relatively simple cybernetic control devices have one equilibrium, or stationary state, in which the systems like to function and to which they tend to return if not gravely disturbed. These are "well-behaved" systems, argues Patten. They do not jump erratically and unpredictably from one equilibrium state to another because they have only one and are similar in this respect to natural ecosystems in which one also usually fails to see big changes from one day to another. "*Ecosystems are stable in the large*" (533, Patten's emphasis). As in the idea of the end of history, evolution comes to an end in the cybernetic ecosystem.

Evolutionary Ecology and Population Dynamics

Evolutionary ecologists reacted negatively to Patten's view of the linearity of ecosystems. Robert May found "the idea that real ecosystems have exactly linear dynamics to be too idiosyncratic to warrant serious attention."[50] Patten himself mentioned only one adversary by name and even then only in passing. This was C. S. Holling, as someone in favor of "nonlinear" and "discontinuous" relationships. Holling favored a view of ecosystems inspired in part by the French mathematician René Thom. In Thom's theory of catastrophes a slight change in a single variable of a system can under certain circumstances give rise to sharp, discontinuous change. Thom's own paradigm examples were taken from chemical reaction kinetics in highly structured cellular environments, and his own work was mainly concerned with biological morphogenetics.[51] Thom held that catastrophe theory might be widely applied—for instance to turbulence in hydrodynamics.

Holling came nearest to using the concept of catastrophe in his explanation of, for instance, sudden outbreaks of insect numbers or sharp falls in fish populations. In particular, he drew attention to the phenomenon that once fish populations had dramatically fallen in numbers as a result of overfishing, they did not return to their original numbers with the end of fishing.[52] In contrast to cybernetic control theory as it existed at the time when Patten published his paper, chemical reaction kinetics allowed for the existence of multiple equilibria. Moreover, the location of equilibria in phase-space is not fixed, and Holling argued that strategies to lock a system in a supposedly advantageous equilibrium can be counterproductive and produce the catastrophe that they tried to prevent. Holling, with another catastrophe theorist, E. C. Zeeman, developed the fold as a graphical representation of discontinuous transitions in a system. The fold visually demonstrated, among other things, the possibility of bifurcation—an extremely small difference in the value of one parameter leading to a dramatically different development of a second parameter.

Holling did not himself explore any of the analogies offered by catastrophe theory through its favored fields of application, such as the turbulent chemical reactions in cells mentioned above. Rather he referred to the imagery of the game, as favored by an evolutionary theorist, Lawrence Slobodkin.[53] He did not develop this imagery in any formal sense. Rather, he meant to promote a particular view on the management of natural systems: "In Slobodkin's terms evolution is like a game, but a distinctive one in which the only payoff is to stay in the game. Therefore, a major strategy selected is not one maximizing either efficiency or a particular reward, but one which allows persistence by maintaining flexibility above all else."[54]

From Holling's point of view Patten assumes the existence of just one domain of attraction (around the one equilibrium that he recognizes in his linear ecosystems) and does not mention the concept of domain of attraction. In addition, the status of metaphor is different in both authors. Patten identifies ecosystems with cybernetic control systems, period. Holling mentions metaphors in a somewhat looser way (such as the game), whereas his more abstract mathematics allows for a number of related metaphors. This suggests that before we conclude with systems ecologists such as Patten that the population dynamicist's approach is reductive, we should bear in mind that to Holling ecological reality is complex and structured and that metaphors that explicitly or implicitly informed his work also stress organization and systemic integration.

Order by Fluctuations

From 1968 Ilya Prigogine added important new insights to his thermodynamic theory of the evolution of complex systems. Whereas in the early 1950s he had argued that systems out-of-equilibrium develop toward a particular steady state with definite features, by the late 1960s he had opted for a much more open and chance-governed evolution.[55] Sometimes, Prigogine argued, a fluctuation around the mean of one of the various variables of a system outside equilibrium would not die out or dampen as fluctuations usually do but would be amplified. "Chance" would then decide which particular fluctuation would amplify and to what new state the system would then be pushed, until a temporary new stationary state would be reached. The important thing to note here is that such amplified fluctuations are not destructive but may create even more complex structures still further from (thermodynamic) equilibrium.

Prigogine's paradigmatic example was an oscillating chemical reaction system, not one that featured evolutionary steps in real time. In 1958 a Russian scientist, B. P. Belousov, had discovered a remarkable chemical reaction involving the oxidation of an organic substance catalyzed by a metal ion in a watery solution. The reaction can be performed and easily observed in a shallow petri dish. Unlike most such reactions it is not homogeneously distributed across space and time. Instead, sudden bursts of chemical activity begin at a random place in the petri dish, and they give rise to propagating colored rings across the surface, like the waves one sees when a stone is thrown into the water but more beautiful. The reaction pulsates like a pendulum, a harmonic oscillator, and therefore is compared to a "clock." This chemical system was subsequently studied by Zhabotinskii in Moscow and, initially through publications in Russian, found its way to the West. The first publication in English by Zhabotinskii appeared in 1970.[56]

In 1968 Prigogine published an abstract reaction system with peculiar characteristics, similar to the Belousov-Zhabotinskii reaction.[57] Prigogine's reaction system, which would come to be called the "Brusselator," is open to the environment, nonlinear (given that it is in part autocatalytic), and is far from equilibrium. Unfortunately, the reaction scheme is physically unrealistic but because of its simplicity has the important advantage that it can be modeled relatively easy on a computer.

Depending on how one chooses the value of the parameters of the reaction, the Brusselator behaves in very different ways. At certain concentrations of the reagents, the reaction proceeds in a steady state, but with one of the reagents raised the Brusselator suddenly starts to function in a limit cycle, oscillating in a similar way to the Belousov-Zhabotinskii reaction. With other parameters changed again the limit-cycle changes shape and becomes what the meteorologist E. N. Lorenz would call a "strange attractor," performing first one oscillation and then another.

Prigogine and his coworkers were quick to point to the biological significance of the Brusselator. The spatial and temporal "organization" that the reaction mass displays is like the gradients of matter that appear in egg yolk and announce the formation of the embryo.

Growth of Complexity without Telos

The Brusselator serves to make a number of interesting points about the behavior and evolution of complex systems. For instance, it illustrates discontinuous development (such as Thom had also addressed in his catastrophe theory) and "bifurcation" points (at which the system may go in either of two directions). Prigogine has outlined a number of philosophical arguments that culminate in the book *La nouvelle alliance* (1979), which he wrote together with the philosopher Isabelle Stengers.[58] Bifurcation points are also of special significance because at such points the system behaves, according to Prigogine and Stengers, as a "whole." This whole is conceived as a population of molecules. At this point we can appreciate the role of fluctuations in creating order. In a model reaction scheme we can simply assign the value of a variable so that a bifurcation point is reached. But in the real world this critical value can be reached by accident, by local random fluctuations around the mean. Once it is reached somewhere, the system as a whole evolves to a new order. This transition is not orchestrated from a coordinating center because there is no center that controls the system as in a cybernetic system or with a governor for a steam engine. Any local change, provided it meets the critical requirements, can induce the rest of the population of molecules to "cooperate" in finding a new mode of behavior. All individuals of the population seem to be informed about each other at the steps of transition. It is a bit like the sudden occurrence of waves in certain mass audiences, for which no conductor is needed. A further speculative argument was derived from the work of the ecologist Robert May: the more complex a system is, the more likely it is that small fluctuations will be just large enough to be critical.[59]

As a last step in understanding Prigogine's position we need to add the notion of "event."[60] We could interpret the "choice" made by a system at a bifurcation point as a singular event, in the sense of a historical event. By itself, neither the Belousov-Zhabotinskii reaction nor the Brusselator can carry the full weight of the notion of event, but if we picture a world in which countless similar reactions hang together, and in which one "event" fulfills the necessary conditions for another "event" to occur, we get a little closer to a historical or a Darwinian view of the development of physicochemical systems. The events that matter cannot be deduced from laws of nature. We now may understand why Prigogine presented the Brusselator, and the Belousov-Zhabotinskii reaction, as a metaphor for the never-terminating evolution of complex systems.

"In General, Succession Never Stops"
In comparison with Eugene and Tom Odum and their use of Prigogine's early work, we have here an almost complete turnaround with regard to the development of ecosystems. In the new view we would expect no climax, no necessary end point for ecological succession, and no relationship between stability and diversity or complexity of ecosystems. Quite the contrary. And instability ceases to be "bad." Rather than an announcement of impending death, it signals the possibility of new forms of complexity.

The later Prigogine did not find an audience among the systems ecologists, who remained faithful to the tenets of stability analysis of ecosystems (many, including the Odums and Patten, to the present day). In fact, Prigogine's position after 1968 is much closer to the evolutionary ecology of C. S. Holling. Another example of this approach is the work of Robert May, whose 1972 article "Will a Large Complex Be Stable?" (to which May's answer was "no")[61] was perceived among systems ecologists as an attack on their basic premises.[62] The article was the first of a series that established chaos theory.[63]

May's sources were quite independent of Prigogine's. And whereas Prigogine made much use of May's work, the reverse does not seem to be the case. May derived his own impressive conceptual system from analysis of the dynamics of a single population (the simplest possible ecosystem, constituting one species only), represented by a single mathematical equation. His mathematical analysis of a small number of such equations revealed a full spectrum of stable points, stable limit cycles and chaos, and the discontinuous transitions (bifurcation points) between them. (Interestingly, May was scathing about catastrophe theory. Admitting that his own findings could be "recast in the language of catastrophe theory," he argued that nothing was gained because it could be done only "*post hoc.*")[64]

May did not simply content himself with theoretical modeling. On several occasions he sought and found support for his own position in the empirical findings of others.[65] He focuses mainly on theoretical problems derived from animal ecology (insect outbursts, analysis of food webs, etc.). The phenomenon of ecological succession, which is a typical vegetational concept (although it has been exported to other ecological domains), does not fall immediately within his scope. Yet, for plant succession too, a number of ecological field studies published in the 1970s do not support the idea of a single climax in Clements's or the Odums' vein. "In general, succession never stops . . ." was the conclusion of one such study and could have been the conclusion to a number of other studies.[66]

THE METAPHYSICS OF FLUCTUATIONS

It is not much of an overstatement to say that to Prigogine "fluctuations" are the essential condition for order on any level of reality. Fluctuations beget the physical universe, life, civilization. Fluctuations—white noise, Brownian movement, etc.—are the most humble aspect of the behavior of matter on the microscopic level. Yet they may lead, via chaotic phenomena, to order on the macro level. But why are there fluctuations?

Fluctuations are a pain in the neck for classical physics. Consider the textbook example of hydrodynamics: the flow of a fluid through a tube. If it proceeds slowly, and if one does not look too closely at the tube's wall, the individual fluid particles proceed straight ahead, as they should, in a so-called laminar flow. It is possible to describe the flow mathematically as if the fluid particles belong to lamina, thinly sliced layers of fluid, that move. But if the flow speeds up, the layers fall apart, and small whirls appear. Is there a natural law that predicts the whirls? No. All we have is the empirical certainty that they will appear. The curling smoke from a cigar or a smokestack is similar.

In spite of the absence of a law, there is a name for it: turbulence. Turbulence is irregular and random. No deterministic approach to turbulence is possible, but we can collect empirical knowledge about it and even make it work for us (as in aircraft).[67] The subject of turbulence is one of those "applied" subdisciplines of physics taught mainly at technical universities and not very high in the pecking order of academic physics.

But it has a history. Around 55 B.C. the Roman poet Lucretius published his *De rerum natura*, a philosophical poem on the nature of things. Lucretius's atomism is not a speculative theory on the nature of matter. Rather, atoms are simply assumed to be the simple microphysical constituents of the visible world, constituents for which Lucretius provides a phenomenological description. The atomism of the Ancients concerned itself with large populations of atoms, their flows and their behaviors. Atoms themselves are below the threshold of perception, but the populations of atoms are not. Lucretius's basic metaphor of nature is a hydrodynamic flow of particles in free fall, in swirls, and in vortexes.[68]

There are two basic aspects to the physics of Lucretius. In principle, atoms fall straight down, as they did at the beginning of the world. Following Michel Serres, we could call this the lawlike, "Newtonian," aspect of the physics of Lucretius. But some atoms behave differently. This is the infamous *clinamen*, the very slight deviation of very few atoms in their fall. The unruly atoms bump against other atoms, and this is the beginning of chains of collisions that finally produce the structures of matter such as they constitute our world.

Lucretius has been much ridiculed by physicists and philosophers because he gave no reasons why deviations from the law would occur. But according to Serres, Lucretius is under no obligation to do so. The clinamen is a basic fact of nature. If nature behaved according to law only, all flows would fall down and end up in an indifferent equilibrium. The swerve prevents that and is responsible for the fact that the world comes into existence again and again. It is as if Lucretius already knew that Clausius's fear of the heat death of the universe was ill founded. Is Serres giving an anachronistic reading of Lucretius? On the contrary, Serres argues that the essential insight of Lucretius was preserved through the centuries of scientific development as a heterodox tradition, a "quasi-invariant de très longue durée."[69]

So the clinamen is a small fluctuation in the movement of matter, but it matters. We may consider it the paradigm case of a small cause leading to disproportional results, of nonlinearity. Of course, small fluctuations are not always of consequence. Many, in fact most, pass unnoticed. But when the circumstances are right, big events may be their result, and in the latter case they are like the "sensitive dependence on initial conditions" developed by the meteorologist E. N. Lorenz. The clinamen has its place in a phenomenological description of nature, a contingent and complex nature, a space for opportunities and events. It is the opposite of the view that reduces nature to Euclidean proportions, that sees general law expressed in every single local instance or event.

CODA

Romantic and baroque complexity are not paradigms that succeed one another in time. Both are discourses on complexity that are available to the sciences and on which the sciences draw. Since around 1800 romantic complexity has been the more orthodox discourse. But in its "overstated" forms (such as *Naturphilosophie*, Smuts's holism, and some of the 1950s systems theories), it met vigorous opposition from scientists. Baroque complexity became a focus of new interest in about 1975, but it is by no means a wholly new conception of reality.

Romantic complexity is the most straightforward conception of complexity. It favors stable structural metaphors, such as the self-correcting cybernetic machine. Romantic complexity is the modern version of *natura naturata*, nature such as it can be known and approached from the point of view of a fixed set of natural laws. Criteria can be established more easily than for the baroque case—criteria by which emergent wholes can be delineated from their environment and recognized as such. Problems reside most often at the empirical level: are there independent ways of confirming the existence of the higher-order individual? This is where directionality of whole systems is brought in.

Baroque complexity favors a very different set of metaphors. Most refer to populations of individuals (or atoms) in turbulent motion. The problem of baroque complexity is conceptual. There may be a higher-order level above the level of swarming individuals, but what is it? In general, it is easier to say what it is *not*. It is not stable patterns of communication—the very concept of pattern is highly ambiguous. If patterns exist at all, they are short-lived. Individuals take part in several wholes rather than in one. The way wholes are delineated depends on situational rather than on abstract criteria. A more solid underpinning of baroque complexity may be found in the concept of reciprocal reference, and this brings the monads into play.

Despite the conceptual problems, from the experiential aspect there seems to be more certainty that something is at stake. We may have the bodily experience of turbulence, even though it is difficult to describe it theoretically. Reflecting on the difficulties of the concept of the baroque, Deleuze remarked that the very idea of "concept" is different in baroque thinking. The usual idea of concept refers to a cosmological order that is grasped by the thinking subject. In the baroque the concept is never severed from the individual. A baroque concept (or *concetto,* which is a literary term) is an allegory, not a symbol of the cosmos. It is a narrative.[70]

Baroque complexity is close to *natura naturans.* Similarly the clinamen is the creative aspect of nature. When we cannot predict the future course of a complex system, it is not because we don't know enough. The world is uncertain. Uncertainty in the baroque case is ontological rather than epistemological.

NOTES

1. These two discourses on complexity share to some extent a common vocabulary (including the word *complexity* itself). But why? In part, the answer is catachresis, the process by which new concepts, lacking a name, draw from what is already known. One example is the word *cybernetics* in Margoroh Maruyama's 1963 article "The Second Cybernetics." This so-called second cybernetics is not, like the first, a steering science, and it has few things in common with the cybernetics of Norbert Wiener. Maruyama needed a word for systems in which deviations become amplified and compared them to the deviation-counteracting systems of Wiener. But Maruyama's cybernetics lack the single integrating center that enforces unity on Wiener's systems of control.

2. See Holling (1966).

3. See Haraway (1976).

4. Smuts (1961, 100).

5. See Rousseau ([1782] 1959, 1063).

6. See Pagden (1993, 48).

7. Pagden (1993, 111).

8. See Leibniz (1986, § 67; English translation from *G. W. Leibniz's Monadology,* trans. N. Rescher (Pittsburgh: University of Pittsburgh Press, 1991), 228.

9. See Martin (1977).

10. See Deleuze (1988, 14).

11. This was pointed out to me by Pieter Schroevers.

12. See Treffers (1995).

13. See Brown (1984, 115).

14. See Deleuze (1988, 7).

15. See Leibniz (1986, § 61).

16. By contrast reductionism is an epistemological strategy rather than an ontology. In one aspect it derives from an analytical frame of mind. It concentrates on the lawlike behavior of relatively simple processes, while holding the rest of the world constant. In a different aspect it holds the simplest laws of nature as the most real. In this respect it is like Platonism. In both cases the results of reductionist research may well be applied to system representations of higher-order entities.

17. See Whitehead (1920, 163).

18. Ibid., 296–97.

19. See Worster (1985).

20. See Whitehead (1920, 163–64).

21. In 1722 Rameau changed the concept of harmony, making it fulfill a different function, as Peter Peters pointed out to me.

22. See Rosen (1976, 111–12).

23. See Buck-Morss (1989, 160, 219, 236).

24. See Benjamin (1985, 48).

25. See Friedman (1989, 53).

26. See Aspray (1990, 125).

27. Ibid., 150.

28. Ibid.

29. See Lorenz (1986, 190).

30. "I don't believe fronts are dead," Jeremy Namias said in 1983 (754).

31. See Darwin ([1859] 1968, 459).

32. See Peel (1971); see also Wiltshire (1979).

33. See Spencer (1894, 517).

34. But we should be careful not to associate Spencer's system as a whole with romantic thought. In particular his theory of the "instability of the homogeneous" (chapter 19 of his *First Principles*), with its almost Lucretian overtones (see below), seems to have no counterpart among his contemporaries.

35. See Kingsland (1985).

36. A. G. Tansley and T. F. Chipp, *Aims and Methods of Vegetation Analysis* (1926), quoted in Golley (1994, 32).

37. See Levy (1939, 203).

38. See Brillouin (1949, 554–68).

39. See Schrödinger (1967, 75–76).

40. In writing this section I benefited from Liesbeth de Ruiter's M.S. thesis (1999) at the Department of Science Dynamics, University of Amsterdam.

41. See Lotka ([1925] 1956).

42. Ibid., 279.

43. On Lotka's significance for ecology see Kingsland (1985).

44. Odum (1969, 262).

45. See Hayles (1990, 94).

46. See Spanner (1964, 254).

47. Prigogine (1955, 85).

48. Ibid., 83.

49. See Patten (1975, 529–39).

50. May (1979, 400).

51. In this context Thom vigorously denied that a cell could be regarded as a "bag of enzymes." See Thom (1980, 43).

52. See Peterman, Clark, and Holling (1979, 321–41).

53. Slobodkin and, before him, Richard Levins pictured species playing a game against "nature." See Smith (1982), who arrived at a more formal concept of game by imagining species playing games against each other.

54. Holling (1976, 83).

55. For a slightly different account of this episode see chapter 4 of Hayles (1990).

56. See Winfree (1974, 82–95).

57. See Prigogine and Lefever (1968, 1695–1700). The Belousov-Zhabotinskii reaction is not mentioned in this article.

58. See Prigogine and Stengers (1979). The English translation, *Order Out of Chaos*, was published by Bantam in 1984.

59. Prigogine and Stengers (1979, 177, 178).

60. See Prigogine and Stengers (1988, 47).

61. See May (1972, 413–14).

62. See Kwa (1993, 125–55).

63. On May, see Gleick (1987).

64. See May (1979, 392).

65. Ibid.

66. See Connell and Slatyer (1977, 1119–44). See also Walker and West (1970, 117–39); Colinvaux (1973, 89); Botkin and Sobel (1975, 625–46); Horn (1976, 187–90); Picket (1976, 107–19).

67. See Tennekes and Lumley (1972).

68. See Serres (1977).

69. Ibid., 200.

70. See Deleuze (1988, 172–74).

REFERENCES

Aspray, W. 1990. *John von Neumann and the Origins of the Modern Computer.* Cambridge, Mass.: MIT Press.

Benjamin, W. 1985. *The Origin of German Tragic Drama.* London: Verso.

Botkin, D., and R. Sobel. 1975. "Stability in Time-Varying Ecosystems." *American Naturalist* 109: 625–46.

Brillouin, L. 1949. "Life, Thermodynamics, and Cybernetics." *American Scientist* 37: 544–68.

Brown, S. 1984. *Leibniz.* Minneapolis: University of Minnesota Press.

Buck-Morss, S. 1989. *The Dialectics of Seeing.* Cambridge, Mass.: MIT Press.

Colinvaux, P. 1973. *Introduction to Ecology.* New York: Wiley.

Connell, J. H., and R. O. Slatyer. 1977. "Mechanisms of Succession in Natural Communities and Their Role in Community Stability and Organization." *American Naturalist* 111: 1119–44.

Darwin, C. [1859] 1968. *Origin of Species.* Ed. J. W. Burrow. Harmondsworth: Penguin.

Deleuze, G. 1988. *Le pli.* Paris: Minuit.

Friedman, R. M. 1989. *Appropriating the Weather.* Ithaca, N.Y.: Cornell University Press.

Gleick, J. 1987. *Chaos.* New York: Viking.

Golley, F. B. 1994. *A History of the Ecosystem Concept in Ecology.* New Haven: Yale University Press.

Haraway, D. 1976. *Crystals, Fabrics, and Fields.* New Haven: Yale University Press.

Hayles, K. N. 1990. *Chaos Bound.* Ithaca, N.Y.: Cornell University Press.

Holling, C. S. 1966. "The Strategy of Building Complex Ecological Models." In K. E. F. Watt, ed., *Systems Analysis in Ecology.* New York: Academic Press.

——. 1976. "Resilience and Stability of Ecosystems." In E. Jantsch and C. H. Waddington, eds., *Evolution and Consciousness: Human Systems in Transition,* 73–92. Reading, Mass.: Addison-Wesley.

Horn, H. S. 1976. "Succession." In R. M. May, ed., *Theoretical Ecology.* Philadelphia: Saunders.

Kingsland, S. 1985. *Modeling Nature.* Chicago: University of Chicago Press.

Kwa, C. L. 1993. "Modelling the Grasslands." *Historical Studies in the Physical and Biological Sciences* 24: 125–55.

Leibniz, G. W. 1986. "Principes de la philosophie ou la Monadologie." Ed. A. Robinet. Paris: J. Vrin.

Levy, H. 1939. *Modern Science.* London: Hamish Hamilton.

Lorenz, E. N. 1986. "The Index Cycle Is Alive and Well." In J. O. Roads, ed., *Namias Symposium.* La Jolla, Calif.: Scripps Institute.

Lotka, A. J. [1925. *Elements of Physical Biology.*] 1956. *Elements of Mathematical Biology.* Reprint, New York: Dover.

Martin, J. R. 1977. *Baroque.* London: Allan Lane.

50   Chunglin Kwa

Maruyama, M. 1963. "The Second Cybernetics." *American Scientist* 51: 164–79.

May, R. M. 1972. "Will a Large Complex Be Stable?" *Nature* 238: 413–14.

———. 1979. "The Structure and Dynamics of Ecological Communities." In R. M. Anderson, B. D. Turner, and L. R. Taylor, eds., *Population Dynamics*. Oxford: Blackwell.

Namias, J. 1983. "The History of Polar Fronts and Air Mass Concepts in the United States: An Eyewitness Account." *Bulletin of the American Meteorological Society* 64: 734–55.

Odum, Eugene. 1969. "The Strategy of Ecosystem Development." *Science* 164: 262–70.

Pagden, A. 1993. *European Encounters with the New World*. New Haven: Yale University Press.

Patten, B. C. 1975. "Ecosystem Linearization: An Evolutionary Design Problem." *American Naturalist* 109: 529–39.

Peel, J. D. Y. 1971. *Herbert Spencer: The Evolution of a Sociologist*. London: Heinemann.

Peterman, R. M., W. C. Clark, and C. S. Holling. 1979. "The Dynamics of Resilience: Shifting Stability Domains in Fish and Insect Systems." In R. M. Anderson, B. D. Turner, and L. R. Taylor, eds., *Population Dynamics*, 321–41. Oxford: Blackwell.

Picket, S. A. 1976. "Succession, an Evolutionary Interpretation." *American Naturalist* 110: 107–19.

Prigogine, I. 1955. *Introduction to Thermodynamics of Irreversible Processes*. Springfield, Ill.: Thomas.

Prigogine, I., and R. Lefever. 1968. "Symmetry Breaking Instabilities in Dissipative Systems, II." *Journal of Chemical Physics* 48: 1695–1700.

Prigogine, I., and I. Stengers. 1979. *La nouvelle alliance*. Paris: Gallimard. Translated under the title *Order Out of Chaos*. 1984. New York: Bantam.

———. 1988. *Entre le temps et l'éternité*. Paris: Fayard.

Rousseau, J.-J. [1782] 1959. *Rêveries du promeneur solitaire*. In B. Gagnebin and M. Raymond, eds., *Oeuvres complètes*. Vol. 1. Paris: Pléiade.

Schrödinger, E. 1967. *What Is Life and Mind and Matter*. Cambridge: Cambridge University Press.

Serres, M. 1977. *La naissance de la physique dans le texte de Lucrèce*. Paris: Minuit.

Smith, J. M. 1982. *Evolution and the Theory of Games*. Cambridge: Cambridge University Press.

Smuts, J. [1926] 1961. *Holism and Evolution*. New York: Viking.

Spanner, D. C. 1964. *Introduction to Thermodynamics*. London: Academic Press.

Spencer, H. 1894. *First Principles*. 4th ed. New York: Appleton.

Tennekes, H., and J. J. Lumley. 1972. *A First Course in Turbulence*. Cambridge, Mass.: MIT Press.

Thom, R. 1980. *Paraboles et catastrophes*. Paris: Flammarion.

Treffers, B. 1995. *Een hemel op aarde: Extase in de Romeinse barok*. Nijmegen: SUN.

Walker, D., and R. West, eds. 1970. *The Vegetational History of the British Isles.* Cambridge: Cambridge University Press.

Whitehead, A. N. 1920. *Concept of Nature.* Cambridge: Cambridge University Press.

Wiltshire, D. 1979. *The Social and Political Thought of Herbert Spencer.* Oxford: Oxford University Press.

Winfree, A. T. 1974. "Rotating Chemical Reactions." *Scientific American,* June 1974, 82–95.

Worster, D. 1985. *Nature's Economy.* Cambridge: Cambridge University Press.

LAURENT THÉVENOT

Which Road to Follow? The Moral
Complexity of an "Equipped" Humanity

A séance where a number of people gathered around a table might suddenly, through some magic trick, see the table vanish from their midst, so that two persons sitting opposite each other were no longer separated but also entirely unrelated to each other by anything tangible . . . a world without things that are between those who have it in common, as a table is located between those who sit around it, a world with no in-between which relates and separates men at the same time.—Hannah Arendt

This essay concerns a "sociologie politique et morale," a political and moral sociology. It is about the way persons are evaluated as moral or political agents and the way things are caught up in such evaluations. We are familiar with the old problem of social ordering or with more recently explored ways of making entities more general, but how can we speak of political or moral evaluations? This is supposed to be a preserve of political and moral philosophers. But I want to tackle the issue with an orientation unusual among philosophers (with a few famous exceptions, including Arendt and Marx) and investigate the moral complexity that results from the "furniture" or "equipment" of humanity.

Much of this essay explores this question in an experimental mode—it is an experiment to see how objects might participate in the moral world. The experiment is actually a challenge, much like Raymond Queneau's *Exercices de style:* I limited myself to one kind of object, roads, and explored variations in the ways these are engaged and evaluated. This is not a fancy experiment. I took each of these numerous states of the road—and human beings—from one empirical case. In this experiment I consider how a road—a particular road in the French Pyrénées—comes to take up political and moral attributes and participate in the construction of some common good or more limited evaluation. And this is also an experiment in complexity, moral complexity—for it is going to turn out that the variations of the road shed light on a range of versions of commonality—and on other characterizations of goodness.

Although the chapter is in some sense a sociology of complex objects, it is also, and more fundamentally, a contribution to a sociology of complex *political and moral ordering.* Thus my fundamental concern is to make a new link between the notion of "the good" (whether from classical political philosophy or from the ordinary grammar of motives) and the notion of "the real" (realism as this is made in science, social science, and everyday encounters with reality). Durkheim made the link in terms of "norms" (the ideal was linked to frequency). Economics makes the connection by talking of "equilibrium." Parts of sociology and political philosophy create it by talking of "meaning" (that is a commonality of understanding demanded by interaction). This chapter makes a link, a new link, in terms of "engagement." Engagement with the world is first a reality test that depends on the way the agent captures the world within a certain type of format (publicly conventionalized, functional, familiar, etc.). But this formatting of a reality depends on a form of evaluation that singles out what is relevant. This evaluation refers to some kind of good, which might be a common good or the fulfillment of a planned action or an even more localized good, governing accommodation with a familiar environment.[1] This essay explores the composition among different moral orders and more local modes of evaluation as these are embodied in objects acknowledged within different regimes of pragmatic engagements with the world. This in turn leads to new insights into different models of activity: a kind of social action that is more collective than others insofar as it is prepared for public critique and justification, an individual and planned action as associated with intentional agents and a functional capture of the world, a familiar engagement as nonreflexive activity guided by embodied atunement with a domesticated and proximate environment.

UNPACKING THE BASIC TOOL KIT OF SOCIAL SCIENCE

A "sociologie politique et morale." Let's start with a warning: this phrase is potentially misleading. This is because it suggests a sociology *of* morals and politics, the study of group beliefs about what is right or legitimate.

54   Laurent Thévenot

This way of thinking fits with the sociological instinct, for sociologists are experts at making people's ideas transparent and unveiling the social interests and social laws that shape their ideas. Indeed French social science developed a series of sophisticated tools to do this in the 1970s (Crozier's "strategic behavior," Friedberg's "negotiated exchange," and Bourdieu's distinctive "habitus" and "unconscious strategies"). Researchers in SSK (the sociology of scientific knowledge) have made use of similar approaches to unmask the ideology of scientific epistemology.

However, the research that I have developed in collaboration with Luc Boltanski over a number of years goes in a different direction (Boltanski and Thévenot 1991). We wanted to account for the way actors place value on people and things in ways that appear to be more legitimate than others, without reducing these evaluations to other factors. The reason is that these evaluations play a central part in the way actors capture the activity of other actors (or of themselves) to coordinate their own conduct (a process that also takes place through conflicts). When sociologists disregard actors' evaluations as illusory or pure a posteriori reconstructions, they miss a significant part of what evaluation is oriented to: that is, coordination.

In this work on critique and justification we studied the relation between generality (which could be reduced to a cognitive necessity) and different kinds of common goods.[2] The tension between the collective and the particular is, of course, both a major preoccupation in everyday life and a crucial issue in social science. And necessarily so, because generalizations and reductions—which tend to become most visible in the critiques and justifications that emerge in the course of disputes—constitute the basic mechanism for making evaluations based on what is common, or communal. They *create* the link—always a matter of tension—between the general and the particular. It is true that some sociological approaches catch aspects of this tension. For instance, to study how "social order" or "common sense" is maintained is also to study ways in which the tension is resolved in favor of the general; conversely, studies of "social conflict" or "breaching experiments" show how what is shared may break down. So these studies are important, but they are also limited, tending to restrict tensions either to conflict between collectives, or, alternatively, to local breakdowns. Few have explored the full width and dynamics of these tensions.

This, then, is the point of our "sociologie politique et morale." Our aim has been to transform basic sociological categories by exploring justifications and critiques and the ways in which these make links among cognitive, moral, and material issues. Of course we have been helped in this work by a number of predecessors: Foucault's insights, in *The Order of Things*, on *epistemic* settings and cognitive operations such as "making similar"; ethnomethodological studies about the maintenance of common sense; Durkheim's and Mauss's version of the sociology of knowledge; and Mauss's concern with practice, which is still influential in Bourdieu's writing. But our aim has also been different because we have neither wanted to "contextualize" and localize collective claims nor directly connect them to "social structures" (even when these were embodied in "social practices" or *habitus*). Instead, our interest has been in the *operations* needed to move toward commonality and generality, together with their requirements and their failures.

POLITICAL AND MORAL ARTIFACTS: WHAT THEY ARE CONVENIENT FOR

How has this sociology of politics and morals developed? A little history and a little context are in order.

Moving from the construction and use of social categories to the larger problem of bringing together and making equivalences and generalities, my first interest was in what I thought of as "investments of form." These are procedures that treat people and objects in homogeneous ways across contexts (Thévenot 1984). For instance, statistical categories, job evaluation scales, or occupational names create *equivalences* between human beings while establishing norms of measurements, standards, or properties that make entities similar. An "investment in form" is costly and demands negotiation, but the cost may be offset by "returns" in coordination, which depend on the extension of the investment's domain within which it is accepted.

In this work cognition was linked to coordination. Objects and objectivity offer strong mediations in making this link. The argument runs so: different investments of forms generate different "forms of the probable," different constraints on what can be proved and offered as relevant evidence. For instance, statistical probability is quite different from evidence based on proximity to a prototype. But both rest in part on material evidence and the involvement of objects, even if what counts as relevant evidence is quite different in the two cases. Objects in series—one after the other—are needed for lawlike probability, whereas personalized and localized things are involved in the kind of plausibility that is anchored in proximity. And this is a crucial move. Coordination depends on cognition, but cognitive forms vary with the way in which people—and other entities too[3]—are treated. This observation leads us to explore different kinds of access to reality and realism.

So how do politics and morals enter the scene? The answer is that they do so if we elaborate on the notion of coordination. For we do not see coordination as a lawlike process mainly determined by forces, constraints, rules, dispositions, habitus, and all the rest. The undetermined, dynamic, and creative aspects of coordination arise instead from the operations of *evaluation,* which actors depend on for the conduct of their action and their selective access to reality. This is the point at which objects and objectivity get deeply connected with morals and politics. Luc Boltanski and I first investigated this connection at the level of the legitimate modes of evaluation involved in large-scale criticism and justification. And a central part of this process is "*qualification*": how people and things are treated and shaped to *qualify for* evaluation. Thus in the way in which we use the term, *qualification* builds a bridge between operations of *evaluation* and the realist conditions for an *effective engagement* with the world.

The connection between *evaluation* (with an orientation toward the good) and *realism* has been obscured by the historical construction of sociology on the model of the nomological sciences. Because the idea that objects and morals are intertwined seems to be something of a blind spot in social science, I want to make a short detour to talk about the eighteenth-century Natural Law theorists. In these writers we find that objects are treated as artificial "moral Entities" endowed with moral capacities. For instance Pufendorf writes: "We may define our moral Entities to be certain Modes superadded to natural Things and Motions by understanding Beings, chiefly for the guiding and tempering of the Freedom of voluntary Actions, and for the procuring of a decent Regularity in the Method of Life" (Pufendorf 1749, I,I,I,3).

In Pufendorf's way of thinking, a moral entity is more than a shared understanding, as it is in contemporary social sciences. Human beings "are endu'd with the Power of producing them [moral entities]," a power that "assigns them such and such Effects" (Pufendorf 1749, I,I,I,1): "Men likewise [Almighty God] were impowered to give a Force to their Inventions of the same Kind, by threatning some Inconvenience, which their Strength was able to make good against those who should not act conformably to them" (Pufendorf 1749, I,I,I,4).

Pufendorf identifies "modes of estimation" according to which "both Things and Persons may be rated and valu'd" (Pufendorf 1749, I,I,I,17). The latter render persons, things, and actions suitable to be "estimated" through a moral "quantity." *Estimation* is the key term here. Pufendorf is concerned to show how persons and things are estimated in similar ways, noting that the Latin word *valor* applies to both (Pufendorf 1749, I,I,I,17).[4] His suggestion is that the "moral quantity" of things relates to price, whereas the moral quantity of persons, their "Degree of the Rate and Value," is measured in terms of "Repute." But in each case the concern is similar. The reason for attaching a certain price to things is chiefly to *compare* them exactly in an *exchange* or a *transport* to someone else. In like manner esteem is used to settle the weight we accord to human beings, the ones relative to the others, and to rank them in a *convenient* order when they find themselves together, given that experience shows that it is impossible to treat them in the same way and not to set up any difference between persons (Pufendorf 1749, II,V,IV,1).

Estimation "frames" moral entities in certain "states" that "contain" them, states in which they perform their operations. These states take place in an artificial "space" devised by humankind, a space of linkages with other things that contribute to "hold and sustain" these states: "Hence a *State* may not improperly be defin'd a *moral Entity fram'd and taken up on Account of the Analogy it bears to Space.* And as *Space* seems no principal and original Being, but is devis'd, to be, as it were, *spread under* other Things, to hold and to sustain them in some particular Manner, so the several States were not introduc'd for their own Sakes, but to make a Field for *moral Persons* to exist in" (Pufendorf 1749, I,I,I,6).

From Legal Moral Beings to Qualifications in Everyday Disputes
So objects and people are jointly involved in the evaluations needed for coordination. Both have moral qualities, and each varies in value. But as

Pufendorf recognizes, this theorem sits uneasily with the idea of equality of human beings in a state of nature, as posited by Natural Law theorists. This concern with equality also features in everyday debates about justice and injustice. And the resolution of the tension between an order of evaluation and equal dignity among human beings lies at the very core of the common requirements met by the range of orders of worth used in these critical debates. In contrast to law theorists, we are also interested in how judgments are made in nonlegal arenas (Thévenot 1992). The kind of moral entities that are commonly used for the evaluations and rankings of everyday life depart in some ways from legal artifacts.[5] Four are particularly important.

1. *From* persona moralis composita *to configuration of the collective.* Pufendorf's construction rests on a theory of *covenant* as the mode of interaction and a theory of the *autonomy* of the *will* as the mode of human agency. The latter is fundamental to the arrangement of covenants. This means that his moral beings presuppose that events should be grasped through "individuals," "individual will," and "individual action." But if we need to question assumptions about the nature of the collective, then we also need to raise questions about the character of the individual and of action. Instead, we need to argue that individuals, wills, and actions, like moral qualities or quantities, are kinds of moral artifacts and that they work only by engaging in certain ways with the material world. For instance, the autonomous intentional individual is usually regarded as a prerequisite for moral agency. But it achieves such moral agency only with the support of other elements—the functional agency of objects— which together characterize a regime of engagement among others. In saying this, I do not aim to unmask the illusions of individual and intentional agency—something that often appeals to sociologists as they struggle with economics or legal theory. Rather I am interested in how this form of agency *works* and what it is *convenient for* (Thévenot 1990b).

2. *From legal enforcement to practical coordination.* This suggests the need for a second move away from Natural Law theory. Reflecting on the efficacy of moral beings, Pufendorf suggests that conformity results from *repressive force.* As such, it is a standard legal account of how qualities are enforced by law, and it also fits comfortably with the perspective of an absolutist state. But our approach to everyday morality needs to be broader, for our concern is not with law but with the various modes of

coordination in everyday disputes. This means that we need to forge conceptual tools that account for the dynamics of evaluation and re-evaluation and for the ways in which evaluations are put to some kind of reality test. What is at stake in everyday disputes is not the determination of actions by values. Instead there is a dynamic and creative process in which new and "qualified" persons and things are grasped. For instance, if we think of "moral quality" as "price," then this implies a particular mode of coordination that is neither war between states nor physical struggle (although violent contests are never far removed). Instead it has to do with general forms of evaluation. The argument, then, is that we will need to extend morality to cover all the standard forms of evaluation, whether or not these are commonly treated as "moral" matters.

3. *The coordinating capacities of qualified beings.* This suggests we need to move from Pufendorf in a third respect, from a focus on instruments of legal and state power and police to the conventions involved in every-day disputes and judgments, to what one might think of as the policing of everyday contests.[6] Enforcing conventions in everyday "policing" is clearly less constraining than enforcement based on a state monopoly of violence. But there are other differences too. First, unlike disputes within the legal arena, those in everyday life are not conventionally closed to the same extent. Second, everyday disputes and coordinations depend on more than the shared "conventions" of background knowledge, taken-for-granted assumptions, or reciprocal typifications that are put forward in *verstehende* or interpretive sociology. For (here are the objects again) the equipment of everyday discipline is largely supplied by the resistance offered by *qualified entities.* For instance, market coordination through price rests on a series of conventions (to do not only with money but also with the identity of the goods). It also, however, depends on the concrete ability to privatize objects, to take them away, to withhold them through private ownership. In short, it is not only that "possession is nine-tenths of the law." It is also a large part of economic coordination.

4. *The multiplicity of general qualifications.* So different objects—or objects that participate in social relations in different ways—may support distinct modes of coordination. But this suggests a final shift from Pufendorf. When he talks of "moral quality," he talks, as I noted above, of "price" for things and "esteem" for persons. But as I have tried to show in work with Luc Boltanski, this terminology is too restricted to account for

evaluations in contemporary disputes. Instead, there are a number of different modes of legitimate evaluation or "orders of worth."[7] Let me suggest a number of points about these orders of worth.

First, each implies a *different configuration of commonality,* which may or may not have to do with what sociologists think of as "social groups" or "communities." Thus, although it may be that "civic" or "domestic" worth and commonality relate to recognizable social collectivities (re-spectively social groups linked by solidarity and communities based on custom), the solidarity of "industrial worth" rests, quite differently, on standardized techniques and technologies; or, another example, the fame of the "worth of renown" depends on signs of recognition and the media that diffuse these.

Second, each links *judgments of worth* to *the common good* as it seeks to resolve the tension between justice based on equal dignity of human beings, on the one hand, and the ordering involved in evaluation, on the other. Not all forms of evaluation can be made compatible with common humanity. Several requirements are shared by all the legitimate orders of worth. A major requirement is the connection between worth and a common good. In other words, people thought to be more worthy are also supposed to sustain some sort of commonality and are taken, in one way or another, to be more "collective" than the less worthy.

Third, each attribution of worth is submitted to *critical evaluations.* Another major requirement for making compatible orders of worth and common humanity is the rejection of any permanent attribution of worth to persons, as would be the case with some kinds of status or innate properties. An order of worth cannot be built on IQ.[8] The attribu-tion of worth should always be open to question because of the risk that ordering raises with regard to common humanity. Stabilized character-izations are regarded as unjust insofar as the attribution of worth is not submitted to critical assessment relating to commonalities and common good. Prices, technical efficiency, reputation, fame, collective solidarity, inspiration—all of these are bases for assessing or denying worth. An-other source of critique comes from the conflicting relationships among different orders of worth. Each kind of worth aspires to a general exten-sion while seeking to reduce the others in *denunciations,* although they may also *compromise* and become compatible within certain limits.

Finally, qualification for worth needs to be *tested.* And this is the key connection between an evaluative orientation toward the good and a realist encounter with the world. Evaluative judgments, in the sense of these orders of worth, are not only *topoï* in rhetorics. They are put to tests involving tangible things. Things are made general and become relevant pieces of evidence in very different ways, depending on the orders of worth that specify the kind of agreement implied by objectivity.

THE REGIME OF PUBLIC CRITIQUE AND JUSTIFICATION: A PLURALITY OF WORTHY ROADS

So how do objects and their arrangements participate in the moral world?

The Somport tunnel was a proposal to build a highway through the Apse valley, one of the high valleys of the Pyrénées, continuing a tunnel through the mountains that separate France from Spain.[9] This is the object I will explore, an object of dispute, debate, and negotiation. And my exploration—and those disputes—is all about what counts, or should count, as a "good road" and what is the reality of such a road.

Aristotelians would argue that to talk of a road is to assume the idea of a good road in terms of *teleological functionality.* They would therefore reject any is/ought distinction (MacIntyre 1984, 58). But in what follows I want to account for a diversity of good roads. To be sure, a kind of teleological regime of *planned action* involves functional agency and intentional agency. Looked at in this way a good road is simply the proper device to allow the action of transportation. We shall return to such a regime in the next section. But disagreements about a fit and proper road raise other kinds of issues about the goodness of the road when conflicting claims aim at generalization. At such moments people involved in the dispute shift to a regime of justification that links goodness to legitimate orders of worth.

And this is precisely the situation for the Somport proposal. As the dispute unfolded, people found that they had to *allocate worth* (and not simply functional value) to the road. And this is where we meet the kind of "moral being" that has to qualify for worthiness. Within the *regime of justification* the evaluation of qualified entities involved many more entities than the object's functional agency and the intentional agency of the planner. Webs of connections with other entities were unfolded, and the grammars that governed these connections started to become clear. For to qualify or to disqualify the road, connections with other already qualified and less controversial beings were made. Entities were arranged and made coherent in terms of worth within different logics of evaluation. And those logics were, or so I will try to demonstrate, relatively constraining.[10] So what are those logics? What are those forms of evaluation? How were justifications made?

A Highway of Market Worth:
Opening Landlocked Areas to Market Competition
The road and tunnel were conceived and backed by the European Council as part of a policy for completing a transport infrastructure to create an "integrated market." The European commissioner responsible for regional policies argued that the decision to support the project underlined "the increasing importance of trans-frontier co-operation in the Community's policies. The tunnel will form part of the overall development of the Pau-Zarogossa region of the E07 motorway." General priorities included the following: to "integrate areas which are either landlocked or situated on the periphery of the Community" and to "reduce costs associated with transit traffic in co-operation with any non-member countries concerned." Once the tunnel was built, "heavy goods vehicles are expected to have their transit crossing cut by 40 minutes." These are the reasons the European Community offered partial funding for the project. It wanted to promote competition and free markets by improving transport. This is a *market qualification* for the road. It works by creating links with other beings that are also qualified in terms of their market worth: customers who make transactions (the moral human being is a customer when viewed in relation to the common good of market competition) and trucks that transport goods. Indeed, the road was designated by the EC as the "E07 Truck Road." The legitimate market connection with heavy and fast transportation results in the design of a road with three and possibly more lanes. The fact that this road is qualified for the market is not simply a matter of labeling or rhetoric: it has significant consequences for the reality of the road—in terms of its width, its gradients, and its potential traffic load.

Here is the conclusion: *a standard "market-qualified" entity is a marketable good or a service that supports evaluation by means of price,* as required for market coordination. For transport, market qualification leads to the division of the road into individual customer services—taking, for instance, the form of tolls. Some EC members questioned the market qualification of the road because it was not itself devised for market competitive procedures. It was intended to be a means of improving competition and lowering prices rather than itself being tested in the market.

A First Compromised Road: A Market-Industrial Infrastructure

Going in this direction, one would argue for a "compromised" road. I use the term *compromise* to mean an attempt to make compatible two (or more) orders of worth within the process of justification (Boltanski and Thévenot 1991). But compromises are not simply juxtaposed justifications. They become solid because they are built up and reinforced over time, being entrenched within material arrangements.[11] And it is because it takes the form of durable infrastructure and not a short-term renewable commodity that the road is a compromised being, meeting the requirements for worth not only in market but also in *industrial* terms.

An Investment of Industrial Worth:
An Efficient Infrastructure for the Future

When they are pushed hard, market and industrial qualifications stand in sharp contrast to one another. They may, for instance, denounce each other in terms of time. Whereas market worth is short-term or even timeless in its pure form, industrial worth is deeply time-oriented. Thus the planners concerned by industrial efficiency conceived the road and tunnel in terms of an infrastructure for the future ("the future needs infrastructure"). This means that investment is a major qualified being or good in a regime of "industrial worth." Technical efficiency is thus connected to a common good through the textures of time and space. Time is future oriented and the increase in industrial worth takes the form of "progress" and "upgrading": "the *upgrading* of the previous road to a section of the European E07 trunk road is intended to provide a *modern* link between Bordeaux and Toulouse on the one side and . . ." To be worthy, an industrial entity is thus one that builds for the future, making planning possible because it will function reliably. Thus "industrial" space is Cartesian and homogeneous. The spatial infrastructure of modern highways is a condition for a territorial homogeneity that has to be achieved despite natural obstacles. And this spatial homogeneity is also secured by standardization, which means that a good industrial road should be both durable and consistent with the design standards for high-quality roads— for instance with gentle curves, gradients, and signposts.

A Second Compromised Road: A Market-Domestic
Way of Communication That Remains Local and Dominated
The market qualification of the road is promoted "from above," by Brussels and its regulations, rather than "from below," by being tested in a decentralized market. However, local actors also use market qualification to support the road and its tunnel, often adopting a *market-domestic* compromise encapsulated in the term *local trades,* which departs from the terms of the European Community integrated market.

Local marketable goods and services primarily have to do with tourism and recreation. I shall return to the complex of potential justifications enclosed in "tourist" identification later. Market worth is clearly one of them: to be qualified for a market, natural areas have to be shaped as "tourist sites." A road is thus an access to tourist sites and part of the arrangement needed to qualify these sites in terms of market worth as an "asset" made out of nature ("capital nature"): "Thanks to the road, the value of tourist activities will be raised because of improved access to the sites."

However, within this market-domestic compromise the road is not an axis for increasing trade (as Brussels wishes) but offers access for local trade and tourist sites. Indeed the locals reject a "truck corridor" (as proposed by the pan-European market argument) and favor a road going to and ending within the valley: a way of entering rather than passing through it. A nicely crafted formula says, "There is a need for a transport network that will remain *in our locale* and which we will therefore be able to dominate (*maîtriserons*)."

A pure market road, a *superhighway,* would undermine rather than contribute to the local tourist trade: "At present the tourist industry is completely integrated into the site and it will suffer from the proximity of a high traffic transit route."

Locals cite the example of the valley of Maurienne, where a small road was connected by tunnel to Italy and the whole valley became exactly the kind of "traffic corridor" that they fear. The road cuts through historic old towns, and the volume of traffic and the frequency of accidents have forced people to leave their homes. Supporters of the market-domestic compromise urge a road that will foster *échanges de proximité* (local interaction), including improved contact with the trades and services of the local town below the valley. One of them mentions the need for such a road if the Aspe bachelors are to find and keep wives: "wives should be able to go [to] town, to a restaurant or the movies, within a half an hour drive and this means improving the present road." This tells us that the compromised road is not simply a form of words. Its material crafting is just as important if it is to withstand a reality test. It should have short three-lane sections to allow overtaking without being a full three-lane highway that would attract heavy traffic.

A Road of Domestic Worth: A Customary Way of Integrating Locals
This compromise leads us to what we might call the *domestic* worth of trust. In contrast with the future-orientation of *industrial* time, *domestic* time is oriented toward the values of the past and its precedents. It relates to and generalizes habitual linkages and customary practices to make a form of trust that is transportable and transitive. If industrial space is Cartesian or generic, mapped out by coordinates, then domestic space is polar, raising proximity and neighborhood into virtues. It is being anchored in a locale, as much as temporal linking, that offers a bedrock for trust. A well-worn path is one of the most basic features of domestic topography, for worth is gained gradually. So the domestic road preserves and consolidates the trails left by customary commerce within an environment. But local and temporal commitments need to be generalized if they are to escape the space of a specific community and be connected to a general common good. This means that the compromise market-domestic road is a delicate balance, which can be split if the test of domestic worth is pushed too far. A local politician declared, "With the Somport case, the McDonaldization of France has reached the front door of Bearn."

A Famous Scenic Route of Worthy Renown
The qualification of people and things through *renown* or opinion is another legitimate order of worth. Entities are shaped in this order as

signs or *symbols*. For instance, roads become material arrangements that render nature *visible* and recognizable. As sight-seeing mechanisms they offer standpoints that present and repeatedly represent distant panoramas, thereby framing nature as landscape. In the Impact Survey of the project we find this: "The road has strong tourist appeal. It offers travellers the opportunity to discover the landscape and, as such, is an asset to the valley." Like the previous qualifications, this is not reduced to a subjective point of view. To be qualified, the road has itself to be "integrated" into the landscape. This involves constraints on its design: "Because of its modest size, the road has been integrated for years into the site and is unobtrusive. Together with the villages and the hamlets, it is the best location for discovering the landscape of the valley." In France we do not talk of "scenic routes" but of "picturesque roads." The term is more inclusive. Qualification refers not only to natural features but also to a landscape of domesticated, cultivated, and inhabited nature.

Following the Route through Other Qualifications:
Civic Accesses, Inspired Ways, Green Paths
I want to conclude this section by touching briefly on two further orders of worth. *Civic* worth is oriented toward general interest, equality, and solidarity among citizens. In this the road is crucial because it creates a basic territorial equivalence among citizens. Such a civic organization of a space of equivalence among citizens extends the revolutionary desire to build a uniform territory by means of legal categories. Compromised with industrial worth in a slogan about *aménagement du territoire* (improvement of territory), it is still a primary justification for road building in France. Weakness in transport infrastructure is denounced in terms of civic worth.

I will not say much about the worth of *inspiration,* although the "path" (whether good or evil) is central to revelation in ways that are not simply metaphorical.[12] Trails and paths are also qualified ways of experiencing the *green* worth of an environment, a primary way of integrating human beings into their environment.[13] But paved roads—and, still more, motorways—are poor candidates for green routes. Instead they are denounced for cutting wildlife trails and migration routes. The response takes the form of compromised green roads: the industrial design includes an additional set of roads for wildlife in the form of bridges and tunnels.

Many have been introduced for frogs, and the Aspe road project includes a "bear-duct," so called by its opponents who named it after aqueducts.

The *green* denunciation of the *market* and *industrial* roads is itself denounced on the grounds of "local development," a compromised common good bringing together *market, industrial,* and *domestic* forms of worth. Thus the decision of the socialist Ministry of Environment to block the construction of the Somport tunnel was criticized by local officials who said that "wider economic concerns were being sacrificed for limited ecological gains." Critics suggested a test using an industrial form of evidence. Another local politician protested that the tunnel would have taken only 3,580 square yards from a total national park area of 370,000 acres. He said, "Under this pretext, they are ready to sacrifice a whole region."

BOUNDED EVALUATIONS AND LOCAL REGIMES OF
ENGAGEMENT: OTHER KINDS OF CONVENIENT ROADS

I have talked about a number of orders of worth and the character of their justifications: market, industrial, civic, domestic, renown or opinion, and inspiration. I have also considered the ways in which human beings and objects achieve moral or political qualification, either within specific orders of worth or in more complex and "compromised" systems where orders of worth are juxtaposed.

In this section I consider the ways in which different kinds of *agency* and capacity are attributed to human and nonhuman entities in what I call *pragmatic regimes of engagement*.[14] My object is to take the notion of agency beyond the regime of justification so far discussed and focus on the different ways human beings *engage with* their environments of artifice or nature. Thus the notion of "pragmatic regime" would include the collective modes of coordination governed by orders of worth but would also cover other kinds of engagements that are approached in one way or another by social scientists in terms of "action," "practice," and "habit." However, my focus is not so much on the human motor for action as on the *dynamics of disagreement and agreement* with the environment. The idea is that these dynamics rest on different forms of "*convenience,*" a notion that implies both a form of evaluation and a format within which the environment is captured in order to fit evaluation. I will situate the character of human *agency* within this larger framework.[15] Therefore, our inquiry into the moral complexity of equipped humanity proceeds by exploring more limited local or personal evaluations.

Different Forms of Agency Related to Modes of "Convenience"
Conventional forms of qualification that derive from worthiness differ from more local evaluations that support other pragmatic regimes of convenience (Thévenot 1990b, 2001). The regime of justification is very demanding with respect to moral infrastructure and emotional involvement (Thévenot 1995c). Fortunately, we only need to attend to such a regime when the engagement is open to public critique.[16] Instead, for more limited coordination we interact with others through more bounded engagements. I shall now introduce an architecture that suggests the way this public regime of justification rests on two regimes of more local engagements: a regime of *planned action* and a regime of *familiarity* that governs proximate accommodation and does not require the kind of strong intentional and autonomous agency attributed in planned action. I will try to cope with the challenge of continuing to illustrate these regimes with new variations of the activity of transportation, of its material support (road, path, track, etc.), and of the kind of human agency involved in each regime.[17]

*The Regime of Justification: A Joint Characterization of Human and
Nonhuman Beings with Conventionalized Capacities* (Qualified Roads)
In the regime of justification human and nonhuman beings are qualified together as conventional moral beings. Thus a *market road* supports human beings qualified as customers who seek to make market relations, facilitating relations between customers and goods that qualify as transactions. An *industrial road* is an efficient infrastructure designed by long-term planners and engineers and competently utilized by professional drivers with reliable vehicles. A *domestic road* is customarily used by locals and other domestic beings, including cattle. A *civic road* is a potential vehicle for equality and solidarity among citizens, in spite of territorial inequalities.

The attempt to qualify or to extend *qualification* links an entity of questionable worthiness with others that are less controversial—although the link itself needs to be qualified and made congruent with an order of worth. Although the discursive verbal expression of the link often takes the form of a verb, the web of connections between entities is more like a network than a narrative sequence, the kind of elementary link being highly constrained by the "order of worth." But what does all this imply for human beings?

Because humans hold a unique position in the process of evaluation, at first sight there is radical asymmetry between humans and other beings. This leads to a second asymmetry: as I noted earlier, the foundation for the construction of a common good is always a "common humanity." This feature is common to the different orders of worth and a common reference point for the sense of justice that sustains them—as is visible when it is challenged by orders of value restricting commonality (as in racism) or extending it (as in certain versions of ecology).

So there is asymmetry between humans and other beings, but closer examination suggests that their joint qualification renders them more similar. Within the regime of justification, the qualification of human being depends on specific ways of engaging objects that are supposed to be beneficial for everyone. Depending so strongly on qualified objects, human beings are themselves *objectified*. This is why worthy people tend to look rigid, "conventional" (in the everyday sense), when they are forced to show their worth, seeming somewhat inhuman when they behave as professional expert, optimizing consumer, grandee, or famous star.

Social scientists use dramaturgical vocabularies (theater, stage, role, play) to capture this rigidity. In doing so they fail to catch the realist involvement of objects that contribute to the maintenance of qualified beings. They reduce the conventional aspect of qualifications to some kind of stage illusion.[18] But conventions also determine the relevance of evidence in public critique and justification. They offer the articulations of a shared sense of objectivity. In that sense conventions are not opposed to facts; both form part of the reality test involved in the collective creation of "forms of the probable." Thus, the technically designed road is a prerequisite for exercise of professional worth in driving; appropriate charges on a toll road are needed if consumer worth is to be performed in buying the right service.

I would like to go one step further: Orders of worth are moral artifacts (one could even call them "political" because of their level of commonality) that bring questions about unjust power into some kind of systematic relationship between human and nonhuman beings, because this relation creates asymmetries of capacities among common humanity. This questioning in terms of justice is prepared by the generalization of some of the ways human beings similarly engage with their "equipped environment." To situate and clarify this process of making public a contest about power abuse, we need to explore more bounded or personal ways of engaging things that do not presuppose such an aggrandizement (*montée en généralité*) of the good. More basic human attachments to the environment, through the accommodation with used and accustomed things and familiar acquaintances or through normal action with objects, are the grounds for the constitution of more public or civil kinds of political and moral agency. Politics and morals of formal human rights and democratic procedures are built in ignorance of these more basic engagements and evaluations. Therefore, they risk fostering mechanisms of exclusion and domination.

The Regime of Familiar Engagement: A Personality Distributed on
Her/His Accommodated Surroundings (A Personal Track)
The exploration of a regime of familiarity is needed to resist the idea that the basic level of human relation to the world rests on individual and autonomous agency—the kind of agency that is assumed in the attribution of interest, intention, and responsibility. By contrast, the sort of human agency that is involved in familiar engagements with a world of proximity depends on numerous idiosyncratic linkages with a customized environment. The familiar handling of used things departs from normal functions or conventional prescriptions. Such dynamics of engagement have nothing to do with conventional forms of judgment or the subject/object divisions implied by normal planned action. They have instead to do with perceptual and kinesthetic clues about familiar and customized "paths" through local environments that involve modifying the surroundings as well as the habits of the human body. Personalized and localized usage composes a habitat as much as it constitutes a personality. Let's call "personality" the kind of agency that is made out of all these accommodations with familiar beings. Such agency is distributed widely through a person's surroundings. The kind of good that governs this cautious handling of human characters and specified things

is not the fulfillment of planned normal action but rather has to do with taking good *care* of this *accommodation*. The proper language to offer accounts of what happens is far from the formal statements offering justifications. It is highly indexical and gestural (Bréviglieri 1997).

The difference between a path and a conventional road appropriately illustrates this mode of engagement between a personalized being and his/her familiar surrounding. A shepherd from the Vallée d'Aspe raises such a familiar engagement and the kind of path and cautious human agency that goes with it, against the plan to build a functional road up to the pastures, although the right to use this road is planned to be restricted to shepherds. The phrase "path dependency" designates, as a general category, a kind of creative learning marked by strong dependence on specific historical conditions and circumstances. The path is a configuration with neither a strong individual intentional nor objective instrumental agency, a primitive figure for familiar commerce with the surroundings. Neither designed nor planned as a functional instrument, the path emerges as a nonintentional result of the acquaintance of human beings with a milieu of human and nonhuman beings. This path is created through habitual frequenting as much as physical topography. Indeed it may simply reflect a pattern of wandering and go nowhere, like a sheep track: if you treat it as a material support to achieve a goal, you are likely to end in a cul-de-sac.

The wandering path is Heidegger's favorite one when he seeks to relativize the subjective being (1962). Sartre, inspired by a phenomenological lineage leading to Merleau-Ponty, tries to capture the notion of familiarity by talking of *entour,* in the sense of close surroundings. But he stays within the vocabulary of intentional action and "project" when he considers failures, although they should bring to light the dynamics of the regime. When Sartre talks of the "unexpected phenomenon" that stops his "project" of bicycling to the next town, he attributes the failure to commonly identified objects: a punctured tire, the fact that the sun is too hot, or the wind blows in his face (Sartre 1956 [1943]). But if I fall while riding on a familiar path, it is difficult to point a finger and blame the irregularity of the road, the wear and tear on the bike, or even a lack of technical competence.

This regime of familiarity is not an archaic way of engaging with the world. Any driver or pedestrian familiar with a modern road "customizes" it in ways that may have nothing to do with the normal action of transportation, and any part of the environment, even highly technical, may be treated in the same way. In such highly localized and diffused familiar arrangements, one cannot attribute failures to specific items, for responsibility is itself widely distributed across the personalities and their personalized surrounding (Thévenot 1994a).[19]

The Regime of Regular Planned Action: Intentional Human Agency and Functional Objects (the Road as a Means to an End)
On the other hand, a road may be planned and deliberately built. Indeed, a road is a paradigmatic case of implementing intentions, a material means for reaching a goal: a "road to follow." Coordination among human beings who do not know one another is impossible if each personality follows his or her own path—or uses roads in a completely idiosyncratic manner. Thus roads (like other commonly identified objects) support the complementary functional agency of allowing normal action from nonpersonalized individuals. Coordination of subjects within a regime of intentional action relies on the separation of subjects and objects in conformity with the classical notion of action. But the capture of objects in a functional format is as much needed as the intentional agency attributed to human beings.

By contrast with the kind of good "care" that governs the regime of familiarity and the conventionalized qualifications that govern the regime of justification, adjustment within regimes of intentional action has to do with successfully achieving regular action. The basic structure of language—with its casual grammar of subjects, verbs of action, and objects—is appropriate for accounts in this regime. It exhibits broad tolerance about the way in which they are defined. A road is a tool for going from one place to another. That is the end of the story. But what happens if shepherds use the highway for their cattle? What if tourists use off-road vehicles on unpaved roads intended only for shepherds to go to their mountain pastures and so to limit the impact on wildlife? When the arguments start, the toleration found within the regime of intentional action is no longer acceptable. The issue has to be settled by talking of conventional qualification and shifts into the regime of justification.

Whereas the familiarity regime fails to attribute responsibility, the regime of regular planned action sustains the individual intentional agency needed for this attribution. The figure of a subject who supports projects and contracts is presupposed by contemporary management and welfare policies. But how are intentions imputed? How are planned actions identified? The answer is—partly in material form.

Examples abound, but this is particularly clear in psychiatry, where, if intentions are unclear, they can sometimes be attributed by detecting regular paths or movements. For instance, in autism observers find it difficult to attribute intentions to the patient. Therapist Fernand Deligny developed a method using graphs rather than language to capture the erratic but "customized" wanderings of those who are autistic. In one of the institutions influenced by Deligny, therapists departed from this recording of idiosyncratic paths and tried to capture the activities of persons who suffer autism in the format of regular planned action. In their view this strategy was needed to coordinate and monitor the interaction of sufferers with nonautistic people (Barthélémy 1990). The idea was to make patterns of regular action, and therefore intentions, explicit by placing regular tools for different actions (picking up food or washing dishes) in separate areas. The visibility of the movements between these areas and the distant instruments meant that it is possible to impute functional and intentional agency—and so to treat persons with autism through their attachments to context.

CONCLUSION: WHAT KIND OF MORAL COMPLEXITY?

I have introduced a diversity of basic human agencies and ways of engaging with the world by focusing on the variation in one kind of material environment: roads. Drawing on the same empirical corpus, I could have introduced more complicated sequential moves involving, for instance, composite strategic plans. John Law has clarified the way material forms support strategies and make possible the "storage" of power (Law 1991). The understanding of this material support of human agency modifies our idea of power and the critical appraisal of power abuse. The classical example that brings us back to transportation devices is the Long Island Parkway, which Langdon Winner uses to illustrate the "politics of artefacts": a low bridge discourages the public transit of black and poor people (Winner 1980). In the case I have looked at here, we find a road that apparently meets a "green qualification" but can also be denounced as hiding a strategic plan that eventually will disregard this qualification. The road has three lanes and therefore escapes the critical four lanes denounced as a high-traffic or "truck" highway. In addition, it is bordered by a bicycle path on each side. However, opponents argue that within this apparently "green" road a strategic plan to enlarge it will be easy to carry out because of the existence of the two bicycle paths.

But how precisely does this attention paid to the material environment of human agency modify our perspective on issues having to do with morality? Bruno Latour has identified how technical objects compensate for the moral failings of human beings and has pointed amusingly to the way moral rules are "inscribed" in safety belts or hotel key rings (Latour 1993a, 1993b). What difference does such inscription make? Will a symmetrical treatment of human and nonhuman beings, and the conception of their relationship as a network, lead us to get rid of the notion of responsibility, a central category in moral issues? John Law rightly observes that liberal political and moral philosophy proposes a figure of the human being that presupposes a series of assumptions about self-interest, language use, or autonomy with respect to his or her surroundings (Law 1998). Following disabled rights activists who denounce discriminatory environments, Law notes that "many, perhaps most, disabled people are substantially disenfranchised in liberal democracies." Technical equipment installed in a portable computer and mounted on a wheelchair might "render them autonomous in certain important respects, and thereby allows them to exercise discretion." Does this mean that this individual and autonomous agency is the only way to raise moral issues, as it is assumed in a broad liberal tradition?

The Moral Questioning of Human Attachments to Nature and Artifacts
In this essay I have outlined a political and moral sociology that aims to capture the complexity of evaluative "formats." This is a sociology of the ways people, but also objects, are caught up in evaluations through their joint involvement in different kinds of engagements. The identification of the nonhuman equipment of our human relations strongly alters our view on moral issues although it does not necessarily undermine the centrality of a reference to common humanity. We are not simply led to integrate a material world into forms of moral questioning that are too often restricted to human relations. This is because it is also possible to

reverse this program and consider how moral or political categories are built to deal with the *attachments* of human beings to their natural and artifactual environments. Human beings clearly take advantage of a diversity of modes of attachment in order to enlarge their capacities. The track is a primitive example of this enlargement, which is not even specific to human beings but also available to other animals. But what is specific to humanity is the way these enlargements of capacities confront the basic assumption of a common humanity. The best place to see this confrontation is in the way human beings *coordinate* their behavior (even in agonistic terms). Among human beings coordination rests on the connection between human behavior and the orientation toward some kind of *good* that delimits the relevant *reality* to be taken into account. This is the way we monitor our own conduct, and this is the way we capture that of others.

But the notions of good that have been elaborated to make sense *and reality* of human conducts are quite diverse, depending on the way attachments to the environment are handled and evaluated. I have argued that "the good" and "the real" are linked together in a variety of ways within what I have called pragmatic regimes of engagement. The argument is that people—but also things—are evaluated through their involvement in different modes of activity and that *evaluation* and the *realist* conditions for an *effective engagement* with the world necessarily go together. The analysis that I have developed in this essay has a number of implications. One is that notions of agency, action, and practice need to be reexamined within the context of these different pragmatic regimes: different regimes imply very different notions of activity. A second, as I have just noted, is that the access to, and capture of, the world—the realist condition of activity—depend on the delineation of some kind of good. The distinction between realism and evaluation is much tighter than is commonly imagined in the social sciences. A third is that objects and people are caught up and evaluated—that is, "engaged"—in a world of multiple regimes.

What Kind of Complexity?
So what kind of complexity of the good *and* the real that are jointly engaged does this framework highlight? First, I want to insist on a sort of "vertical" complexity. At the basic level, within the regime of familiar

engagement, the scope of evaluation is quite local. A local good governs proximate accommodation with circumstances and the environment, and it does not involve individual or autonomous agency at all. However, this localized and personalized shaping of attachment does not lie outside moral and political questioning. Familiar engagements sustain the reality and the good of personal usages. They constitute a habitat, a home, that supports the capacity of a human *personality.* The language of rights usually presupposes a more generalized and detached figure of *individual* agency that corresponds to the regime of planned action. But this upper level collapses if it is not built on the prior maintenance of a personality. The claim for a fundamental right to housing points to this priority, but, again, one should realize that the artifacts of law are usually erected at the level of individual agency and largely ignore the prerequisite of this agency. When law integrates more familiar engagements, it presupposes their transformation into collectivized "customs." In the regime of planned action, which has to do with successfully achieving regular action, some other definition of "the good" is involved, which is linked both to the human agency of a subject intending a project and to the objective separation of objects that are captured through their function, that is, their capacity to support the project. No more erring tracks and paths, no more personalities, but regular roads for regular transport and the separation of human individual and autonomous subjects.

In the regime of justification the confrontation between enabling attachments to the environment and common humanity is more demanding in terms of the common dignity of human beings. Actually, the enlargement of the scope of the evaluation results from the fact that certain modes of attachment have been widely generalized and offer the possibility of equivalence. This is typically induced by standard artifacts or new standard links with things (in terms of information exchange, for example). Equivalence opens up the possibility of measuring unequal capacities and creates a tension with an orientation toward equal human dignity. It raises issues of injustice and power abuse. Evaluations in terms of legitimate orders of worth have been specifically elaborated to deal with this tension. Different orders of worth are ways in which the *furnishing* of the world is integrated with common humanity. Each mode of integration links human and other beings in its own specific way, and each implies a specific form of human ability or capacity, which may be unequally distributed. Thus the bond generalized in private ownership and the sale of goods is not like that based on habit and precedent that guarantees trust. And the two differ from bonds that rest on visibility and the common identification of signs or on the chains through which living creatures depend on one another. "Green" critiques or justifications are not new insofar as they integrate nonhuman beings into evaluations but rather because they rest on a different kind of generalized linkage.[20] Each of these orders of worth that govern critiques and justifications shapes its own way in which humans and human dignity properly link to and depend on natural or artificial objects—in what we might think of as a "compound humanity."

The plurality of orders of worth introduces another sort of "horizontal" complexity, one I have studied with Luc Boltanski. Each of the general *justifications*—and I have mentioned a number of these, including the *industrial*, the *market*, the *civic*, and the *domestic*—has its own measure of "the good," its own general order of worth. Because there are a number of different orders of justification, the people and the objects they discover or presuppose are also caught up in *compromise:* thus the road that I discussed above embeds and presupposes not one but several such justifications or versions of the good. Responding to the reproach that we ignore the fact that "impure" arrangements are more powerful than "pure" ones (Law 1991, 173; Law and Mol 1995, 285), I would say that coherent qualification is required in the movement of critique, whereas compromises are constantly arranged to organize complexity.[21]

Which Approach to Responsibility?
The attribution of responsibility takes place in such a movement of critique. Therefore, it requires the delineation of a kind of good. At the level of familiar acquaintance, the careful attention to being attuned to one's surroundings does not allow a strict allocation of capacities and responsibilities—in the classical sense—among human or other entities. Careless handling is not necessarily the result of deliberate intention; it ordinarily results from the lack of accommodation with the peculiarities of a particular human and nonhuman environment. At the other end, the construction of moral beings through the qualifications and moral artifacts of the regime of justification means that it is possible to ascribe responsibility and achieve general agreement in ways compatible with an idea of

a common humanity. This is not the case for the regime of planned action, which is mainly designed to detach human agents from objects in their environment and treat each of them as the proper source of responsibility for failure. The difference means that morality crafted in terms of worthiness is quite different from the individual agency of autonomous actors presupposed in most studies.

From these variations of the notion of responsibility, one can see that the identification of regimes of engagement does not contribute to the relativization of the notion nor to its distribution among a network of connected entities. The idea is rather to differentiate among the ways human attachments to the environment are submitted to critical evaluation, without being limited by a simple dichotomy between public and private.

EPILOGUE

Having said this, let me end with a story. It is a story that reveals the complex ways in which people shift between different pragmatic regimes and moral treatments of their attachments to the world.

Jean Labarère is a shepherd. He is not the biblical shepherd who "maketh me to lie down in green pastures," "leadeth me beside the still waters," and "restoreth my soul" (Psalm 23). Neither, like the ancient shepherd, does he set the wilderness against the civilization of the city. Instead, he is a contemporary shepherd with complex relations to nature. Although he lives for much of the year in the wilderness and is one of the few people who might actually meet a Pyrenean bear, the way he lives is also technological—indeed one might say technicized. In the high pastures where he lives with his flock for several months a year and produces cheese, his home is a rather comfortable cabin with modern domestic appliances and a solar-powered radio-telephone. Indeed, some of his equipment and his food arrives not by traditional mules climbing on steep trails but by helicopter.

What kind of bizarre hybrid shepherd is he? And here is the paradox: he has all his state-of-the-art equipment because of those archaic and nonhuman creatures, the bears. He is funded and sponsored by a voluntary association, whose charter seeks to promote harmonious "cohabitation" and to "let shepherds and bears live together in the Pyrenees."

Pyrenean bears, the "last of their kind," are "endangered by new roads." Helicopters and radio-telephones spare the construction of roads. The justification or the test is that of green worth: as a member of the association puts it, "The bear is an *integrator*. We cannot care for bears without taking care of the forest and the pastures, for the bears are demanding. They are very demanding about the quality of their habitat. If you want to protect bears then you always have to care for the whole mountain environment." The aim is to avoid both a "human reservation—like an Indian reserve"—and a zoo for bears.

But Jean Labarère is something more, for he is also inspired by nature. He is a shepherd-poet celebrating the mountains, "stone giants, clothed in red, who, since eternity, have looked at one another as if a couple in love." And he has also written a poem to honor his sheepdog. In this poem he extends the moral vocabulary of selfless love—the regime of agape described by Luc Boltanski (1990)—to domesticated animals. For the poem tells a true story about the legendary stray sheep, a "foolhardy ewe" who left the paths of the flock and moved toward the steep precipice. But the dog was watching and quickly joined the sheep:

Mes que cadon tots dus, era aulha e eth can.
Qu'entenoi eth truquet trebucar ua lia,
Eth men can que hamà, eth son darrèr hamet.
Tà deth qu'èra eth son darrèr dia,
Que pensarèi a tu qu'èras un bon canhet.
Si ès partit aciu haut rejuénher quauqua estela,
Que sèi qu'averàs causit "l'Etoile du Berger."
E s'i as rencontrat aquera praube oelha,
Que l'as de perdonar, tu mon brave canhet. (Labarère 1994)[22]

NOTES

The first version of this essay, "A Paved Road to Civilised Beings? Moral Treatments of the Human Attachments to Creatures of Nature and Artifice," was presented at the presidential plenary "Relating Nature, Objects, and the Social Challenges of a Knowledge Society" at the joint meeting of the European Association for the Study of Science and Technology and the Society for the Social Studies of Science, Bielefeld, October 10–14, 1996. I am grateful to Karin Knorr for her invitation and for further stimulating conversations with her. Peter Meyers was a strong help in the English formulation of my statement, both as an English-speaking native and as a colleague with whom I enjoy regular discussions. Later presentations at the Institute of French Studies, New York University (1997), and at the Sociology Department of the University of California Berkeley (1998) helped me to refine it. I especially thank Ann Swidler and Craig Calhoun for their valuable comments. I am extremely grateful to John Law for his patient and enduring efforts to shape the previous version of this paper into its present form. He is obviously not responsible for the limits of this enterprise.

1. In French the word *engagement* works still better because the notion of both material and moral engagements is highly developed. The key is "engaged" in the lock, just as two parties are "engaged" in a contract (and not just when they are married).

2. Boltanski and Thévenot (1991, in translation at Princeton University Press). For an introduction in English, see Boltanski and Thévenot (1999); for a short presentation of this turn and of the collective research that sustains it see Thévenot (1995a). For a discussion of this trend and its more recent extensions see Wagner (1999); for a comparison with Callon's and Latour's framework and a contrast with Bourdieu's, see Bénatouïl (1999).

3. This concern with the involvement of "nonhuman" beings has been influenced by the research program at the Centre de Sociologie de l'Innovation at the Ecole Nationale Supérieure des Mines de Paris (Callon and Latour 1981). However, the connection with morals is quite different, as will become clear in what follows.

4. Barbeyrac adds, in his earlier French translation, that the French word *valeur* "never applies to persons in order to indicate the esteem they are given" (Pufendorf [1771] 1989, III,21). This observation is no longer valid. I thank Abbigail Saguy for having made available to me the English translation of Pufendorf's *The Laws of Nature and Nation.*

5. Or "fictions" or "fable," as Pufendorf says, and Locke, following him. See Locke, *The Second Treatise of Government* ([1690] 1966).

6. On "Convention theory," which has informed a whole series of French studies in socioeconomics, see "L'economie des conventions" (1989), Orléan (1994). For English reviews of this literature, see Wagner (1994), Wilkinson (1997).

7. In *On Justification* Boltanski and I brought together two types of texts. On the one hand, we looked at some of the classics of political philosophy that we treated as works by *grammarians of the political bond* seeking discursive solutions to the problem of agreement: Augustine, Bossuet, Hobbes, Rousseau, Smith, Saint-Simon. On the other hand, we considered a series of contemporary handbooks or guides to good behavior.

8. Alexis Carrel tried to build the common good of a *cité eugénique;* see Thévenot 1990a.

9. The French survey of this conflict was done with the collaboration of Marie-Noël Godet and Claudette Lafaye. For a more complete analysis in French, see Thévenot (1996a, 1996b). This survey was continued by a comparative one, conducted with

Michael Moody, focusing on a conflict raised by the project of a dam in a California Sierra river. This comparative survey took place in a more general four-year program of comparative research on forms of justification and repertoires of evaluation in France and the United States. Michèle Lamont and Laurent Thévenot were responsible for this project; see Lamont and Thévenot (2000). On the comparison of the two environmental conflicts and differences between French and U.S. politics, see Moody and Thévenot (2000); Thévenot and Lamont (2000); Thévenot, Moody, and Lafaye (2000).

10. Here we differ from actor-network theory insofar as we focus on the coherence required by the critical testing of arrangements, the critical tensions raised by composite arrangements, and the kind of compromising needed to make different orders of qualification compatible. We view organizations as devised for such compromises. For an approach of the incoherence of organization with respect to different "ontological regimes," see Law (1996).

11. One might fruitfully parallel this notion of compromise, and compromised device, with the concept of "boundary object" (Fujimura 1992; Star and Griesemer 1989). The focus on "translation" also highlights the role played by such intermediaries (Callon and Law 1989).

12. Revelation is the crucial test here. For instance, Rousseau experiences a kind of "road to Damascus" event when he sees the light on the road to Vincennes and finds the inspiration to write his *Discours sur les sciences et les arts.*

13. The path consolidates wildlife trails, although Simmel noted that the animal "does not create the miracle of the path, i.e., coagulate the movement into a solid structure which gets beyond him" (Simmel 1988).

14. This introduces the part of my research agenda that followed the work on justification with Luc Boltanski.

15. The different kinds of agency (*agence*) that I tried to identify are not reducible to a distinction between human and nonhuman entities. The common use of the term (which offers in French the relational *agencement*) unfortunately points to the first pole of the opposition active/passive. By contrast, I want to encompass both these poles in a range of characterizations of the way entities are engaged. For a subtle analysis of the "ontologies of organisms and machines" in experimental arenas and of different "epistemic practices," see Knorr-Cetina (1995, 1999). For stimulating proposals about "material agency" and a comprehensive discussion of this issue (including the "Epistemological Chicken" debate initiated by Collins and Yearley [1992]) see Pickering (1995).

16. John Law draws a salient comparison between the "cost of justification" (we spoke of "sacrifice" in *De la justification*) and the cost of audit and of the apparatuses of surveillance and reporting that have been put in place for anyone who has to deal with the British state (health service, teachers, universities, etc.).

17. In this essay I cannot explore the notion of the pragmatic regime in detail. I have documented this approach in several papers and grounded it in empirical studies (Thévenot 1993, 1994a, 1994b, 1995b, 1996c, 2001). In particular, different investigations have been dedicated to following the "same" object, some consumer good, in different regimes, from the situation of personal and familiar usage in a domestic arena to the most public treatment, such as what we observe in European committees in charge of setting safety standards, through the methods and implements of the laboratories that certify their achievement of standardized properties (Thévenot 1993).

18. I shall not here enter into a detailed discussion of competing theories of convention. This notion is at the center of a recent trend in French socioeconomics called the "Convention theory," to which I contribute. Instead of considering conventions as mere collective agreements that bring the convergence of expectancies, whether explicit in contracts or tacit in customs, I would rather look at conventions as more complex *coordinating devices* that deal with the limits of more localized engagements, when there is a need for third-party assessment. A convention is not a broad convergence of shared knowledge. It is nothing more than a limited agreement about selected features people use to *control* events and entities. What is most important in the convention is not only a rather negative agreement about what is *inconvenient* but the common acceptance of what is left aside as irrelevant. This acceptance is grounded on the common knowledge that there is no hope for a more complete alignment (which is assumed in classical group collectives).

19. I studied this problem on a more consequential domain. I compared organizations that deliberately encourage this familiarity regime in their management to organizations where the workplace is, by contrast, arranged to facilitate a justification regime and the imputation of failures either to human or nonhuman qualified beings (Thévenot 1996c).

20. This development aims at answering Bruno Latour's question about a possible emerging seventh order of worth, "green worth" (Lafaye and Thévenot 1993; Latour 1995); for more on this issue, see Thévenot (1996a).

21. Such compromises constitute the skeleton of organizations (Thévenot 1989). Stark developed an approach of complex organizations based on the ability to combine evaluative principles to manage a "portfolio of justifications" and produce multiple accounting (1996).

22. The literal translation in English is the following:

> They both fell down.
> I heard the sheep bell hit the stones.
> My dog gave his last bark.
> My dear dog, I will think of you.
> If you have gone on high, and reached some star

I know you would have chosen the "shepherd star"
[in French, in the text, the "evening star" is called the
"shepherd star"].
And if you met this poor sheep there,
then you'll forgive her,
My brave little dog.

REFERENCES

Barthélémy, M. 1990. "Voir et dire l'action." In P. Pharo and L. Quéré, eds., *Les formes de l'action,* 195–226. Série Raisons pratiques, no. 1. Paris: Editions de l'Ecole des hautes études en sciences sociales.

Bénatouïl, T. 1999. "Comparing Sociological Strategies: The Critical and the Pragmatic Stance in French Contemporary Sociology." *European Journal of Social Theory* 2, no. 3, special issue, "Contemporary French Social Theory" (August): 379–96.

Boltanski, L. 1990. *L'amour et la justice comme compétences.* Paris: Métailié.

Boltanski, L., and L. Thévenot. 1991. *De la justification: Les Économies de la grandeur.* Paris: Gallimard.

———. 1999. "The Sociology of Critical Capacity." *European Journal of Social Theory* 2, no. 3, special issue, "Contemporary French Social Theory" (August): 359–77.

Bréviglieri, M. 1997. "La coopération spontanée. Entraides techniques autour d'un automate public." In B. Conein and L. Thévenot, eds., *Cognition et information en société,* 123–48. Série Raisons pratiques, no. 8. Paris: Editions de l'Ecole des hautes études en sciences sociales.

Callon, M., and B. Latour. 1981. "Unscrewing the Big Leviathan." In K. Knorr-Cetina and A. Cicourel, eds., *Advances in Social Theory and Methodology,* 277–303. Boston: Routledge and Kegan Paul.

Callon, M., and J. Law. 1989. "La proto-histoire d'un laboratoire ou le difficile mariage de la science et de l'économie." In *Innovation et ressources locales,* 1–34. Cahiers du Centre d'Etudes de l'Emploi no. 32. Paris: PUF.

Collins, H., and S. Yearley. 1992. "Epistemological Chicken." In A. Pickering, ed., *Science as Practice and Culture,* 301–26. Chicago: University of Chicago Press.

Conein, B., N. Dodier, and L. Thévenot, eds. 1993. *Les objets dans l'action: De la maison au laboratoire.* Série Raisons pratiques, no. 4. Paris: Editions de l'Ecole des hautes études en sciences sociales.

Dumont, L. 1983. *Essais sur l'individualisme: Une perspective anthropologique sur l'idéologie moderne.* Paris: Seuil.

"L'économie des conventions." 1989. *Revue économique* 2, special issue (March).

Elias, N. 1975. *La dynamique de l'Occident.* Trans. Edmund Jephcott. Paris: Calmann-Levy. Originally published 1939 as volume 2 of *Über den Prozess der Zivilisation.* Basel: Haus zum Falken.

Fujimura, J. 1992. "Crafting Science: Standardized Packages, Boundary Objects, and

Translations." In A. Pickering, ed. *Science as Practice and Culture,* 168–211. Chicago: University of Chicago Press.

Heidegger, M. 1962. "L'époque des 'conceptions du monde.'" In *Chemins qui ne mênent nulle part.* Trans. Wolfgang Brokmeier. Paris: Gallimard.

Knorr-Cetina, K. 1995. "The Care of the Self and Blind Variations: An Ethnography of the Empirical in Two Sciences." In P. Galison and D. Stump, eds., *The Disunity of Sciences: Boundaries, Contexts, and Power.* Stanford: Stanford University Press.

———. 1999. *Epistemic Cultures: How the Scientists Make Knowledge.* Cambridge, Mass.: Harvard University Press.

Labarère, J. 1994. *Poète et berger.* N.p.: Association Los Caminaires.

Lafaye, C., and L. Thévenot. 1993. "Une justification Écologique? Conflits dans l'amenagement de la nature." *Revue Française de Sociologie* 34, no. 4 (Oct.–Dec.): 495–524.

Lamont, M., and L. Thévenot, eds. 2000. *Rethinking Compartive Cultural Sociology: Repertoires of Evaluation in France and the United States.* (Submitted to Cambridge University Press.)

Latour, B. 1993a. "Les cornéliens dilemmes d'une ceinture de sécurité." In *La clé de Berlin et autres leçons d'un amateur de sciences,* 25–32. Paris: La Découverte.

———. 1993b. "Le fardeau moral d'un porte-clefs." In *La clé de Berlin et autres leçons d'un amateur de sciences,* 47–55. Paris: La Découverte.

———. 1995. "Moderniser ou Écologiser? A la recherche de la 'septième' cité." *Ecologie Politique,* no. 13: 5–27.

Law, J. 1991. "Power, Discretion, and Strategy." In J. Law, ed., *A Sociology of Monsters? Essays on Power, Technology, and Domination,* 165–91. Sociological Review Monograph no. 38. London: Routledge.

———. 1996. "Organizing Accountabilities: Ontology and the Mode of Accounting." In J. Munro and J. Mourtsen, eds., *Accountability: Power, Ethos, and the Technologies of Managing.* London: International Thompson Business Press.

———. 1998. "Political Philosophy and Disabled Specificities." ⟨*http://www.comp.lancs .ac.uk/sociology/soco26jl.html*⟩. Accessed July 30, 2001.

Law, J., and A. Mol. 1995. "Notes on Materiality and Sociality." *Sociological Review* 43: 274–94.

Locke, J. [1690] 1966. *The Second Treatise of Government (An essay concerning the true original, extent and end of civil government), and, A Letter Concerning Toleration.* Edited, with a revised introduction, by J. W. Gough. Oxford: Blackwell.

MacIntyre, A. [1981] 1984. *After Virtue.* Notre Dame: University of Notre Dame Press.

Moody, M., and L. Thévenot. 2000. "Comparing Models of Strategy, Interests, and the Common Good in French and American Environmental Disputes." In M. Lamont and L. Thévenot, eds., *Rethinking Comparative Cultural Sociology: Repertoires of Evaluation in France and the United States,* 273–306. Cambridge: Cambridge University Press.

Orléan, A., ed. 1994. *Analyse économique des conventions.* Paris: PUF.

Pascal, B. 1954. *Oeuvres complètes*. Bibliothèque de la Pléiade. Paris: Gallimard.

Pickering, A. 1992. "From Science as Knowledge to Science as Practice." In A. Pickering, ed., *Sciences as Practice and Culture*, 1–26. Chicago: University of Chicago Press.

———. 1995. *The Mangle of Practice*. Chicago: University of Chicago Press.

Pufendorf, S. 1749. *The Law of Nature and Nations; or, A General System of the Most Important Principles of Morality, Jurisprudence, and Politics*. Trans. from the French by Basil Kennet. London: J. and J. Bonwicke.

———. [1771] 1989. "Le Droit de la Nature et des Gens, ou, Système général des Principes les plus importans de la Morale, de la Jurisprudence, et de la Politique." Trans. from the Latin by Jean Barbeyrac. *Revue économique* 2, special issue, "L'économie des conventions" (March).

Sartre, J. P. [1943] 1956. *Being and Nothingness: An Essay on Phenomenological Ontology*. Trans. Hazel E. Barnes. New York: Philosophical Library.

Simmel, G. 1988. *La tragédie de la culture et autres essais*. Trans. Sabine Cornille and Phillippe Ivernel. Paris: Editions Rivages.

Star, S., and J. Griesemer. 1989. "Institutional Ecology, 'Translations,' and Boundary Objects: Amateurs and Professionals in Berkeley's Museum of Vertebrate Zoology, 1907–1939." *Social Studies of Science* 19: 387–420.

Stark, D. 1996. "Recombinant Property in East European Capitalism." *American Journal of Sociology* 101, no. 4 (January): 993–1027.

Thévenot, L. 1984. "Rules and Implements: Investment in Forms." *Social Science Information* 23, no. 1: 1–45.

———. 1989. "Equilibre et rationalité dans un univers complexe." *Revue économique* 2, special issue, "L'économie des conventions" (March): 147–97.

———. 1990a. "La politique des statistiques: Les origines sociales des enquêtes de mobilité sociale." *Annales E.S.C.*, no. 6 (Nov.–Dec.): 1275–1300.

———. 1990b. "L'action qui convient." In P. Pharo and L. Quéré, eds., *Les formes de l'action*, 39–69. Série Raisons pratiques, no. 1. Paris: Editions de l'Ecole des hautes études en sciences sociales.

———. 1992. "Jugements ordinaires et jugement de droit." *Annales E.S.C.*, no. 6 (Nov.–Dec.): 1279–99.

———. 1993. "Essai sur les objets usuels: Propriétés, fonctions, usages." In B. Conein, N. Dodier, and L. Thévenot, eds., *Les objets dans l'action*, 85–111. Série Raisons pratiques, no. 4. Paris: Editions de l'Ecole des hautes études en sciences sociales.

———. 1994a. "Le régime de familiarité: Des choses enpersonnes." *Genèses*, no. 17 (Sept.): 72–101.

———. 1994b. "Objets en société. Suivre les choses dans tous leurs états." *Alliage*, no. 21, *Pour penser la Technique*, 74–87.

———. 1995a. "New Trends in French Social Sciences." *Culture* 9, no. 2: 1–7.

———. 1995b. "L'action en plan." *Sociologie du Travail* 37, no. 3: 411–34.

———. 1995c. "Emotions et évaluations dans les coordinations publíques." In P. Paperman and R. Ogien, eds., *La Couleur des pensées: Emotions, sentiments, intentions,*

145–74. Série Raisons pratiques, no. 6. Paris: Editions de l'Ecole des hautes études en sciences sociales.

——. 1996a. "Mettre en valeur la nature; disputes autour d'aménagements de la nature en France et aux Etats-Unis." *Autres Temps. Cahiers d'éthique sociale et politique,* no. 49: 27–50.

——. 1996b. "Stratégies, Intérêts et justifications. A propos d'une comparaison France–Etats-Unis de conflits d'aménagement." *Techniques, territoires, et sociétés,* no. 31: 127–49.

——. 1996c. "Les formes de savoir collectif selon les régimes pragmatiques: Des compétences attribuées ou distribuées." In J.-P. Dupuy, P. Livet, B. Reynaud, eds., *Limitations de la rationalité et constitution du collectif.* Paris: La Découverte.

——. 2001. "Pragmatic Regimes Governing the Engagement with the World." In T. R. Schatzki, K. Knorr-Cetina, and E. von Savigny, eds., *The Practice Turn in Contemporary Theory,* 56–73. London: Routledge.

Thévenot, L., and M. Lamont. 2000. "Exploration of the French and the American Polity." In M. Lamont and L. Thévenot, eds., *Rethinking Comparative Cultural Sociology: Repertoires of Evaluation in France and the United States,* 307–27. Cambridge: Cambridge University Press.

Thévenot, L., M. Moody, and C. Lafaye. 2000. "Forms of Valuing Nature: Arguments and Modes of Justification in Environmental Disputes." In M. Lamont and L. Thévenot, eds., *Rethinking Comparative Cultural Sociology: Repertoires of Evaluation in France and the United States,* 229–72. Cambridge: Cambridge University Press.

Wagner, P. 1994. "Action, Coordination, and Institution in Recent French Debates." *Journal of Political Philosophy* 2, no. 3: 270–89.

——. 1999. "After *Justification.* Repertoires of Evaluation and the Sociology of Modernity." *European Journal of Social Theory* 2, no. 3, special issue, "Contemporary French Social Theory" (August): 341–57.

Wilkinson, J. 1997. "A New Paradigm for Economic Analysis?" *Economy and Society* 26, no. 3 (August): 305–39.

Winner, L. 1980. "Do Artefacts Have Politics?" *Daedalus,* no. 109: 121–36.

MARILYN STRATHERN

On Space and Depth

In the final analysis, everything is suspended in movement.—Tim Ingold

The substance of this essay takes a commonplace technique of interpretation and suggests circumstances under which it produces a kind of complexity. The technique is that of figure-ground reversal as it is applied to
artifacts that are visually present,[1] a technique that by itself simply draws
on habits of perception. It may, however, be combined with certain
conceptions of the act of interpretation itself.[2] The result is then an
oscillation between perspectives that appear to summon quite different
approaches to the world.[3] My own interest in this as a complex phenomenon stems from attempts to apprehend the effects of scale in social life
(Strathern 1991, 2000), a connection that I hope will become evident as
the chapter proceeds.

One set of conceptions of the act of "interpretation" became commonplace among twentieth-century observers and commentators. It
takes a divergent form: at some moments it seems as though there is
nothing beyond interpretation, for there is nothing that is not amenable
to human comprehension and in that sense the product of it, whereas at
other moments one appears to see through the practice of interpretation
for the very artifice it is.[4] At times this divergence has been the subject of
controversy, and writers on social life, including those within anthropology, may accuse one another of holding one or other perspective as an
extreme position or absurd theory.

Consider, for example, a pair of complaints that stems from this divergence. On the one hand it may be argued that any one act of interpretation is invariably selective: because we can grasp an object in multiple
frames all at once, this or that particular teasing out seems reductionist.
We have not let in "enough" interpretation through the nets of our

attention. On the other hand, attempts to imitate the simultaneity of perceptions by piling on exegesis can give rise to the equally orthodox complaint of "too much" interpretation, from which comes one very predictable appeal, namely to bypass interpretation (selection) altogether and respond directly to the world.[5] It is the apprehension of lack or surfeit that gives rise to such complaints (as though one could have too little or too much meaning! [see J. Weiner 1995]) and gives a kind of momentum to the oscillation of views. Although there may be moments when practitioners in interpretation hold one or other view, there are always some elements that summon the counterview.[6] Movement between the two moments can be (so to speak) set in motion through commonplace figure-ground reversal.

Interpretation implies taking something—an event or location or artifact or whatever—and specifying its singular qualities. It is the resultant singularity of the entity that encourages the divergence in comprehension. For the entity in question is being made apparent both in its particulars and as inevitably summoning a context of a kind, a whole field of possible (further) particulars and understandings. Think of all the coordinates through which one might address one's interpretation of a photograph, for instance, from its chemical composition to its aesthetic impact. Yet (obvious and mundane observations) to consider the particular quality of the photographic reproduction is to sidestep the subject matter; to focus specifically on the way a face is angled within the frame is to slide past the effect of the smile. The singularity of the selection reveals it as a choice among many. The specific instance appears as only a moment out of an infinite universe, and the universe that contains the many cannot be reduced to any one of them—it is a phenomenon of a different order.[7]

I suggest that there is a kind of generalized figure-ground vision here. Certainly the notion that there are always many choices, coordinates, or perspectives to adopt gives a scale to the object at issue, for it is enlarged or diminished by reference to these other orders of things.[8] But that effect is not just anyone's perception; there is a particular set of conceptions here. This movement between viewpoints belongs to a Western or Euro-American but certainly modernist tradition that takes as axiomatic the idea of a continuum of characteristics as the background (ground) to any singular or specific one (figure). Verran (1998) offers a vivid example of a space-time continuum, one that compels ecologists to produce interpretations ("models") of specific conditions set within a wider understanding of environmental and human universals. Some recent discussions from social/cultural anthropology address the singularity of moments apprehended as moments in space and time, and to these I will shortly turn.

This essay considers "interpretation" in the modernist tradition as an act of singularity, that is, one that makes singular the subject of interpretation, and hence gives rise to an oscillation of view(point)s. However, rather than describing the writings in this tradition, it describes certain experiences of it. To this end I examine four photographs. The point is that when all is said and done—whether there seems too much or too little interpretation—these puzzles in the pictures remain. (Producing such "remainders" is one of the hallmarks of the anthropologist's kind of ethnography.) A question follows about what we might learn by interpreting interpretation this way. The answer seems to be that we do not add much to the art of interpretation that has not already been discussed countless times. However, we do perhaps learn about some effects of oscillation and thus about effects of "scale."

FIGURES, GROUNDS, AND CONTINUA

Casey (1996) has addressed the phenomenon of singularity or particularity in respect to certain prevalent (Euro-American, modernist) views about places. The particularity inherent in the idea of "a place" lends itself to naturalistic or scientistic descriptions that suppose it is carved out of an encompassing and generalized "space." That generalized space is regarded as abstract and amorphous, thereby requiring concrete and localized expression, as well as being the general condition and source of universals in human experience. We thus arrive at the naturalistic view of space as the prior background against which we are invited to see individual places "in" it. Concerned with the reported priority that many of the anthropologist's subjects give instead to place itself (Casey quotes Myers's observation that to the Australian Pintupi "a place with its multiple features is logically prior or central" [1996, 15; after Myers 1991, 59]), he proposes a phenomenological reversal. The anthropologist needs to retrieve a sense of place, and with it local knowledge, as a matter of embodied perception: "we are never without emplaced experiences" (1996, 19). We are, he says, in place because we are in our bodies. That concreteness is phenomenologically prior, and we should reorder our postulates about generalities and particularities. "Space and time are contained in places rather than places in them" (1996, 44). Far from being suspended in space, then, a place contains space within itself, as it does time, journeys, and histories. What was most natural (space) thus comes in this description to appear the most artificial: in Casey's words, universals are mere planes of abstract perfection abstracted from concrete perceptions. He is much happier with the idea of the particular place as a gathering point for, in his words, the "complexities and dirty details" of experience (1996, 45).

The reference to time is apposite, Greenhouse (1996) would observe, given that the idea of intervals of time being carved out of some infinite expanse belongs to the same Euro-American repertoire as the idea of places within space. Less a matter of philosophical stance than of historical epoch, however, she would point to the idea of event-filled time as a modernist creation. Her argument is precise here. We encounter modernities, she says, when we encounter efforts to *overcome* the heterogeneity of specific moments through summoning a grand temporal narrative. Linear time is a way (not the only one) to distribute powers and agency; it orders multiple particulars. And linear time, in Greenhouse's view, is already itself an ordering: it is "the time of the nation-state" (1996, 179). Part of its meaning in turn lies in its reference to the larger infinity or eternity, the "shapeless matrix" (1996, 181) of which it is imagined to be a natural segment, and it reproduces itself in creating further natural segments. Individuals, albeit on a smaller scale, thus find their personal histories being "constructed out of the same elements as the collective story of progress [that] modern nation-states claim for themselves" (1996, 180). In Greenhouse's description particularity is predicted by the ordering functions of linear time, for linear time produces particular segments, intervals, and moments as descriptions or exemplifications of itself.[9] Diversity, difference, and plurality might appear outside that ordering process. Yet it is because different worlds are seen to be carved ultimately out of the same universal realities (naturalistic time and space) that they are amenable to ordering.

That recursive possibility is already there in Casey's description. The particular (place) cannot have been grasped "in the first place" without coordinates (space). Summoning "depths" and "horizons" from Merleau-Ponty and Husserl, he writes that "there must be an ingredient in perception from a start, a conveyance of what being in places is all about," so that depth already situates perceptions in a scene of which we form a part, and the "coherence of perception at the primary level is supplied by the depth and horizons of the very place we occupy as sentient subjects" (1996, 18–19, italics omitted). Because he or she is surrounded by depths and horizons, "the perceiver finds herself in the midst of an entire teeming place-world rather than in a confusing kaleidoscope of free-floating sensory data" (1996, 17). The (general) frame is already within the (particular) picture, so to speak, just as (universal) linear time is imagined to be intrinsic to everyone's (individual) biography. Or, as one might say apropos Casey's own description, the frame is already within the picture just as his reversal of space and place evokes a language of depth, of everything already understood as being inside something else.[10] Both the idea of intervals of time being carved out of some infinite expanse and the idea of places within space can be imagined in terms of figure and ground (Ingold 1993). Indeed the very vocabulary of expanse evokes a kind of landscape with potential figures within (see, among others, Hirsch 1995). Casey deliberately effects a reversal of the expected order. Space is within places, not the other way around: the ground has become the figure. His description works, in short, because of the figure-ground reversal of his own interpretive move.

Like present moments in time, it is possible to say of places that a place is both a point along a scale—as one travels from one to another, places seem separated by distance that can be measured—and is also the only point at which one can ever "be"—the place from which all distances are calculated. We can borrow from such space-time coordinates the concept of scale to describe the aggrandizing and diminishing effects of figure-ground reversal. For this kind of reversal has a quantifying or measuring effect. The moment a figure is seen in relation to its ground, it is bound to appear encompassed by the larger entity. This is an enduring hierarchy or asymmetry. However much a figure is enlarged by putting it into a "wider context" of understandings, it inevitably falls short of that context itself.[11]

Figure-ground reversal involves an alternation of viewpoints.[12] Now although ground by definition encompasses figure, what is to count as figure and what is to count as ground is not a definitive matter at all, and here the values to be attached to particular phenomena are unpredictable. Figure and ground promote, we might say, unstable relationships. I further speak of oscillation, a tied divergence, when what are summoned are worlds or value systems at once seemingly different from yet also comparable to each other. Here the freight of "quantity" introduces an asymmetry. When there can be too much or too little of something, when vastness appears to overwhelm, or when a single perspective appears to miss so much, then scale can give a particular impetus to the very decision of what is to be rendered as figure and what as ground. Ground acquires the value of an unmarked category. So when the greater (unmarked) value can be expressed in terms of an appropriateness of quantity—neither too much nor too little—then *that* is what locates the entity in question as ground. An excess, in either direction, becomes a (suitably grotesque) figure against the ground (the natural world) of appropriate and reasonable description. Quantity thus turns out to have a (re)stabilizing effect.

Stability and instability coexisting in a correlative relationship, each implicated in the other, produce complex phenomena.[13] Stabilizing and destabilizing effects similar to that sketched above appear between and within modes of interpretation themselves.

I have said that one kind of world is laid out by those who refuse to see beyond interpretation, another by those who claim to see through it.[14] Both may project a larger, natural world of "real-life" experience.[15] For the former, reality lies in the fact that everything is a product of interpretation and is thus in the texts, the rhetoric, the strategies by which analysis moves from one position to another yet always has to occupy a position. What is significant is the persuasiveness of the interpretation, which then becomes subject for further interpretation. (Ground becomes figure: a figure is to be understood in relation to its ground, which then appears as the figure.) If this sensibility exaggerates interpretation, dispensing with everything implied in the term *representation*, namely, the idea that there is anything beyond interpretation, then the counterpart sensibility would instead wish to see through it. (Figure becomes ground: the ground, being taken for granted, naturalizes the figure, which merges with it as part of the ground.) Here reality is what you get after you take interpretation away; all you need are methods of discovery.[16] In other words, this form of interpretation claims that no interpretation is necessary. Far from being all encompassing, interpretation seems to deflect attention away from the real world; deep models are held in suspicion, and the commonsense understandings on which people manage to communicate with one another instead rise to the surface. Yet nothing holds these two positions apart but the acts of perception that slip between them: the relationship between them is in that sense unstable.[17]

There is still some common ground between the two. If interpretation "stops" movement in the attention to the movement around it, then in that attention the world also appears full of stopped, singular things, such as "things" or "events" or "relations." The effect of any interpretive intent is to then make those things seem to move *subsequently,* that is, as a result of attention to them. Discrimination and distinction, connection and relationship, all make the object of attention move. So anthropological analyses play off subjects against objects or imagine centralized and uncentralized polities or specify divisions of labor, and anthropologists make diagrams out of boxes with directions on them or devise flowcharts with arrows. The act of interpretation is understood as bringing entities, human or abstract, into play with one another. Whether we describe transactions between persons or types of political systems or lives segregated into different spheres, description creates a sense of movement in the data, pushing this information up against that. Such a search for animation holds whatever mode of understanding is at issue; we may regard it as a point of stability on which all interpretive exercises are bound to come to rest.[18]

To illustrate some of these points I set up a field of singularities: four photographs. (There are no tricks in the examples, but although the choice was countless, the order is deliberate.) Of interest perhaps is less the quality of understanding to which this particular sequence gives rise than the rapid-movement effect of following through the sequence at all. The photographs comprise two pictures taken by anthropologists in Papua New Guinea, interpolated with two from a classic by the life-science photographer Lennart Nilsson.[19] I make interpretation explicit with two Papua New Guinean examples. Although I have to remain interpreter myself throughout, the other two make visible the modernist Euro- · American oscillation between the position that everything is interpretation (so one always has "too little" of it) and the position that one can see through interpretation (so one always has "too much"). In commenting on the mutual persuasiveness of both positions, I also want to ask whether paying attention to these two strategies—"interpreting" them— adds to what I already see in the ethnographic data from Papua New Guinea. The voice throughout is that of a Euro-American modernist committed to understanding the world in which he or she lives.

WOMEN CARRYING BILUMS

This photograph is taken from Maureen Mackenzie's (1991) study of peoples from the Mountain Ok region of Papua New Guinea mediated through the particular attention she pays to the string bags or *bilum* that women make, whether for themselves or their menfolk (fig. 1). Men's bilums are worn typically on the nape of the neck or shoulders and are used not for carrying children but for carrying hunted meat and personal possessions. The bag that bulges across a woman's back curves over it as her belly curves in front. Women use these bags to carry everything from babies (the cover of Mackenzie's book shows a child curled up asleep in a bilum like a cradle) to the taro stalks in these bilums (cf. 1991, 140), taro tubers being likened to children who have to be coaxed to grow. Women have to have a feel for their craft in making these bags, she says (1991, 136); one's hands must be light "and flow like running water." These three women are walking upstream, to a garden no doubt. The photograph appears on the same pages as that remark but is not particularly intended to refer to it. What are we looking at?

Mackenzie's caption is simply "A good bilum must be strong and capable of hard work," a nice attribution to the bags and perhaps to the capabilities of those who carry them. Although communities keep to their own style of bilum, distinguished by overall shape, type of handle, and decoration on the opening or "mouth," all domestic bilums are made to be strong. The photograph could have appeared anywhere in the book—it is a generic picture of such strength.

The photograph, then, has the status of an illustration. Mackenzie does not make it an object of interpretation but deploys it to exemplify what is elsewhere in the book an interpretation of the bilum's significance. If the illustration foregrounds one of its specific qualities—the carrying capac- ity of the bag—that works because the capacity is described elsewhere,

Figure 1. "A good bilum must be strong and capable of hard work." From Maureen Mackenzie,
Androgynous Objects: String Bags and Gender in Central New Guinea *(Chur: Harwood*
Academic Publishers, 1991), plate 88. Reproduced by permission.

and the reader's attention has already been cultivated. The photograph
serves as "background" evidence by momentarily foregrounding all the
personal knowledge of the area that we assume is at the back of Mackenzie's analysis. It invites attention to the fact that the analysis draws on
firsthand fieldwork—the report of what women told her about hands
having to be light like running water comes from someone who has not
only heard but seen (photographed) the fast Mountain Ok streams. In
short, we can move the figures against *their* background, paying attention
now to the bilum and now to the stream up which the women are
walking, or displace those with the fact that the women's description of
bilum making draws on images they create out of their own surroundings. As we carry on reading the text, the photograph as a whole assumes
the position of ground against the figure of the analysis (Mackenzie's
explication of the bilum).

To perceive figure and ground together implies constant eye movement. The space we create by this roving attention gives the photograph
internal depth, even as the figures literally move away from the camera,
the distance being marked by the tiny size of the woman in front. The
anthropologist's interpretive strategies thus "see" spaces within spaces,

and a single figure can be placed against one of a number of grounds. So although the camera apparently "stops" the women at a point on their journey, the interpreter can create his or her own movement and animate them in then locating the figures against other diverse grounds. As Mackenzie does, we can consider the women in the context of their roles as mothers (the bilum is referred to as "mother of us all"), or we can consider the bag in the context of looped-string techniques found over large parts of Papua New Guinea. Each contextualization presents a fresh configuration of figure and ground for attention. Exactly such interpretative procedure has characteristically given depth to ethnography.

The anthropologist's figure-ground strategies may of course cut across those of the people whose own strategies otherwise provide him or her with depth to the material. Mackenzie can use a picture of a bilum as an example of a generic quality she was told about, manifested by three generic women. Yet for the Mountain Ok, that quality is always created out of the context of specific relationships between persons, who have names, whether in the form of a gift to a relative, as women may make bilums for their male relatives, or in the way women acquire from particular others the skill that animates their work. This is another context for the anthropologist to consider.

Now the anthropological concept of context is, in turn, an open invitation to engage in figure-ground reversal of the most obvious kind, for it is provided by making obvious the act of observation itself (data and analysis, ethnography and theory, and so forth). Let me put some of these observations from the Mountain Ok into the context of interactions between persons. Meta, a young woman from Eliptamin, talked about how she acquired looping skills:

> Before, when I was little I didn't know anything. I used to watch my mother. . . . One day I saw her put the bilum she was working on safely in the rafters while she went to the garden to work. I'd been watching her hands carefully and wanted to try myself, so I took her bilum. But I didn't really know how to loop. I was only pretending to loop and I messed up her looping. I saw I'd done it all wrong and was frightened and put her bilum down. Then I ran away at top speed . . . to hide in the bush. Later, when my mum came back it was really hard work for her to undo what I had done and she wanted to hit me. But she told

me, "You must start a training bilum of your own, you want to make a bilum but your hands are heavy. You must practise to get the proper feel of looping. When you've made your first bilum it will be cranky but then we'll throw it in the river. The river will carry your wonky bilum away, and it will wash away your heavy handedness. Then your hands will be good at making bilums, your hands will move like running water." (Mackenzie 1991, 102)

ULTRASOUND SCAN

The next example—a visual translation of an ultrasound scan of a woman's uterus—is altogether different (fig. 2). Whereas I am reasonably confident about my interpretations of Mackenzie's material—that is, I know what her analysis is doing, even if at the end of the road I do not know what the Mountain Ok are doing—here I am at the edge of my world of knowledge. As an interpreter I can of course contextualize the image with reference to the previous material and thus give it a movement of sorts. Take the visual analogy with the bilum. The Ok bilum is already analogous to a womb; it specifically recalls the woman's role as mother. But we need more information than that, for at the same time, the anthropologist's too hasty identification of the Ok figure with "mother" may create quite misleading connotations. That ascription needs further interpretation; for a start, the English-language supposition that a mother is intrinsically female does disservice to the complex gender of the Ok mother. (The ideas and qualities embedded in the Telefol concept of mother, Mackenzie says, are not simply ideas of achievement in "the female realm" but positive values in "the male realm" too.)[20] The interpreter might begin to feel that there is nothing but interpretation in the world. That is just what this photograph implies.

The use I want to make of the picture, as in the case of the Mountain Ok illustration, also cuts across other people's interpretations. Ultrasound scans can be treated like photographs of persons. For the parents this is the picture of a relative—it may go into the family album. If they focus on its particularity, an ultrasound scan taken on such and such a day of the baby at so many weeks old, they have no problem of interpretation. These scales are all containable within the one image.

But there is a sense in which the photograph seems all scale; ground

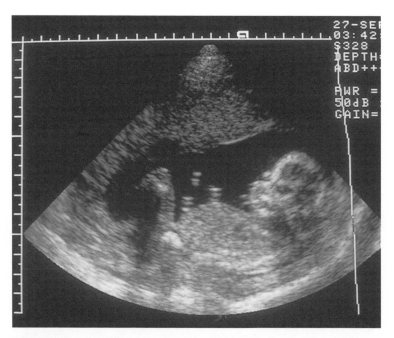

Figure 2. From Lennart Nilsson, A Child Is Born *(London: Doubleday, 1990). Reproduced by permission. The accompanying description reads: "Until the 16th week the whole fetus is visible on the screen of the ultrasound device. The pictures are a visual translation of the ultrasound echo registered by the device" (104).*

has become figure. Look at the space the image fills. There is nothing but the results of the scan in the frame. Although it is a rendering of the insides of a woman's body, that information has to be supplied by what lies outside the picture. Of course, we could say that it shows the fetus "within," but the image of the fetus within the womb is doubly mediated. What we are looking at is not, so to speak, a photograph of a fetus but a photograph of the scan, that is, the movement that produces that image is the movement of the scanner. We are looking at what the scan did. At various points the scan picked up particular features, and it is those that its sweep marks, a whole fan of "interpretations," elements recorded at different moments (cf. Nilsson 1990, 104).

What exactly is the record of?

Using diagnostic ultrascanography, implanted embryos and developing foetuses can be visualised externally on a screen, as if separate from the pregnant woman. A beam of very brief pulses of high-frequency sound, generated by a transducer placed in contact with her skin, is directed through her body and partly reflected by soft tissues and follicular, embryonic and foetal structures. The echoes from the reflections are visualised as an image on a screen for the operator to interpret. The developing foetus thus becomes observable. (Price 1990, 124–25)

The picture is composed, then, of a series of moments that interpret echoes as images, and that is what the picture is of. The whole sweep gives a configuration of sorts, but the movement is between these points of interpretation. There is no ground by which to contextualize this image: it is, as it were, all figure. The movement of the eye is rendered invisible by the visible movement of the scan.

As a result, these "interpretations" require interpretation; in fact, those who look at the ultrasound scan can do nothing but interpret it. "Interpretation is all," say the authors of *Tomorrow's Child:*

Ultrasound . . . is apparently safe, although there are still debates about whether we have enough information to assess its possible effects on young embryos in the long term. In experienced hands, an "anomaly scan" at about twenty weeks can undoubtedly detect many major congenital defects, such as anencephaly, where no brain develops. Yet interpretation is all, given the fuzzy images of ultrasound, and many medics are sceptical of some of the claims made by ultrasound enthusiasts. . . . [Some] researchers claim to be able to detect 82 per cent of Down's fetuses during the second trimester through ultrasound.

Yet other doctors stress how misleading ultrasound can be, finding false positives (i.e. results that appear to indicate a positive result for, say spina bifida, when the fetus is normal) commonplace. (Birke et al. 1990, 170)

Because abnormalities can be diagnosed this way, the scan is searched for diagnostic clues, putting the spectator into a world of ever-receding uncertainty.[21] The clinician or parent is directly confronted with the realities of what interpretation means. Has the scan picked up the abnormality? If it has, will the abnormality be read by the experts?[22] If it is read by the expert, will it be relayed to the layperson? Rayna Rapp (1986) has recorded one mother's response:

> I saw the sonogram of the twins and I was thrilled. But I really couldn't read it, I didn't know what it meant. They had to interpret it for you, to say "here's a heart, these are arms." Afterwards, it made me queasy— *they made the babies real for me by telling me what was there.* If they hadn't interpreted, it would have just been grey blobs, and now, I'm more frightened to get the results of the amnio back. (10, my emphasis)

There is "not enough" information, and "more" interpretation is needed.

PEOPLE AND THEIR CELLS

Here is another incorporation of space (fig. 3). The frame appears to contain the spectators. Acting as interpreter, I could say that in the picture we see a "nurse" in the background who looks at the couple while in the foreground the couple gaze at each other. But the three persons locked in their attention to one another are also mere ground to the figure that is the subject of the photograph: (a photograph of) a magnified embryo. The fertilized ovum has been cultured for two days outside the body and now, having reached the stage of four-cell division, is ready for insertion into the woman (Nilsson 1990, 200). This is the point, at the four- or eight-cell stage, when it is also available for preimplantation diagnosis (a single cell may be removed for diagnostic procedures without apparently affecting the development of the embryo).

However, this is not a picture of a diagnostic procedure. Unlike the ultrasound photograph, which *was* the diagnosis, this simply shows what is potentially available for diagnosis. The picture itself is about what has come from the bodies of the couple and will be returned to the body of the woman. The cells that she has inside her have been figuratively brought outside, and indeed their picture is propped up so that—were the couple to turn their heads—they would see it. It presents the reader of the book with an illustration of, and apparently unmediated access to, things as they really are.

Figure 3. From Lennart Nilsson, A Child Is Born *(London: Doubleday, 1990). Reproduced by permission. The accompanying description reads: "The nurse shows the hopeful parents an enlarged image of their own fertilised ovum immediately before insertion into the woman's uterus. The ovum has been cultured for two days in a nutrient solution, and has now divided into four cells" (200).*

At this moment no interpretation is necessary. Of course, various methods have to be used to obtain the photograph, including an exquisite camera technology. Yet those methods are self-evident: you know you are looking at a photograph because photographic technique has made it possible. The coloring, the magnification, and the two-dimensional presentation are directly attributable to the method. But you could, so to speak, discard the method, and you would still have the cells as they are available for other forms of visualization. Contrast ultrasound, where each interpretive moment depends on the last; if you began undoing the scan you would undo the sequencing on which the whole visualization process rests. Nilsson offers just this contrast. He elsewhere juxtaposes ultrasound and photograph ("a fetus in the 16th week of pregnancy, visualised through ultrasound [and] a fetus of the same age, in a photograph" [1990, 105]). It is clear that the latter is intended to show the embryo "as it is." So too with the cells.

The reason that we know we are looking at cells lies in all the conventions by which we "recognize" them, so although we may have to be told these are the cells of a developing embryo, we don't have to be told that they are cells. And while the Euro-American viewer would not know without being told that they belonged to that particular couple, he or she already knows that that is what the insides of the body are like. In this sense there is no distance between the subject of the photograph and the observer. That gives this picture its distinctive space. I referred fleetingly to the relationship between the photograph of the cells and the people around it in terms of figure and ground, but such a cultural interpretation is superfluous to our immediate understanding of the subject. In fact, although one could do the same kind of exposition on it as for the Ok women and their bilums, giving the picture depth in that way is also unnecessary. Indeed, "too much" interpretation may simply get in the way. The modernist spectator does not have to labor over focusing on this or that as figure to ground because there is one very evident "depth" already there that appears not to depend on interpretation at all. It comes, instead, from the taken-for-granted background "continuum" of universal biological process.

What are the people with on that screen? In their shirtsleeves and neat haircuts they are company to a picture of what they understand to be inside them. Again, I delete the specific identities—the fact that it matters absolutely to the couple that this is an embryo that will shortly be within one and not the other woman. If these are persons and the cells of their bodies, they are already set within a naturalistic background that makes them part of an existing order. In this sense the figures of both person and cell have become ground. Thus the people there no doubt think that this (the cells) is what they are made up of and that this is how things really are. Of course they would say that such a view is only one perspective. They are also made up of many other things, all the way from the wrist, to which a watch is attached, to the molecules that make up their cells. Cells, in any case, form tissue, and tissue forms internal organs, and the organs are hung on a frame of bones that is covered by skin, and before you know it, there are Mr. and Mrs. So-and-So. Again, this knowledge depends on innumerable techniques of discovery and description, mobilizing the methods of different disciplines even, but no interpretation is required to see the depth.

In this worldview the bones are inside the skin, and there is marrow within the bones: the order is fixed. Whether talk is of molecules or of whole organisms, the mode of analysis is summoned by the scale of the phenomenon. So the nesting of different types of knowledge within one another follows the natural sequence. Any one of them may require our attention, and will push others into the background, yet unlike the interpretive depth exemplified through figure-ground movement, the relative emplacement of these orders is quite simply not open to interpretation. All you need is method; the photograph of the cells indexes a specific knowledge gained by specific techniques. The very process of magnification (method) tells us that the cells are smaller than the woman; the penetration of the optic machinery tells us that they are inside her body. In the same way, the viewer knows that the photograph of the cells is inside the photograph of it, not the other way around. So although the cells are here brought to the surface in order to be seen or manipulated, that does not alter their essential position as bodies within a body.

Now those cells on the screen there don't look anything like the people they belong to. They are made apparent as a distinct order of phenomenon created by distinct methods of inquiry. And these are regarded as contexts that can exist independently of human intervention. In fact, these people and their cells can occupy the same visual space—both can be on the surface—only by appearing as entities of quite different order. Anthropologists can exhort themselves to treat data on the same level only because the data are naturalized as already different (this is an informant's statement, that is the fieldworker's opinion).[23] It is already scaled. Consider again the quite different visualization of the Ok woman and her bilum (fig. 1). Ok perceive (so Mackenzie implies) an isomorphism between the curve and burden of the bilum and the curve and the burden of the woman's body, especially when she is pregnant. She has on her back, outside, a version of what she also carries on her front, inside. She carries both at the same time, and both are thus equally available to the sensibilities of the observer. In the way the two body forms are perceived, they already occupy the same space. You do not bring the baby artificially to the surface because it is the very surface that is conserved in the way attention is drawn to the body within.

But have we learned anything? Has this traverse added new knowledge? Let me take the fourth photograph (fig. 4), a man decorated in dance attire from Mt. Hagen, also in Papua New Guinea, and ask what kind of space one might create for it.[24]

First, although the face more or less fills the frame, it seemingly offers interpretive depth. Indeed, it seems presented as such in the way the nose is highlighted and the cheeks recede into darkness, and one could add endless exegetical depth. I would have no problem in contextualizing and recontextualizing it—drawing attention to the finery that indicates this is a dancer at a ceremonial exchange display, or to the pigmentation that indicates to him that his ancestors are clustered around the nape of his neck, or to the glistening fat and oil that indicate the health and prosperity he proclaims by decorating at all. One could focus and refocus on each item in turn and, as in the case of the Ok ladies, recontextualize each. Thus the modernist interpreter would appear to "find" depth through relationships between figure and ground seemingly offered by the data themselves.

Second, I could do something closer to the dispersed possibilities of the ultrasound scan. Supposing one started with the bilums that Ok ladies make for men and that men additionally decorate with feathers. One might then look at the feathered plaque in the man's wig that is called in Mt. Hagen by the same term used for *bilum* and *womb*, as well as for jackets and jerseys. These plaques are made by men entirely and made of feathers, always after the same mode. Such a plaque is atop this dancer's wig, its bright red center within a darker surround, just as the man has highlighted his nose in red so it stands out against his darkened ancestor-protected face. Now the occasion of the dance is a display of wealth, brought into the open from having been hidden away, literally in people's houses, metaphorically inside their persons, in the same way that children emerge from the wombs of their mothers. The analogy is an indigenous one. The man himself is, so to speak, an everted mother: he is

Figure 4. A dancer from Mt. Hagen, Papua New Guinea, has painted his face in disguise. The nose is highlighted in red, catching the sun, as does the shell on his forehead, whereas the rest of the face is blackened so that it merges with shadows cast by the dark wig. Photograph by the author (1967).

the child that was born. And he in turn gives birth to the wealth that on this occasion is brought outside, just as the feathers are brought outside and just as he has painted the red color of his inside body on its surface.

Unlike the first set of interpretations, these are not stabilized by a series of "external" contexts. Rather, each depends on the other. (All is interpretation.) Thus, seeing significance in the plaque depends on having thought about the Ok bilums; seeing the red as the inside made outside depends on interpreting the whole occasion as "bringing outside" what is otherwise kept within the house, and so forth. One could produce a string of intertextual sequences, but each interpretative moment would both take from the last and anticipate the next, leaving behind a trail of erased significances. In other words, every ground in turn becomes figure. Incidentally, while the ever-receding horizon of signification also worries Hagen men—especially with regard to the political motives of those around them—they do have strategies for "stopping" the flow, for instance, taking omens to try to comprehend the effects of their acts before they have taken place.

Third, I could also create space in the alternative modernist mood. Figures merge into their ground. (No interpretation is needed.) We know what we see, namely that someone has dressed up and painted his face for what is therefore obviously an important occasion. What we might call the diagnosis is irrelevant—that is, how the person will be judged later by others—as are the details of the finery. "We" (Euro-Americans) wear fine clothes on occasion and swathe ourselves in gowns and regalia, and there is nothing exceptional in that. In fact, there is nothing exceptional about this kind of explanation, except that were it to be proffered these days, it would be deliberately set against other modes of an overtly interpretive kind. That is, it would be used to say that elaborate interpretation is not necessary. In this view, then, the spectator is looking at a familiar kind of human behavior, even though the local form may be unfamiliar. There is no depth to the interpretation of the picture because there is no distance between picture and spectator. The same goes for the rationale of the display. The desire of people to show things off, just as the desire for possession, can be taken as self-evident.

There is a parallel here with figure 3. In the same way as Euro-Americans assume there is a natural linear scaling that puts the cells into the body, and not the other way round, so too in this view there is a scaling among all those traits that are taken as the common characteristics of human beings, wherever they live, and the cultural forms that differentiate their habits and customs.[25] The former, in this view, underlie all human activity, whereas the latter is a superstructure of elaboration that can, so to speak, be discarded—take away the (singular, particular) culture, and you have the commonsense (background) understandings out of which all culture has come. So the observer has immediate access to the basic information presented by the Mt. Hagen dancer: this is someone dressed up for an audience, recognizable in terms of the kinds of motives observer and observed share.[26]

Let me return to the question of movement. The fourth picture obviously "stops" the Mt. Hagen man's movement; in the dance he is deliberately bobbing up and down in order for his feathers and apron to swing back and forth, animating the whole assemblage of decorations. In this he is drawing the attention of the audience less to himself than to his decoration. (The entire assemblage is supposed to conceal his personal features.) What he is striving for is an effect, and the diagnosis of the effect gets enveloped in an ever-receding interpretation of how people have interpreted his display. In the end he never knows the final judgment. But he does know that he will make an effect of some sort, and he dances on the basis of what he presumes are commonsense (Hagen) understandings he shares with the spectators. By focusing analytical attention on the movement, then, I can simultaneously recapitulate all the modes I have been talking about—recontextualize the picture (give it depth like the Ok ladies); show how the dancer is caught in an endless speculative spiral of interpretation and counterinterpretation (like the ultrasound scan); or suggest that he only dances at all on the basis of understandings he shares with those who look at him and which he would no doubt politely extend to any anthropologists who were around too (like the persons looking at the cells).

A FINAL OSCILLATION

Can one move on from these previous positions? One feature about the fourth photograph recalls Verran's account of the Australian aboriginal landscape. Mirrored in the Mt. Hagen dancer's gesture, eyes ahead, is another person, the spectator. However flawed or criticizable the stance that the observer-interpreter takes, he or she knows him- or herself as a person. So the reason my attention is caught by these people is because they catch me. Recall figure 1. Whether the anthropologist had to maneuver herself into a position to photograph three women walking away from her, or whether a painted dancer seduces the spectator, there is the movement of mutual orientation. To look at these photographs again is to create afresh a space that the onlooker knows as a social space. One person's movement provides a measure for another's.

In attributing interpretive intentions to other people, a Euro-American modernist might well say that each also provides an interpretive moment for the other. The two onlookers are caught in what they know, or do not know, about one another. They are also caught in an inevitable compromise—the understanding each has of the other is compromised by the understanding each imagines for the other but cannot know. Here is a quotidian oscillation indeed. That unfulfilled expectation—the incomplete knowledge each has—is what simultaneously compels and makes disappointing attempts to interpret what people mean by what they do. Perhaps Euro-American appeals to "reality" arise when you are able to take the persons away, as I have done at moments in all four photographs; two of them (figs. 2 and 3) are meant to illustrate the process here. Then the person of the observer has to be his or her own source of regard and his or her own measure of things. What you see instead of a world filled with other persons is a world on which this or that human, individual, interpreter offers his or her particular and singular perspective. That perspective can always be dwarfed by phenomena of a quite different order. I have not done much more than point to certain effects of scale and ponder its presence in some current projects of "understanding" the world. Either figuring, that is, when ground becomes figure (all interpretation), or grounding, that is, when figure becomes ground (no interpretation), may seem the more important activity, either depth or surface as the greater approximation to reality. At the same time, and obviously, interpretation always falls short of whatever is used to measure it; as we have long known, it always brings the realization of everything that has not yet, or already has, been interpreted.[27] Yet this is more than an autonomous or self-generating outcome of hermeneutic method or semiotic theorizing or philosophical endgames. It is of a piece, I have been suggesting, with certain modernist and Western (Euro-American) projections at large, including particular notions of space and time, and the idea that in specifying a singular condition one enlarges a figure only to reduce it against its wider background.

NOTES

A version of this chapter was originally given to the International Centre for Contemporary Cultural Research seminar series at Manchester University, "Creative Social Space," in 1993. My thanks to Pnina Werbner (and see 1993, 1997) for her illuminating comments.

1. The clumsy phrase is meant to cover much more than paintings, photographs, and the like, which obviously demand visual attention; see Wagner (1986a, 1986b), the inspiration for the present exercise.

2. I mean primarily the elucidation of meanings, including the processes of analysis and explanation by which an observer makes meanings ("understanding") for him- or herself, in short, reading, explication, making sense (Mailloux 1995, 121).

3. Law and Benschop (1997), who also take a set of four visual depictions, comment on the kind of world depicted, so to speak, beyond the depictions.

4. This is a particular description of a divergence found in numerous guises. See, for example, Hirschman (1987), who begins by quoting a journal article that argued against the collection of empirical materials with insufficient attention to theoretical analysis to determine the criteria of selection and goes on to say that there can be circumstances where a work "explains far too much" (he cites the case of a "paradigm" that spawns—his term—thirty-four hypotheses) (1987, 179). Robert Cooper's (1997) review of Gianni Vattimo's *Beyond Interpretation* points to the relentless questioning of certainties, which leads to having to notice everything and thus to "over-interpretation" by contrast with the denial of complexities in conveying understanding ("interstanding"), which leads to "under-interpretation."

5. The appeal is regularly made in social anthropology at moments when its paradigms and models seem to make more rather than less complicated the effort of understanding strange phenomena.

6. See, for example, Davis's (1992, 28) comment on how "to describe exchange in a way which accepts natives' experiences that there are different kinds of exchange; [while at the same time wanting] to explore an underlying reality which is, so to speak, consistently at the same level." In effect Davis argues that different orders of knowledge are flagged both by people's different categorizations and by the difference between them and those (anthropologists) who explore what it is they say, yet these differences are ones that analysis ought then to treat all on a par. The former statement implies interpretive work that has already taken place (minimally, in discerning what the relevant categories are), whereas the latter claims that there is nothing the anthropologist's interpretations can add that has any special purchase—his or her commonsense observations are on a par with those of the people under study.

7. "Order" both in the sense of scale (order of magnitude) and in the sense of different orders (families, species) of phenomena. The "space" and "depth" in my title belong to different orders in the second sense (space-time/depth-surface).

8. At the same time there is a "complex" relationship here, of the kind anthropologists have referred to in the analysis of kinship systems, for example, in the juxtaposition of different orders (second sense) of phenomena.

9. Compare Gell (1998) on styles in art: "The notion of 'individual style' implicitly depends on the existence of collective, undifferentiated, period styles against which individuality emerges as a 'figure' against 'ground' " (159).

10. However, one could equally well make the concept of "space," as a historically

modernist invention, do all the gathering and particularizing work of the concept of "place" (after the Derridean move that makes speech a form of writing).

11. These conceptions are of course criticized and upturned, as Casey does, within the Euro-American tradition. See, for example, Ingold's (1992, 1993, 1995) several expositions on the different epistemological renderings of *environment*. It may be seen now as an arena within which the individual organism is contained, now as itself contained within the organism's individual capacity to make of its surroundings the environment in which it survives.

12. One could see these viewpoints as simultaneous expansions of a relationship between literal and figurative constructions. Figurative perception yields an image, an entity momentarily precluded from further explanation and thus "self representing," whereas literal constructions open out relations, are discursive, point to definitional properties, and act as a set of reference markers (Wagner 1986a).

13. See, for example, Parker and Cooper (1998), after Ilya Prigogine. To borrow the language of complexity theory, systems pushed away from equilibrium and thriving in oscillation between order and disorder are known as complex.

14. Rabinow and Sullivan's (1987) magisterial introduction to the earlier interpretive turn provides for this very partial statement a much wider context, namely a history of interpretive standpoints. They distinguish interpretivist analysis from deconstruction and theories of communicative rationality, as well as from neoconservatism, with Taylor's contribution being taken as a strong reading of the interpretive tradition. My project is quite different (has its own singular character) from this history of ideas. Thus my apparent reduction of an otherwise complicated field to a simple axis is given, very simply, by the scale of "too much" and "too little" interpretation.

15. Itself the subject of criticism. Compare Thomas's comment (1996, 16), almost in Casey's words, that we mistakenly proceed as though uninterpreted material phenomena were primary and had (secondary) interpretations added to them—phenomena that first show up in the world have in fact to be "unworlded" (decontextualized, deinterpreted) in order then to be the object of explicit interpretation.

16. For example, Davis, in his observations on exchange, is concerned to exemplify the "underlying pattern to exchange in all cultures" (1992, 27), including its complex social meanings, but looks on analyses that attend to *meanings* (the term is his) as displacing what people say they do with a false sense of depth. "I find it difficult to argue that it [the pattern] lies deeper in some instances than in others or that it is more real than people's intentions and their statements about their actions." To concentrate on symbols and meanings renders all else unreal (1992, 8). In his view this is at worst obfuscating, at best only to be laid on a par with what is apparently immediately accessible—"the reality of the natives' understandings of what they do" (1992, 27).

17. For example, models may become suddenly visible for "what they are": a heap of

painted metaphors, boxes, and arrows that are no more than lines on paper. In that moment of doubt what is "stopped," so to speak, is a willingness to carry on with interpretation. Yet every stopping place brings a new constellation of things into view. When one seeks ways to make new knowledge, the novelty of each particular (individual) becomes a driving motor of further interpretive endeavor.

18. Animation in the social sciences is most evident when observers produce "models" of what they observe, as-if mechanisms with working parts that show what happens when this variable is moved against that. On animation effects in patternings, see Gell (1998, 77–79).

19. With warm thanks to Sarah Franklin for providing me with these two examples.

20. Thus Mackenzie (1991) argues that the very different-looking and decorated bilum worn by male initiates also connotes aspects of motherhood.

21. See, for example, Price's (1990) cautionary remarks:

> Rapid developments in ultrasound equipment yield not only more and more data but also uncertainties about interpretation. Newly identified features extend both the range of normality at each stage of gestation and the stock of knowledge about the natural history of developmental conditions. . . . A misdiagnosis or an intervention following diagnosis may lead to the termination of a wanted and normal pregnancy. Overdiagnosis of foetal abnormality is but one example of the cascade effect in clinical care where one medical intervention leads to another with an unwanted outcome for the woman. (137)

22. By "experts" I mean the radiographer who operates the scan and the medical consultant to the patient/client (see Price 1990, 137–38).

23. In fact, the photograph could almost illustrate Davis's (1992, 28) statement about the anthropologist's comparative approach to exchange (note 16 above).

24. A version in color can be seen in Strathern and Strathern (1971, plate 11). I took this photograph in 1967, in the Central Melpa area of Mt. Hagen, Papua New Guinea. I trust it conserves anonymity; dancers do not like to be recognized through their decorations. It is the decorations that are the subject of the dancer's display and, here, the subject of the photograph.

25. For example, Annette Weiner (1992, 154) writes, "Although local solutions [to a certain universal paradox] are spectacularly diverse—a tribute to human ingenuity and imagination—they are also poignantly distressing [i.e., we share common feelings in relation to them]."

26. This style of argument has been explicitly applied to Papua New Guinea. I quote further from Annette Weiner's work on exchange, which aims to show that "all exchange is predicated on a *universal* paradox—how to keep-while-giving" (Weiner 1992,

5, my emphasis, author's omitted). What follows is presented as self-evident, beyond the need for interpretation. "Some things . . . are easy to give. But there are other possessions that are imbued with the intrinsic and ineffable identities of their owners which are not easy to give away. . . . [And then the reassurance] *We are all familiar with the crowns of queens and kings*—the signs and symbols of authority and power—or antique furniture and paintings that proclaim a family's distinguished ancestry. . . . When a Maori chief brandishes a sacred cloak . . ." (1992, 6, my emphasis). Weiner makes her connections here explicit: "My references . . . to examples from Western history are specifically directed to overcoming these divisions [between primitive and rational worlds] and to show how the sources of difference and hierarchy are profoundly similar because they arise out of the universal paradox" (1992, 154).

27. It was a writer's complaints that "much more needs to be said," that his endeavor at interpretation was incomplete and full of missing links, which led to my reflection on the kind of infinite worlds presupposed by modernist notions (and I take notions of society as a case in point) (Strathern 1992).

REFERENCES

Birke, L., S. Himmelweit, and G. Vines. 1990. *Tomorrow's Child: Reproductive Technologies in the Nineties.* London: Virago Press.

Casey, E. S. 1996. "How to Get from Space to Place in a Fairly Short Stretch of Time: Phenomenological Prolegomena." In S. Feld and K. Basso, eds., *Senses of Place.* Santa Fe: School of American Research Press.

Cooper, R. 1997. "Millennium Notes for Social Theory." Review of *Beyond Interpretation: The Meaning of Hermeneutics for Philosophy,* by G. Vattimo. *Sociological Review* 45, no. 4: 690–703.

Davis, J. 1992. *Exchange.* Buckingham: Open University Press.

Gell, A. 1998. *Art and Agency: An Anthropological Theory.* Oxford: Clarendon Press.

Greenhouse, C. J. 1996. *A Moment's Notice: Time Politics across Cultures.* Ithaca: Cornell University Press.

Hirsch, E. 1995. "Landscape: Between Place and Space." In E. Hirsch and M. O'Hanlon, eds., *The Anthropology of Landscape: Perspectives on Place and Space.* Oxford: Clarendon Press.

Hirschman, A. O. 1987. "The Search for Paradigms as a Hindrance to Understanding." In P. Rabinow and W. M. Sullivan, eds., *Interpretive Social Science: A Second Look.* Berkeley: University of California Press.

Ingold, T. 1992. "Culture and the Perception of the Environment." In E. Croll and D. Parkin, eds., *Bush Base: Forest Farm. Culture, Environment, and Development.* London: Routledge.

——. 1993. "The Temporality of the Landscape." *World Archaeology* 25: 152–74.

———. 1995. "Building, Dwelling, Living: How Animals and People Make Themselves at Home in the World." In M. Strathern, ed., *Shifting Contexts: Transformations in Anthropological Knowledge*. London: Routledge.

Law, J., and R. Benschop. 1997. "Resisting Pictures: Representation, Distribution, and Ontological Politics." In Kevin Hetherington and Rolland Munro, eds., *Ideas of Difference: Social Spaces and the Labour of Division*. Oxford: Blackwell.

Mackenzie, M. 1991. *Androgynous Objects: String Bags and Gender in Central New Guinea*. Chur: Harwood Academic Publishers.

Mailloux, S. 1995. "Interpretation." In F. Lentricchia and T. McLaughlin, eds., *Critical Terms for Literary Study*. Chicago: University of Chicago Press.

Mosko, M. 1985. *Quadripartite Structure: Categories, Relations and Homologies in Bush Mekeo Culture*. Cambridge: Cambridge University Press.

Myers, F. R. 1991. *Pintupi Country, Pintupi Self: Sentiment, Place, and Politics among Western Desert Aborigines*. Berkeley: University of California Press.

Nilsson, L. 1990. *A Child Is Born*. London: Doubleday.

Parker, M., and R. Cooper. 1998. "Cyborganization: Cinema as Nervous System." In J. Hassard and R. Holliday, eds., *Organization-Representation: Work and Organizations in Popular Culture*, 201–28. London: Sage.

Price, F. V. 1990. "The Management of Uncertainty in Obstetric Practice: Ultrasonography, *In Vitro* Fertilisation and Embryo Transfer." In M. McNeil, I. Varcoe, and S. Yearley, eds., *The New Reproductive Technologies*. London: Macmillan.

Rabinow, P., and W. M. Sullivan, eds., 1987. *Interpretive Social Science: A Second Look*. Berkeley: University of California Press.

Rapp, R. 1986. "Translating the Genetic Code: The Discourse of Genetic Counselling." Paper presented at American Ethnological Society meeting.

Thomas, J. 1996. "Time, Culture and Identity." *Archaeological Dialogues* 1: 6–21.

Strathern, A., and M. Strathern. 1971. *Self-Decoration in Mt. Hagen*. London: Duckworth.

Strathern, M. 1991. *Partial Connections*. Savage, Md.: Rowman and Littlefield.

———. 1992. "Writing Societies, Writing Persons." *History of the Human Sciences* 5: 5–16. Reprinted in M. Strathern. 1999. *Property, Substance, and Effect: Anthropological Essays on Persons and Things*. London: Athlone Press.

———. 2000. "Environments Within: An Ethnographic Commentary on Scale." In K. Flint and H. Morphy, eds., *Culture, Landscape, and the Environment*. Oxford: Oxford University Press.

Verran, H. 1998. "Managing Australian Lands through Burning: Learning from Yolngu Aboriginal Knowledge Traditions." Department of History and Philosophy of Science, University of Melbourne. Mimeographed.

Wagner, R. 1986a. *Symbols That Stand for Themselves*. Chicago: University of Chicago Press.

———. 1986b. "Figure-Ground Reversal." In L. Lincoln, ed., *Assemblage of Spirits*. New York: George Braziller.

Weiner, A. B. 1992. *Inalienable Possessions: The Paradox of Keeping-While-Giving.* Berkeley: University of California Press.

Weiner, J., ed. 1995. *Too Many Meanings. Social Analysis* 38 (special issue).

Werbner, P. 1993. "Essentialising the Other." Department of Social Relations, University of Keele, Keele, Staffordshire. Manuscript.

———. 1997. "Essentialising Essentialism, Essentialising Silence: Ambivalence and Multiplicity in the Constructions of Racism and Ethnicity." In P. Werbner and T. Mahood, eds., *Debating Cultural Hybridity: Multi-Cultural Identities and the Politics of Anti-Racism.* London: Zed Books.

JOHN LAW

On Hidden Heterogeneities:

Complexity, Formalism, and Aircraft Design

You don't have a map in your head, as a child. Later, you have the globe—the seas and the shapes—and you can't ever get back to that emptiness, that mystery. Knowing that there are other places, but not knowing where they are, or how to get there.—Penelope Lively, *City of the Mind*

. . . mimesis fuses brilliantly with alterity to achieve the connection necessary for magical effect, the connection I have earlier alluded to as a kind of electricity, an ac/dc pattern of rapid oscillations of difference. It is the artful combination, the playing with the combinatorial perplexity, that is necessary; a magnificent excessiveness over and beyond the fact that mimesis implies alterity as its flip-side. The full effect occurs when the necessary impossibility is attained, when mimesis becomes alterity. Then, and only then can spirit and matter, history and nature, flow into each others' otherness.—Michael Taussig, *Mimesis and Alterity*

FIRST STORY

It was to be eighty-four feet long, twenty-three feet high, and thirty-five feet from wing tip to wing tip. It was called the P.17A. And it was—it is—the design for an aircraft, a military aircraft, submitted by the aircraft manufacturer English Electric Company to the British government in 1958.

I will talk about its wings, about the design of its wings.

Like a paper dart, these were to be delta shaped, their leading edge swept back at 50°. They were to be thin—their thickness only 2.5 percent of their breadth at the tip. They were to be short and broad—their aspect ratio (the span from wing tip to wing tip divided by gross surface area) was to be 2.77. And their gross surface area was to be 597.3 square feet.[1]

So why were they to have this shape? What was the reasoning that lay behind them? This is the topic of this essay: it is a study in design, in complexity as heterogeneity, and, in particular, in the multiplicity of heterogeneity.

The story starts with a formalism that helps to express or explain, or to impose exigencies on the shape of the wings. However, this formalism also does a lot more. Look at the following, which comes from the English Electric brochure on the P.17A:[2]

$$G = \frac{(\text{velocity} \times \text{lift slope})}{\text{wing loading}} = \frac{M \cdot a_t}{W/S} \quad (1)$$

Let me define the terms, for these are terms that can be linked to the words that appear in the less formal part of the expression.

- M is Mach number, the speed of sound, so M = 2 would be twice the speed of sound, and so on.
- a_t is transonic lift slope, of which more in a moment.
- W is the weight of the aircraft.
- S is the wing area.
- G is a measure of the response of the aircraft as it flies through vertical gusts of wind.

The expression is a way of expressing what aerodynamicists call "gust response." It is a quantification of the susceptibility of an aircraft to vertical buffeting. The aircraft, or so the expression tells us, will be buffeted less if it weighs more, and it will be buffeted more if it flies faster, if it has a larger wing, and if its lift slope is higher.

DIFFERENCE

This wing, and the formalism from the English Electric brochure, have much to tell us about complexities, particularly with the complexities that come with absences that are also presences, those complexities that come with Othernesses that are both expelled and drawn in. It has much to say about the complexities of that which is not pure or clean or homogeneous but rather carries what is different within. I will think of these as the complexities of heterogeneity.

The tools that I will use to think about this derive from semiotics. A reminder: semiotics is the study of relations. More specifically, it is the argument that terms, objects, entities, are formed in difference between one another. The argument is that they don't have essential attributes but instead achieve their significance in terms of their relations, relations of difference.

It is easy to apply semiotics to a formalism such as the one above, for this is the distribution of a visible set of relations, a set of differences that helps to determine the significance or role of the terms that are linked together. For instance, it establishes the difference between gust response and velocity. There are, as they say, "variables" that intervene between these, such as lift slope and wing loading. If everything else were equal, if these variables were not to intervene, then gust response and velocity would vary together—which they don't, because it is rare for everything to be equal.

But is everything there? To pose the question is to suggest the answer. Something, indeed much, is missing. In one way this is blindingly obvious, for the distributions made by formalisms don't stand alone. But what is missing? This is my concern, the point of an inquiry into complexity as heterogeneity. It is an inquiry that requires that we turn up the magnification of the stories and look in more detail at their terms with the hope of exposing and investigating a list of heterogeneities.

SECOND STORY

If we magnify the formalism then what we see depends on what we choose to magnify and where we look. I'll magnify it in various ways in the course of this essay, but I'll start with the term that I left hanging in the air, the term *lift slope*. We already know something about lift slope. We know that it is related to, but different from, gust response and the other terms in the formalism. But outside the formalism the term is idle, a shortcut. It doesn't tell us anything. So what happens if we magnify it? What do we discover?

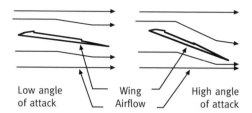

Low angle
of attack

Wing
Airflow

High angle
of attack

Figure 1. Relationship between angle of attack and lift. If the increase in lift with increase in angle of attack is small, then lift curve slope is low.

The answer is that it decomposes, turning from a single term into a relation between two further terms. So this is another difference, another specified difference. And the new terms are *lift* and *angle of attack*.

Some definitions:

– Lift is the lifting force of a wing as it moves through the air. In engineering this is usually written C_L.
– Angle of attack, written α, is (roughly) the angle between the wing and the air through which it is traveling (see fig. 1).
– And lift slope is the slope of the curve that links the two for a given wing if they are laid out as the two coordinates of a graph (see fig. 2).

All of this means that if lift slope is low, then lift doesn't change much as the angle of attack alters and the curve is flattish, and if it is high, then it does.

HETEROGENEITY/SIMPLICITY

If we magnify the term *lift slope* in this way then we introduce a further set of differences. We might write them into expression (1) to produce something like this:

$$G = \frac{\text{velocity} \times (\text{change in lift coefficient}/\text{change in angle of attack})}{\text{aircraft weight}/\text{wing area}}$$

$$= \frac{M \cdot (dC_L/d\alpha)}{W/S} \quad (2)$$

We might work at this formalism to rearrange its terms and simplify it a little. But let's make another point. This new formalism is more complicated than the old although it's not unmanageable, at least not yet. But if we were to expand the other terms—for instance unpacking the calcula-

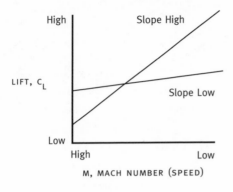

Figure 2.
Curves relating lift to speed.

tions that lead to Mach number, M—it would grow still further. And, no doubt, it could be expanded in other directions too.

What might we make of this? One answer is that design is all about distributing relations of difference but that only some of these are relations of presence (fig. 3). Only some of them crop up together on the page. The corollary is that the making of this center, this formalism, performs many other relations, including links that are relations of absence. In one way or another, and for one reason or another, there are limits to the relations made present.

I want to suggest that there are several logics of absence or alterity, and I will point to some of these shortly. But, looking at the formalism above, there is a straightforward and immediate version of the logic of absence. This is the fact that it is easier to handle formalisms with fewer terms than those with more (although the same logic applies to nonformalisms). So this, perhaps, is a basic design principle, a basic feature of the character of making centers, of making designs—that present complexity is self-limiting.[3]

I'm going to call this heterogeneity/simplicity. If we put *heterogeneity* on one side for the moment, then by *simplicity* I mean, straightforwardly, that there is not enough room for everything. Not everything can crowd into a single place, and implosion, or, perhaps better, condensation, is impracticable. Perhaps this is a general principle, but, linked to concern with design and control, it's what the actor-network theorists point to when they tell of "punctualization."[4] That which is complicated comes in simple packages—like lift slope—that can be used to make sense.

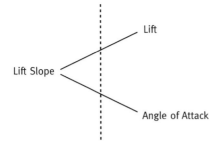

Figure 3.

In the paragraph immediately after the formalism in the brochure we read the following: "By comparing several aircraft, of known characteristics, which have been flown in low altitude turbulence, it is possible to decide a maximum value for this parameter which will ensure a comfortable flight."[5] "This parameter" is G, gust response again.

HETEROGENEITY AND ABSENCE/PRESENCE

On the one hand the two paragraphs are contiguous. It is reasonable to imagine continuity, copresence, and more relations of difference. But as we read on and a moment passes, so the field of presence starts to shift. Before, it was a matter of formalisms, terms that stood in quantifiable relations with one another. Now it is something different.

When we looked at that formalism we already knew that something was absent. We knew that there was one kind of logic at work, a logic of absence. We also knew that this absence was an engineering/algebraic logic, one of pragmatic simplicity, the business of limiting complication in order to secure ease of manipulation. But there were other kinds of absence too. Indeed, in order to make the narrative work, I let slip a clue, for by referring to lift slope as "idle" I traded on another absence: the suspicion that the reader would "know" what was meant by such terms as *weight* or *surface area*—which, by implication, were not idle. This, then, was another logic of absence.

The second paragraph, the one that makes my "third story," takes us in another direction. It tells us new kinds of relations are being performed, relations that no longer have to do with formalisms but rather with the flying of aircraft. I will delve into this shortly, but first let's focus on the changing relations of presence. For the effect of the new paragraph is to perform a subtle shift. It "reminds" us what is absent from the formalism, but this is a double effect. First it reminds us that there is no reference to "the real world," to what "actually happens" (as opposed to what might happen). But second, it also inserts that absent "real world" into the formalism, which means that after the new paragraph the real world is, as it were, both present and absent from the formalism and that the formalism has started to acquire extra weight. It has started to acquire this weight in the impossible interference between absence and presence.

This, then, will be my definition of *heterogeneity*—heterogeneity in design and heterogeneity elsewhere. I will say that heterogeneity is an oscillation between absence and presence. It is about the way in which whatever is not there is also there but also how that which is there is also not there. Heterogeneity, then, is about the differences that reside in connection and disconnection, or, more precisely, it is about the ambivalent distributions entailed in dis/connection. Which means that simplicity not only creates absence, but it also depends on presence. Hence the term *heterogeneity/simplicity.* Now we are in a position to ask whether there are other forms of absence/presence, other heterogeneities.

FOURTH STORY

If we stay with the aircrew a little longer and search through the pile of documents we find this:

> The state of the pilots is variously described as "tired," "bathed in sweat," "weakness in limbs," "headache." The main factors causing fatigue appear to be several. There are oscillations in the higher frequencies to which various portions of the human anatomy respond . . . , moderate impacts which continually jar the pilot and throw him about, and occasional large gusts which frighten him by giving the aircraft a violent movement. In addition the pilot had the strain of carrying on with his job, and the worry whether the aircraft structure would stand up to the treatment.[6]

This paragraph is taken from an internal English Electric memorandum.

Observing next that the pilots are "near the limit of their endurance," it continues by noting that "the navigator, who has his eyes on his instruments, will be more prone to sickness than the pilot who looks at the horizon. At the same time he will be trying to extract precise information from a variety of electronic equipment requiring fine adjustments to be made by hand."[7]

Here we have a second form of absence. This isn't a matter of simplicity— or if it is, then it is a new form of simplicity, for this is material absence. Removed from the flat space occupied by the formalism, we find ourselves in the sweating world of the aircrew. We discover pilots who flew their creaking aircraft too low, pilots who worried about whether the wings would break off, pilots who were thrown about their cockpits, pilots who climbed shaking from their aircraft at the end of these flights.

If we are imaginative, then perhaps we can smell the fear, feel the sweat on the bodies, the taste of vomit. For this is another set of presences, another set of relations, another syntax, another set of differences— different presences that are absent from the space of algebra.

The corporeal or, if we include the aircraft, the corporal-and-the-technological—these are absent from the space of the page, from the formalism about "G," gust response. This is the absence of a form of materiality. In the way they write the P.17A brochure, there is no room for vomit; it does not fit. There is no room for sweat in formalisms. In the documents that are sent to the government ministries there isn't enough space for Meteor aircraft, so they are removed, not simply because there isn't enough room but also, or more, because they are materials that do not perform themselves in the differences of the page, within a logic performed in algebraic difference.

Yet these are absences that are also present, for G is there on the page (fig. 4). Gust response is fixed not by the other parameters that occur in the formalism (although these are fixed in their relations with one another) but rather in a set of relations of absence/presence to do with the suffering of aircrew. "By comparing several aircraft, of known characteristics, which have been flown in low altitude turbulence" (I quote the sentence again), "it is possible to decide a maximum value for this parameter which will ensure a comfortable flight." This is a parameter to do

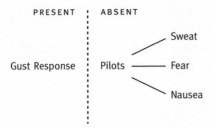

PRESENT : ABSENT

Gust Response : Pilots ——— Fear

Sweat

Nausea

Figure 4.

with comfort of particular aircrew, comfort that will allow them to perform the task of piloting the aircraft efficiently, properly.

Absence/presence, the absence of materiality that is also a presence—
no doubt this is what those who write actor-network studies intend when
they talk of "translation" and "chains of translation."[8] And this is a second oscillation in the distributions of heterogeneity: the absent presence
of materiality, the Otherness of materials that don't fit in but also do.

FIFTH STORY

Before I go on with this story of what is absent—about the absence, for
instance, of fear—I need to go back to the formalism to understand what
is happening to G and to forget, for the moment, the crew. "If the gust
response parameter, G, is fixed to give a certain response level, and the
operational Mach number and the aircraft weight are also fixed, then
from (1) it is clear that $a_t \cdot S$ becomes constant." What is happening here?
Let's deal with formalism first.

If G (gust response), M (speed), and W (weight) are fixed, then this
means that the only terms that still have freedom to move are a_t and S. It's
easier to see what's going on if we rewrite the first expression

$$G = \frac{M \cdot a_t}{W/S} \quad (1)$$

as

$$G = \frac{M \cdot a_t \cdot S}{W} \quad (2)$$

But if G, S, and W are now fixed, then equation (2) reveals that a_t multiplied by S is (now going to be) a constant. When one goes up, the other

goes down. It's a nice simplification: speed is inversely correlated to transonic lift slope.

But what of W and M, weight and speed? How come these have been fixed? Let's think first about speed. The previous page of the English Electric brochure tells us that "the essential design compromise implied by OR 339 is between high speed flight at low level, and operation from short airfields. The intermediate choice between a high-wing loading with a low aspect ratio to minimise gust response, and a large wing area assisted by high lift devices to provide plenty of lift at low speeds, must be resolved."[9] Here there are a lot more complications, but let's focus on the phrase "high speed at low level." Where has this come from? The answer is in "OR 339," an Air Ministry document, an Operational Requirement written by officers of the air force and telling a story about what a new aircraft is supposed to do. Part of paragraph 10 of OR 339 runs as follows: "In order to minimise the effect of enemy defences, primary emphasis will be given to penetration to, and escape from, the target at low altitude."[10] And part of paragraph 16 reads: "The penetration speed is to be in excess of $M = 0.9$ at sea level, with an ability to make a short burst at supersonic speed."[11]

So speed, M, is fixed "in order to minimise the effect of enemy defences." But if we push the paper chase one stage further, we can ask, Who is the "enemy"? And what are its "defences"?

Here is the opening paragraph of OR 339: "By 1965 a new aircraft will be required by the Royal Air Force for tactical strike and reconnaissance operations in limited war using nuclear and conventional weapons. Such an aircraft will enable the Royal Air Force to continue to make an effective contribution to the strength of SACEUR's shield forces, as well as to our other regional pacts."[12] SACEUR: this is an acronym for Supreme Allied Commander Europe, which tells us, as if we didn't already know, that we have encountered another looming absence/presence: "We shall wish to consider whether there is a requirement for a low level weapon, either manned or unmanned, in case the Russian defences become effective against high flying aircraft and ballistic missiles."[13]

Here it is at last, made present, not in OR 339 but in the correspondence of government ministers. Taking the paper chase one step further into a background document to OR 339 that describes the earlier Canberra, we at last begin to learn about the likely defenses of the Russian enemy: "The Canberras, operated strictly at a low level, may continue to be effective until the enemy develops an efficient low level surface to air guided weapon."[14] If an attacking plane is to get away from a defensive, surface-to-air, guided weapon, then it needs to fly fast ("high penetration speed") and very low—but the Canberra can't do this.

HETEROGENEITY/OTHERNESS

This chain of differences is long-winded, ramifying endlessly and growing many branches. But we don't need to look into all of its ramifications. Retracing one line will do, one set of dis/connections.

Gust response, G, was fixed in a relation of material heterogeneity, the absence/presence of the sweating pilots. And M, Mach number, was also fixed because OR 339 sought to minimize the effect of enemy defenses. In the final set of dis/connections the enemy turned out to be "the Russians" and the defenses "an efficient low level surface to air guided weapon." So "fear" and "the Russians" were also within the formalism, not simply outside it.

None of this is empirically extraordinary. In tracing this chain we're not learning anything startling about the design of the P.17A. But I think we've learned something more about heterogeneity. We've learned that the enemy is within, that it is within the design, within the formalism. And the chain spells out the way—one of the ways—in which the enemy has been incorporated or assimilated.

This is another form of heterogeneity, another oscillation in differences that are both absent and present (fig. 5). For the enemy and its surface-to-air guided weapons are a part of the formalism, a part of the wing design, rigorously present. At the same time, like the extended formalism, and the bodies of the pilots, they are just as rigorously absent. So the argument is that this is a third form of heterogeneity; another version of the alternation of absence/presence, the heterogeneity of tellable Otherness. The enemy excluded, the foe that is necessary, necessarily included, necessarily a part of the center, necessarily other.

"The Other" is a threat. The air force officers who write operational requirements talk in just those terms, speaking of "the threat." This means that "the Russians and their surface to air guided weapons" are like Edward Said's Orientals.[15] They are necessary to the West, to its making

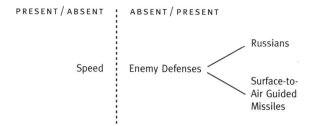

PRESENT / ABSENT   ABSENT / PRESENT

Speed   Enemy Defenses   Russians   Surface-to-Air Guided Missiles

Figure 5.

of itself, because they are dangerous, different, antithetical. They play a similar ambivalent role, for they are indeed a threat, a danger, something apart and something to be kept apart. They deserve to be forbidden, excluded, kept at the periphery. Or, in the language of defense, they deserve "interdiction." So Otherness is a dangerous absence, but at the same time it is a promise, a seduction, a necessity, an incorporation, a need incorporated in its absence into the semiotics of presence. It is incorporated, for instance, into speed, M, and into the formalism linking gust response, G, to M; for without this incorporation M might take any value, the wing of the P.17A might take a different shape, and the RAF need for "a new aircraft" would also look different or perhaps disappear altogether.

Heterogeneity/Otherness is a third form of heterogeneity. It says that the forbidden, the abhorrent, sometimes even the unspeakable, are both present in and absent from whatever is being done, designed, or said.[16] Fear is distributed as an absent presence in the center, in the formalism.

SIXTH STORY

Let's go back to the fixing of parameters. Remember: "If the gust response parameter, G, is fixed to give a certain response level, and the operational Mach number and the aircraft weight are also fixed, then from (1) it is clear that $a_t \cdot S$ becomes constant." So G and M are fixed, but how has weight, W, been fixed? Here's English Electric's brochure again:

> It is desirable both from the point of view of development time and cost, that a proposed aircraft to any given specification should be as small as possible. For any project study the optimum size of aircraft is obtained by iteration during the initial design stages. The size of air-

craft which emerges from this iteration process is a function of many variables. Wing area is determined by performance and aerodynamic requirements. Fuselage size is a function of engine size and the type of installation, volume of equipment, fuel and payload, aerodynamic stability requirements and the assumed percentages of the internal volume of the aircraft which can be utilised.[17]

So there are many variables, too many to magnify. Let me stick with engines.

Aircraft size (and therefore weight) isn't simply a matter of the "size and type of installation" but is also, and even more immediately, a function of the number of engines. Here is OR 339 again: "The Air Staff require the aircraft design to incorporate two engines."[18] But why two engines? The English Electric brochure offers an insert in the course of writing about another aircraft, the P.1B:

> Abandonment of twin engines would be the only other way of achieving a smaller aircraft and this also involves a large reduction in the sortie pattern. This arrangement has not however been considered, due to the overwhelming pilot preference of a twin-engined arrangement even in the P.1B. This is because of the very high accident rate of supersonic aircraft following total engine failure, due to their very high rate of descent and the limitations of emergency power control systems. The argument for two engines in the present case is reinforced by the need to operate several times further from base than the P.1B and for a substantial time at low altitude where the glide capability would be much reduced.[19]

The pilots are back again. This time they are not being frightened by oscillation or being made nauseous, but they are worrying about another difference that is absent but present, for the worry is that supersonic aircraft are more likely to crash, and the OR 339 aircraft has to travel a long way from home.

But there are other possible differences. Here is Vickers Armstrong. Vickers was a competitor of English Electric and had submitted its own design, the Type 571. One of these designs was for a single-engined aircraft:

> From the very beginning of our study of the GOR we believed that if this project was to move forward into the realm of reality—or perhaps

more aptly the realm of practical politics—it was essential that the cost of the whole project should be kept down to a minimum whilst fully meeting the requirement. This led us towards the small aircraft which, by concentrating the development effort on the equipment offers the most economical solution as well as showing advantages from a purely technical standpoint.[20]

And again: "Overseas sales. The cheaper this aircraft is, both in first cost and operating cost, the wider it's [*sic*] overseas sales potential will be. This would seem to favour the single engine system."[21] The argument was that a small aircraft would sell better, be more lethal per £ spent, and might even be attractive to the Royal Navy because it might fit on their aircraft carriers.[22]

HETEROGENEITY/NONCOHERENCE

Aircraft safety, pilot worry, the need to fly far from base—this was one set of relations, one set of differences, one set of considerations that tended to fix W at a higher value, make the aircraft heavier. Cost, cost-effective lethality, naval use, practical politics, and sales make up a second set of relations, of differences, of considerations that tend to fix W at a lower value and so make the aircraft lighter.

So there are two sets of connections, two sets of relations of difference. This is old territory for technoscience studies. It's a controversy. The Air Ministry is going to disagree with Vickers and stick with its large aircraft: "The reply by D.F.S. to D.O.R.(A)'s request for a study on the single versus twin engined aircraft was received 16th July. It showed fairly conclusively that the twin engined configuration is the less costly in accidents."[23] But if it is a controversy, it is also another form of absence/presence, for controversy and disagreement are absent from W. They are absent from the formalism—there is no room for controversy in formalisms. There is space for trade-offs, reciprocal relations, all kinds of subtle differences and distributions yes, but controversies no, and noncoherences not at all.

If the arguments about the size of the aircraft, about W, about the number of engines it should carry, are a form of controversy, they are also an expression of noncoherence, dispersal, and lack of connection (fig. 6).

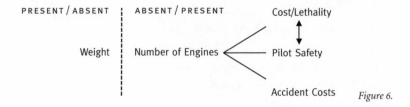

Figure 6.

This is because the Air Ministry is talking about one thing, Vickers about another:

> We must be perfectly clear as to what is the principal objective of the design. It is to produce a tactical strike system for the use of the Royal Air Force in a limited war environment, or a "warm peace" environment, and should thus be aimed at providing the maximum strike potential for a given amount of national effort. It is not—emphatically not in my view—to produce a vehicle to enable the Royal Air Force to carry out a given amount of peace-time flying for a minimum accident rate.[24]

Vickers is talking about cost/lethality, and the Air Ministry about accident costs. This is a dialogue of the partially deaf. It is also a dialogue in which the Ministry decides—in which it "has" the power. But there is something else, a point to do with absence/presence, about the absence/presence of noncoherence. What is present encompasses, embodies, connects, makes links that are absent—except that they aren't connections at all because they aren't coherent. And they aren't joined up into something consistent—except that they are nevertheless brought together, in their noncoherence, into what is present. (Present) coherence/(absent) noncoherence, like jokes, or the performance of jokes in Freud's understanding, noncoherence or interference is a fifth version of heterogeneity.[25]

SEVENTH STORY

Gust response, speed, and weight are fixed, so we are left with a_1, lift slope, the slope of the curve that tracks variations in lift against changes in angle of attack, and the hope that it will be flat. But there is more. For instance, the stories are about transonic flight: how the wing will behave at roughly the speed of sound. But there are other questions. For example, how will it act at low speeds? So here's another complication, one that I chose to ignore earlier. This is the quotation again, from the English Electric brochure: "The essential design compromise implied by OR 339 is between high speed flight at low level, and operation from short airfields. The intermediate choice between a high-wing loading with a low aspect ratio to minimise gust response, and a large wing area assisted by high lift devices to provide plenty of lift at low speeds, must be resolved."[26]

So gust response is important, but so too is takeoff—which means the need for plenty of lift at low speeds. The brochure says:

> Another convenient parameter is one which gives an indication of the relative response to gusts while achieving a given take-off distance. This may be expressed as P say, where

$$P = \left(\frac{a_t}{C_{L_F}} \right) \quad (3)$$

where C_{L_F} is the maximum trimmed C_L, flaps down, in touch-down attitude. P must be a minimum for good design.[27]

We've met these terms before. A reminder:

- C_L is lift coefficient, roughly the lifting force of a wing: here, the lifting force of the wing as the plane comes into land with its flaps down.
- And a_t is lift curve slope, change in lift against change in angle of attack.

This means that P quantifies a hybrid relationship, the hope, that it is possible to find a wing with low transonic gust response and high lift at landing—but how to find a wing of the right "planform," or shape? The brochure continues: "In the absence of comprehensive data on the effects of flaps on low aspect ratio wings, a comparison replacing C_{L_F} by C_{Lmax} indicated that delta wings were superior to trapezoidal and swept wings."[28] The terms here are as follows:

- C_{Lmax} is the aerodynamicist's way of talking of maximum lift.
- Low aspect ratio wings (a reminder) are wings that are short in relation to their area.

- Delta wings are triangular, like those of a paper dart (fig. 7).
- A trapezoidal wing is shaped like a trapezium. That is, although its tip is parallel to its root, the leading and trailing edges converge toward that tip (fig. 7).

The paragraph continues to talk about planform:

Since it was thought possible that by using leading edge flaps on trapezoidal wings, higher values of C_{L_F} might be obtained than those from delta wings, wind tunnel tests were carried out using a trapezoidal wing-body combination. In the event, these tests confirmed that the delta gave higher values of C_{L_F}. The delta planform was also expected to have better transonic characteristics, and again high speed tests in our 18" tunnel on a family of aspect ratio = 2 planforms confirmed the unsatisfactory characteristics of trapezoidal wings, with sudden large aerodynamic centre movements at transonic speeds. This confirmed the choice of the delta planform.[29]

To understand this we need to know about aerodynamic centers. As it moves through the air, a wing lifts, but it does so by differing amounts in different parts of the wing. However, it's useful to sum the effect of all these separate parts to create something called the "aerodynamic center." Roughly speaking this is the place in the wing where the changes in overall lift occur as it flies faster or slower or its angle of attack changes. Above stalling speed the location of the aerodynamic center doesn't shift much: for most wings it is about one-quarter back from the leading edge at subsonic speeds. But as the plane flies faster, at around the speed of sound the aerodynamic center tends to move backward. This isn't a disaster unless it moves quickly and jerkily, in which case the aircraft can be difficult to control—which would take us back to pilot sweat and fear.

So the English Electric engineers were looking at two things. One was aerodynamic center. Here the trapezoidal wing was a problem. The movement of the aerodynamic center was "sudden" and "large," whereas the delta wing was better behaved. The second was C_{Lmax} (*max*, here, means maximum lift). Here there was a surprise: the delta wing was better again. On both counts the trapezoidal wing came off worse.

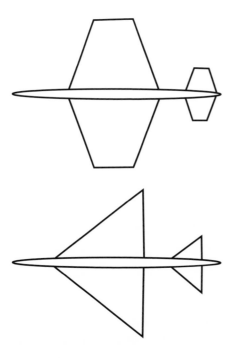

Figure 7.
Trapezoidal and delta wings.

HETEROGENEITY/DEFERRAL

There are two sets of relations: the link between planform, the shape of the wing, and C_{L_F}; and the link between planform and aerodynamic center. The delta wing is better—better, that is, in the wind tunnel.

The wind tunnel is another instance of heterogeneity/materiality, of distribution between absence and presence. On the one hand there are the flat surfaces of the drawing office that work to pull everything together, to center it; and on the other there are the three-dimensional models, materials, and measurements of the wind tunnel. So the wind tunnel is absent from the formalisms of the design office, yet it is present too. But there is something more, something more subtle about the differences that emerge in that distribution. This is the fact that the differences are produced in movement, in a continuing process of displacement, in a continuing displacement between materials and sites.

Perhaps one way of saying this is that it isn't possible to "sum up" the wing in the design office. The representation that appears in the design

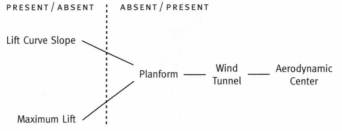

Lift Curve Slope

Planform —— Wind Tunnel —— Aerodynamic Center

Maximum Lift

Figure 8.

office, the sets of formalisms and the drawings, is incomplete, unfinished. It is not centered, not drawn together, because it needs the wind tunnel. It needs the differences that will be generated in the move to the wind tunnel (fig. 8). But so, too, is the version of the wing that appears here. It is also incomplete and needs further attention by the design office, stress engineers, machinists, metallurgists, and, later, by maintenance engineers and mechanics.

This is another ambivalence of absence/presence. This is because the wing is present, all there, drawn out. But those lines also embody absence, the absent/presence of differences that are deferred, of relations that are still to come and have still to be made—relations that are not present, are not now. So the distributions here, the absent/presences, are differences in movement involving displacement through time in what Jacques Derrida calls *différance*.[30] They involve an oscillatory distribution between the present/now and the absent/future or the absent/now and the present/future. They work in the heterogeneous interferences of time, in what we might think of as heterogeneity/deferral.

EIGHTH STORY

In English Electric's summary brochure there is a section at the beginning called "History." Here's part of the first paragraph: "Several widely-differing designs for a Canberra replacement aircraft were studied at Warton towards the end of 1956, and, by early 1957, calculations and wind tunnel tests had shown the optimum design to be an aircraft resembling the P.17 configuration. The merits of this configuration were confirmed by further tests, and the design was found to meet GOR 339 requirements as these became known."[31] This paragraph is accompanied by three drawings of the P.17A that give an overall view of its geometry (see fig. 9).

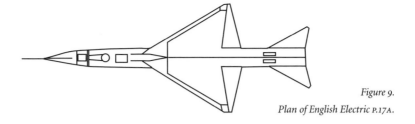

Figure 9.
Plan of English Electric P.17A.

The full brochure offers a more abstract account: "The design process of a modern aircraft, especially a versatile one, could be summarised as obtaining the best combination of a large number of variables each one of which reacts on many of the others. The final product must meet each of its requirements roughly in proportion to the emphasis placed on the relevant role."[32] This is a sentiment that echoes those of a government White Paper:

> An aircraft must be treated not merely as a flying machine but as a complete "weapons system." This phrase means the combination of airframe and engine, the armament needed to enable the aircraft to strike at its target, the radio by which the pilot is guided to action or home to base, the radar with which he locates his target and aims his weapons, and all the oxygen, cooling and other equipment which ensure the safety and efficiency of the crew. Since the failure of any one link could make a weapons system ineffective, the ideal would be that complete responsibility for co-ordinating the various components of the system should rest with one individual, the designer of the aircraft. Experience has shown that this is not completely attainable, but it is the intention to move in this direction as far as practical considerations allow.[33]

THE ARCHITECTURES OF HETEROGENEITY

We move, then, from the wing back to design—to design, as they say, "in general." Design is heterogeneous; this is the argument. It enacts distributions in the form of an oscillation between absence and presence, and oscillation is one of the conditions of its possibility. This means that from the point of view of the center it is ambivalent and incomplete. It also means that it embodies and expresses a set of tensions between what is present on the one hand and what is absent but also present on the other. Simplicity, materiality, Otherness, noncoherence, and deferral—these are the tensions and ambivalences I have listed. No doubt there are others, many others, and no doubt they are heterogeneous too, these distributions.[34] Heterogeneity is just that: heterogeneous.

This is the point of my argument. I want to recover the ontological heterogeneity of this term, *heterogeneity*. I want to understand the tensions that are made in design, in centering, in drawing things together. This is difficult, itself a process full of tension. For the risk is that when we talk of it, we also lose the oscillatory and unassimilable character of heterogeneity: "I am arguing . . . that the stability and form of artifacts should be seen as a function of the interaction of heterogeneous elements as these are shaped and assimilated into a network."[35]

This comment comes from an article that I wrote in 1987. There heterogeneity had to do with what I am now calling heterogeneity/materiality. The concern was with system building: the manipulation of all kinds of materials, technical and human. No doubt this is fine, but it also needs to be nuanced. We need, or so I am suggesting, to avoid the flattening effect of imagining that there is on the one hand a great designer, a heterogeneous engineer, and on the other a set of materially heterogeneous bits and pieces. Instead, we need to hold on to the idea that the agent—the "actor" of the "actor-network"—is an agent, a center, a planner, a designer, only to the extent that matters are also decentered, unplanned, undesigned. To put it more strongly, we need to recognize that to make a center is to be made by a noncenter, a distribution of the conditions of possibility that is both present and not present.

These, then, are tropes with which we might play in technoscience studies of complexity. For the differences are small. There are many narratives with a center of one kind or another in technoscience studies and in large technological systems.[36] Electricity systems, weapons systems, technoscience systems—the performances are similar, and the resonances between these 1987 words from technoscience studies and those words penned by the anonymous author of the 1955 government policy statement about weapons systems cited above are more than coincidental.

But why this similarity? Why this common cultural bias? Here is a hypothesis. The notion of "heterogeneous engineering" may be understood in two ways. It may be treated as a way of thinking about oscillation, absence/presence, uncertainty, and the necessary Otherness that comes with the project of centering. In short, it may be treated as a feature or an aspect of complexity as this is understood by the contributors to this volume. Alternatively, it may be used to describe and perform an architecture of modernism.[37] No doubt there are different versions of this "modern project." No doubt they do different things. But, to put it too quickly, perhaps we might say of this that it is a way of being that seeks to improve the world, to engineer it, to build a better society by knowing, by gathering knowledge together, and then by deploying it in the attempt to order relations in the best possible way. This is an architecture that seeks to impose a specific and optimum distribution on its materials, human and otherwise.

The second version of "heterogeneous engineering" resonates with the benevolent and centering intention of this modernism. It catches something important about each of the "modernist" quotations above: the historical talk of the aircraft design and its "merits"; the "best combination of variables" cited in the English Electric statement of design philosophy; Vickers's systems talk with its trade-offs between cost and lethality; and the "combination" of elements mentioned in the government statement about weapons systems. In each it catches the utopian need to deal in different kinds of materials, technical and social, to center them, to handle them, to manage them. It does it with the characteristic modernist lack of concern with things in themselves—with, for instance, the distinction between human and nonhuman—for the perfect society involves both human and technical innovation. In each it catches the concern with simplification, with bringing materials together to optimize the outcome. It catches, that is, the need, the desire, to combine them at a privileged place, that of the designer. In each it catches the "semiotic" impulse that underpins the combination of somewhat pliable bits and pieces: the idea that components are a more or less malleable effect of a set of relations of difference, a set of relations that can be engineered to produce a better world. Perhaps, too, it also catches in each of these citations an acknowledgment of deferral, the deferral implied in the process of experiment, the trial and error, the iteration toward utopia.

The "modernist" version of "heterogeneous engineering" plays on all these notions. It resonates with them. But it misses the complexities of heterogeneity. It misses those places that don't fit so well with the control impulse, that have forgotten that even the control impulse, the possibility of centering, is made by distribution into heterogeneity. This means that it doesn't catch the heterogeneities of noncoherence, the fact that things don't add up, the oscillations that make the mirage of the perfect center.

What happens if the heterogeneous distribution and its interferences are reclaimed from the flattening that comes with the modern project? What happens if they are detached from its utopianism, removed from the concern to center? For as it is, heterogeneity is only recognized, when it is recognized at all, from a place of homogeneity, a design/control place, where whatever does not conform becomes a technical obstacle, an irritant, something to be managed, limited, and controlled.

Are there alternatives? If so, what might the alternatives be? Perhaps we might acknowledge that the conditions of possibility are lumpy and different, multiple in character. Perhaps we might remember that heterogeneity is, indeed, heterogeneous, an expression of complexity. Perhaps we might imagine that absence/presence comes in indefinitely many forms and then investigate some of those forms, live with them. But what would happen if the ambivalences of absence/presence were no longer treated as something to be commanded and constrained, to be controlled from a single center? For it may be that there are ways, various ways, of welcoming their alterity. Not in the form of a large project that will finally, at the end of the day, at the end of history, improve society. Not as yet another grandiose utopia for ordering the social, for remaking it in a better way. But neither in the form of the resignation of quietism. Such are the questions that start to flow if we once recognize the heterogeneity of heterogeneity.[38]

NOTES

I am grateful to the Nuffield Foundation for Fellowship support that made possible the collection of data; British Aerospace, the North West Heritage Group of British Aerospace, and the Brooklands Museum for permission to explore and cite British Aircraft Corporation files; to Brita Brenna, Michel Callon, Claudia Castañeda, Bob Cooper, Mark Elam, Kevin Hetherington, Bruno Latour, Ivan da Costa Marques, Ingunn Moser, Bernike Pasveer, Vicky Singleton, Marilyn Strathern, Sharon Traweek, and Helen Verran for their intellectual support; and in particular to Annemarie Mol, for a sustaining collaboration and friendship over nearly a decade.

1. The figures are taken from English Electric (1959). This was a short brochure pro-

duced by English Electric for senior RAF and government personnel. The figures quoted differ marginally from the full-length brochure (English Electric/Short Bros. [1958]), but the differences do not affect the argument.

2. English Electric/Short Bros. (1958, 2.1.9).

3. The point is developed by Marilyn Strathern (1991).

4. See, for instance, Callon (1991).

5. English Electric/Short Bros. (1958, 2.1.9).

6. See English Electric (1957).

7. Ibid.

8. See, for instance, Latour (1993) and Callon (1995).

9. English Electric/Short Bros. (1958, 2.1.8).

10. Air Ministry (1958).

11. Ibid.

12. Ibid.

13. AIR 8/2167 (1957).

14. AIR 8/2014 (1956).

15. See Said (1991).

16. The argument is developed in technoscience studies by Donna Haraway (1991). A further point: like others who have written in Science, Technology, and Society (STS), I should observe that the analysis is impartial with respect to (what is sometimes called) truth and falsity. I am neither saying that the Russians were or were not an enemy.

17. English Electric/Short Bros. (1958, 2.1.8).

18. Air Ministry (1958), par. 9.

19. English Electric/Short Bros. (1958, 1.S.6). Consider also this: "Only the most phlegmatic and unimaginative individual can fail to take a keen interest in the running of his only engine when he is a few hundred miles from the nearest land or the nearest area of population or line of communication" (Vickers Armstrong 1958a).

20. Vickers Armstrong (1958b, 2). This is a short, glossy version of the Vickers Armstrong submission in response to GOR 339.

21. Vickers Armstrong (1958c, 3).

22. Ibid., 2–3.

23. AIR 8/2196, par. 43.

24. Vickers Armstrong (1958a, 1).

25. The importance of noncoherence for the cohesion of the U.K. cervical smear program is explored by Vicky Singleton. See Singleton and Michael (1993).

26. See note 9 above.

27. English Electric/Short Bros. (1958, 2.1.9).

28. Ibid.

29. Ibid.

30. See Jacques Derrida (1978); see also Fredric Jameson's (1991, 38–45) discussion of movement in representation, where he writes about the Westin Bonaventure Hotel.

31. English Electric (1959).

32. English Electric/Short Bros. (1958, 2.1.8).

33. Her Majesty's Stationery Office (1955, 9).

34. For discussion of tension in a related context, see Robert Cooper and John Law (1995) and John Law (1998).

35. Law (1987, 113).

36. See Michel Callon (1986), Thomas P. Hughes (1983), and Bruno Latour (1988).

37. Zygmunt Bauman (1989).

38. As, for instance, is argued in Gilles Deleuze and Félix Guattari (1988).

REFERENCES

AIR 8/2014. 1956. Future Tactical Air Bombardment/Reconnaissance Policy. Document drafted by Operational Requirement Branch, Air Staff, October 19. Public Record Office.

AIR 8/2167. 1957. George Ward, Minister for Air, to Duncan Sandys, Secretary of State for Defence, February 26. Public Record Office.

AIR 8/2196. 1958. Historic Diary Tactical Strike Reconnaissance Aircraft. Undated note attached to letter from G. W. Tuttle, D.C.A.S., to C.A.S., August 1, 1958. Public Record Office.

Air Ministry. 1958. Air Staff Requirement No. O.R. 339. Tactical Strike/Reconnaissance Aircraft. London: Air Ministry.

Bauman, Z. 1989. *Modernity and the Holocaust.* Cambridge: Polity Press.

Callon, M. 1986. "The Sociology of an Actor-Network: The Case of the Electric Vehicle." In M. Callon, J. Law, and A. Rip, eds., *Mapping the Dynamics of Science and Technology: Sociology of Science in the Real World,* 19–34. London: Macmillan.

———. 1991. "Techno-economic Networks and Irreversibility." In J. Law, ed., *A Sociology of Monsters? Essays on Power, Technology, and Domination,* 132–61. Sociological Review Monograph no. 38. London: Routledge.

———. 1995. "Representing Nature, Representing Culture." Paper presented to the Centre for Social Theory and Technology, Keele University.

Cooper, R., and J. Law. 1995. "Organization: Distal and Proximal Views." In S. B. Bachrach, P. Gagliardi, and B. Mundell, eds., *Research in the Sociology of Organizations: Studies of Organizations in the European Tradition.* Vol. 13: 237–74. Greenwich, Conn.: JAI Press.

Deleuze, G., and F. Guattari. 1988. *A Thousand Plateaus: Capitalism and Schizophrenia.* London: Athlone.

Derrida, J. 1978. *Writing and Difference.* London: Routledge.

English Electric. 1957. Note on Crew Fatigue due to Low Altitude Flying for G.O.R. 339. Warton: English Electric.

———. 1959. Project 17. Warton: English Electric.

English Electric/Short Bros. 1958. Aircraft Project P.17; Tactical Strike/Reconnaissance Aircraft to G.O.R. 339. 3 vols. Historical Retrieval Information Centre, Public Relations Department, British Aerospace, Warton Aerodrome, Warton, near Preston, Lancashire. Mimeographed.

Haraway, D. 1991. "The Biopolitics of Postmodern Bodies: Constitutions of Self in Immune Systems Discourse." In D. Haraway, *Simians, Cyborgs, and Women: The Reinvention of Nature*, 203–30. London: Free Association Books.

Her Majesty's Stationery Office. 1955. The Supply of Military Aircraft. Cmd. 9388. London, February.

Hughes, T. P. 1983. *Networks of Power: Electrification in Western Society, 1880–1930.* Baltimore: Johns Hopkins University Press.

Jameson, F. 1991. *Postmodernism, or, the Cultural Logic of Late Capitalism.* London: Verso.

Latour, B. 1988. *The Pasteurization of France.* Cambridge, Mass.: Harvard University Press.

———. 1993. *We Have Never Been Modern.* Brighton: Harvester Wheatsheaf.

Law, J. 1987. "Technology and Heterogeneous Engineering: The Case of the Portuguese Expansion." In W. E. Bijker, T. P. Hughes, and T. Pinch, eds., *The Social Construction of Technical Systems: New Directions in the Sociology and History of Technology,* 111–34. Cambridge, Mass.: MIT Press.

———, ed. 1991. *A Sociology of Monsters? Essays on Power, Technology, and Domination.* Sociological Review Monograph no. 38. London: Routledge.

———. 1998. "After Meta-Narrative: On Knowing in Tension." In R. Chia, ed., *Into the Realm of Organisation: Essays for Robert Cooper,* 88–108. London: Routledge.

Said, E. W. 1991. *Orientalism: Western Conceptions of the Orient.* London: Penguin.

Singleton, V., and M. Michael. 1993. "Actor-Networks and Ambivalence: General Practitioners in the UK Cervical Screening Programme." *Social Studies of Science* 23: 227–64.

Strathern, M. 1991. *Partial Connections.* Savage, Md.: Rowman and Littlefield.

Vickers Armstrong. 1958a. G.O.R. 339: One Engine Versus Two Engines: A Proposal for a Small Working Party to Study Available Statistical Records. Internal memorandum from J. K. Quill to H. Gardner, May 5.

———. 1958b. Study of G.O.R. 339. Weybridge, Surrey: Vickers-Armstrong (Aircraft).

———. 1958c. G.O.R. 339. Letter from J. K. Quill to H. H. Gardner, July 1.

ANDREW BARRY

In the Middle of the Network

The metric system provides us with one image of modern government. In the modern political imagination, standard systems of measurement are often thought to play a key role in the eradication of differences and in the reduction of complexity. The consolidation of the political and territorial unity of the nation-state has, it is thought, depended on the capacity of standardized systems to make things comparable and calculable across the whole territory of the nation. And the development of modern forms of government has often been thought to rely not just on bureaucrats with the necessary ethical disposition but on the creation of a political and economic space that could, with the appropriate instruments, be measured, uniformly.[1]

POLITICAL ORDER

If we consider complexity as an index of irreducibility, then one of the intended and imagined effects of government has been to reduce complexity and to produce a unified political and economic order, an order that can be summed up. The very popularity of the idea of "the state," conceived of as a functional and indivisible unit, attests to the prevalence of this view.[2] That which is complex is, in this view at least, that which the state has failed to encompass or reduce

But does government, in practice, lead to a reduction in complexity or to an increase? And is there a way of governing that is able to invoke and utilize complexity rather than simply oppose it? It is possible to be irreductionist in government, or is governing an inevitably reductionist enterprise? In thinking about these questions, Europe is an exemplary object for analysis.[3] Why? First, because European integration is so often taken to be the clearest contemporary example of a reductionist and technological political project: a metric political system writ large. In this view "Brussels" is a bureaucratic machine, driven by an intent to erase all technical and social differences, oblivious to what they mean to those living in the different regions of Europe. It is a superstate in the making. There is a small element of truth in this common image. It is certainly true that the process that political scientists call integration has been a remarkably technical one. Indeed, in comparison to the extraordinary concern with technology, financial regulation, and the law in the development of the European Union, there has not been much effort to foster what one might call a European public sphere or, in many parts of the Union, a strong sense of European citizenship.[4] Here in London, Brussels is still considered part of a foreign country, and the bureaucracy is viewed as faceless bureaucrats. But to think of Europe as a huge bureaucracy is mistaken. For what has developed across Europe is a whole range of regulations and devices, governing and monitoring everything from the cleanliness of beaches to the design of electrical equipment and the safety of toys.[5] The European Union has surprisingly few bureaucrats, no teachers, no prisons, and no doctors. It has few human representatives with which it is possible to identify. But it does possess an array of procedures, regulations, and standards that govern the behavior of human and nonhuman devices throughout its territory and, indeed, beyond. The European Union, one might say, is an unusually heterogeneous arrangement of elements.[6] At the same time, however, it lacks a common political culture within which the details of this arrangement could be addressed in public.[7] In these respects it bears some resemblance to many other, more and less well known, contemporary institutions of transnational governance that have come to play an increasingly important part in international politics in the period since the end of the cold war.[8]

But Europe is important and interesting for another reason. For because the European Union is a relatively new political entity, its attributes are still, as sociologists of science would say, controversial and unstable.[9] It offers ample scope for those wishing to explore the art of government-in-the-making, a process of ordering rather than an achieved political order.[10] In particular, as we shall see, there is a lively debate within European institutions about whether Europe should, or should not, be unified through the reduction of complexity. The public image of the European

Union is of an uncompromisingly reductionist political enterprise, a bureaucratic monolith that continually seeks to promote the common and the standard against the local, the customary, and the traditional. But inside the political apparatus other versions of the European project are articulated, ones that contest that this is or should be the case, ones that, moreover, explicitly talk not just about complexity but about the complexity of science and technology.

This essay explores this debate through an ethnography of a particular part of the European Commission. In doing so it does not offer an analysis of a particular feature of complexity or a critical assessment of a particular theory of complexity. Rather, I am concerned with how accounts of the complexity of science and technology themselves form part of an effort to reorder the world and with how such accounts figure in efforts to develop policy that takes proper notice of complexity. The case is of more than local ethnographic interest to students of European integration. For it suggests how, insofar as government today itself has come to rely on technical devices, a concern with the complexity of science and technology has come to have some considerable political significance.[11] In this way the essay is also a modest exercise in reflexivity if by reflexivity we mean a consideration of the circumstances and conditions of our own work.[12] Talk of complexity is sometimes regarded, in sociology and anthropology, as a somewhat marginal and intellectual activity of little direct relation to policy. But this is to abstract it from its own historical formation. Here we see it in an impure hybrid form, enmired in current political controversies, subject to conflicting uses and interpretations. This is a discussion about the political significance of writing about complexity and the complexity of its political and historical significance.

NETWORKS AND STANDARDS

So has the formation of "Europe" led to a reduction in complexity? Is there an emerging European political order—a European state? Can devices designed in Toulouse really now be applied in the same way in Scotland and Sicily? Has the development of the European Union led to what we might call, following Deleuze and Guattari, a new striation of space, an ordering based not around the nation-state but a transnational political entity?[13] Not quite. Partly this is because the ideal of standardization has, in practice, simply proved impracticable. No doubt, the idea that "the modern nation-state" relies on the foundations of a standardized technical base was always a political myth, albeit an extraordinarily potent one. But in Europe today, attempts to standardize all forms of regulation and measurement, along the lines of the model of metrication, have been recognized as unrealizable. Some years ago a pragmatic decision was made. The European institutions abandoned the idea of standardization and embraced the more limited project of harmonization, in which different member states would agree to recognize the practices of others and agree on minimum standards while accepting the continuing existence of differences.[14] Yet even the modest ambition of harmonization has proved difficult to achieve. Different countries and agencies have chosen to interpret what the European authorities say in different ways, or chosen to formally adopt them but not apply them, or subverted them. And when introduced across Europe, common standards sometimes turn out to refer to different things.[15] "Bad air" in London is not the same as "bad air" in Paris, even when it is measured against the same European standards. The British authorities have four ways of classifying the quality of air; the French have ten, which do not correspond with those across the Channel.[16] Quite simply, the European institutions' attempts to draw Europe together on the basis of common standards have been, at various levels, resisted. Harmonization has leveled out many barriers and filled some cavities in Europe's political surface, but it also made visible all kinds of subtle fractures and dislocations that might not have otherwise been noticed. In turn the existence of these variations has demanded further technical labor, constant repair by committees of experts. In some cases they have provided the occasion for public political conflict. Consider, for example, the emergence of BSE ("mad cow disease") in cattle, which revealed differences in the hygiene of abattoirs across Europe, although the precise character of these differences has been hard to determine. Harmonization is an ongoing process. The situation should be immediately recognizable to students of thermodynamics. Reducing complexity is costly. Achieving complete uniformity is impossible.[17]

But there may be another reason why the formation of Europe might not involve any straightforward reduction in complexity. In the European institutions it was routinely said Europe was marked by diversity and would remain so. There would be "unity in diversity." Without doubt this slogan has often been simply empty rhetoric, and many European Community policies appear to have paid lip service to diversity. It is perhaps not surprising that the idea of unity in diversity had, according to one observer, moved "from optimistic ideal to virtual self-irony" for some of those employed in the European institutions.[18] Yet for a variety of reasons and motivations, and in a number of ways, the long-standing concern with diversity was invested with a novel kind of importance in the 1980s and early 1990s. Instead of seeking to reduce variation, it was said that Europe could and should try to mobilize it. Europe should not just be a frame within which diversity was preserved, despite the existence of common interests, but a zone in which variation had a value. Europe's identity could be defined less in terms of its unity, after all, than in terms of its irreducibility.

One version of this new concern for diversity was the idea that Europe could be governed simply through the operation of the market and the creation of an enterprise culture.[19] Seen in these terms the idea of a European "state," based around the Brussels bureaucracy, could be an obstacle to European government rather than its precondition. Deregulation, competition, and privatization were to be the key elements to this political strategy. Europe would become, in this vision, a space in which the mobility of capital and labor would be maximized and the technical distortions in the operation of the market removed. The knowledge that "the state" could obtain about the economy was always going to be impoverished in comparison to multiple and shifting visions available to participants in the market. Liberal political thinkers had recognized this is in the nineteenth century. The sum of many partial perspectives would always add up to something more and something of an entirely different order from the view available to the center.[20] Certainly. But were there not many obvious contradictions to this particular vision of a liberal order, and didn't its formulation overlook some obvious points? The creation of a "single European market," after all, would entail a process of reregulation rather than deregulation per se. And would not the formation of a genuine single market lead to the progressive transfer of regulatory responsibilities to European institutions?[21] Would not the opening of Europe's borders to the free movement of capital and technology lead to the eradication of national differences, just as surely as any state-imposed directive? The effect of such a project would surely lead simply to more uniformity.

But along with the idea of the market economy, and in many respects as an antidote to its dominance in political debate, the key term in the development of European government in the early 1990s was the network. In the Commission president's own response to the neoliberalism of the 1980s, the 1993 white paper on growth, competitiveness, and employment, great stress was placed on the political and economic importance of so-called network industries such as telecommunications, energy, and transport, the construction of which required coordinated action at a European level.[22] There was little original in this. This was a traditional sense of network that, since the nineteenth century, had provided a justification for action by the authorities in the national public interest. And a justification for international technical standardization. Europe, in this view, required an information and communication infrastructure—an information motorway—in a way that was analogous to the national public interest in the telegraph and railway networks of a century earlier and that also would be able to compete with information superhighways of North America. The continent would be united by wires and lines.

But elsewhere the idea of the network was used in quite different ways and referred to different objects. For in the European institutions it also came to signify a decentralized form of organization and intervention that was less organized yet more coordinated than the invisible hand of the market. A network in this sense was a more or less loose association, not an infrastructure at all. In this sense it was associated not with standardization, nor with centralization, but with an acknowledgment of complexity.[23] In this sense the notion of the network became more than just a metaphor for Europe. It was an instrument for acting on the constitution of Europe and in a way that might realize the multiple potential links among knowledge, research, and government across the continent.[24] Perhaps through networking Europe could be drawn together without any direct imposition of an order but through a steady process of reordering. Thus complexity would not be reduced but reproduced.

MILITANTS

There are many different stories that could be told about networks and networking in Europe today, some of which use the terms as a way of thinking about complexity. I want to tell one—about a particular part of the European Commission's bureaucracy in Brussels, a section (Directorate A) of DG-XII (the Directorate General for Science, Research, and Development)[25] devoted to research strategy and supporting measures, "which basically means studies, evaluations, reports and foresight studies and so on."[26] Here the idea of the network figured as one element of a broader story told by some researchers about the complexity of science, technology, and their relations to the economy. For some in DG-XIIA the assessment of science and technology policy was necessarily a complex matter, and talk about complexity figured in opposition to two reductionist ways of talking about the value of technology. On the one hand, an assessment of the value of technology should not be reduced to a consideration of the technical quality of the scientific or technical work (and therefore left to scientists themselves). Value was always something more than a technical matter.[27] On the other hand, it could not be reduced to a consideration of market value and therefore assessed in narrowly "economic" terms. It had to involve, among other things, a concern with societal needs, with geography, with regulation, and with the role of users in innovation. In this view any assessment of the value of technology was potentially open-ended.

Bureaucracy may be an inappropriate word to describe some of the work of Directorate A, if by bureaucracy we mean an organization governed by a commitment to political neutrality and the impartial execution of formal procedures. For at least a few members of this directorate did not identify themselves as bureaucrats but as intellectual outsiders seeking to act on the workings of the Commission from the inside, through the deployment of expertise. One researcher, who worked for a unit called FAST (Forecasting and Assessment of Science and Technology) in DG-XIIA, had been interested in labor process theory, in Gramsci, and in ethnomethodology. He expressed his institutional position in the following terms: "[Individually] we have an awful lot of autonomy, which makes it important for us to go through the whole hierarchy and especially to jump between institutions and promote the viewpoints of each of us [in FAST]. We have our own networks, and we write our syntheses and we promote our own recommendations for Community policies."[28] Another senior figure's intellectual and political position derived, in part, from Marxism and systems theory but was also, in his view, comparable to the position adopted by Ilya Prigogine, the Nobel Prize winner in chemistry and coauthor of *Order Out of Chaos*. FAST was a "scientific militant about the human and social utility of science. . . . A scientific militant like Prigogine is [a] militant for the new alliances."[29] Its function was to open up controversy about social dimensions of science and technology in the Commission and to conduct a "resistance" against dominant positions, including, above all, the "competitiveness ideology" that conceived of the function of scientific and technological activity in narrowly economic terms. Elsewhere in the Commission the role of the intellectual existed even at the highest levels of the organization. A senior official in the research unit working under then Commission president Jacques Delors, the Cellule de Prospective, suggested that his group functioned as an intellectual animator operating through interservice discussion groups that cut across the formal boundaries of the Commission bureaucracy.[30] Thus, it had influence: "The role of the Cellule is to act as an outsider . . . to influence those engaged in drafting [for] the power in any bureaucracy is held by those who draft."[31] Without doubt the sense of "militancy" and autonomy of FAST and the Cellule and their commitment to certain intellectual doctrines was, as Bourdieu would say, a strategy of distinction. But it was also intended to have effects. The proposals and research reports written by DG-XIIA did not function just as a form of legitimation, nor were they merely "intellectual."[32] They were intended to bring together the "social" and the "technological" elements of the European project. Although the members of the Cellule and FAST did not consider themselves future researchers, they were concerned with *la prospective*—an orientation toward the future. But what was the justification for the particular orientations they adopted? What problems did they pose, and what problems might an attention to the complexity of science and technology be expected to address?

Bruno Latour has written of the perfect symmetry between the dismantling of the Berlin Wall in 1989 and the first conferences on the global environment in the same year. Both indicate a need to rethink the binary oppositions that informed the twentieth-century political imagination: between nature and culture, between the material and the social, and between liberal market economies and state socialism.[33] This observation had some resonances in the European Commission. For one, justification for the need for work on the complexity of science and technology was the structural position of the European Community itself, or rather its shifting position in the New World Order. One DG-XIIA official, Jean, framed his understanding of the position of Europe in terms of a historical sociology that drew explicitly on the actor-network theory of Callon and Latour.[34] The problem for Europe, in his view, was to replace the highly organized network of allies created in the period after 1945 by a much more complex set of connections demanded by a new historical situation. Science policy was, in his view, not so much about making decisions but, in actor-network terms, mobilizing alliances to take account of new social and environmental realities.[35] In this context science policy had to be seen as a process of reconstructing networks—a process of reordering—not a decision that somehow determined how everything else should develop. He expressed his view of the changing position of Europe in these terms:

> JEAN: I would say the decision [about science policy] is not a decision; it's how you can make so many allies, and this process [in Europe], which has been very successful up to now, is maybe less successful right now. . . .
>
> ANDREW: So how have the allies been created or mobilized in the past?
>
> JEAN: One of the major solutions was the East-West direction. The second one was space. And the third one was with the help of a strong national industrial policy: big support and organization of market and prices. So you could recover a high investment in all these cases quite easily. Today, things are moving. Things are more complex. We are not in a protected market. . . . We're losing allies, [but] we still have a budget and the solution will be how we will adjust to globalization [and] the interaction of many more actors in the process, societal needs and so on.

But if the European Commission had to confront the complex reality of Europe in the period after 1989, it also had to confront the legacy of its own institutional and technological history: the marks and residues left by earlier interventions. The European institutions had once displayed a remarkable commitment to nuclear power in general and nuclear fusion in particular. Indeed, the Commission's own laboratories, run by DG-XII, had once been primarily devoted to civil nuclear research.[36] Yet seen in terms of Europe's emerging interest in the complexity of the social and

150   Andrew Barry

the technical, such a commitment was misguided. For nuclear fusion research was highly centralized, and the generation of power by nuclear fusion, if it ever proved possible, would necessarily be concentrated in a few facilities. Michel Foucault had once noted that social and political thought had yet to cut off the king's head. But in political terms, nuclear fusion was undoubtedly an absolutist solution: a technology in which all power flowed outward from a central source. It was the antithesis of the kind of politicotechnical regime favored by the proponents of complexity in DG-XIIA. One FAST researcher expressed the opposition between the economists and sociologists of DG-XIIA and the view of others in DG-XII thus: "None of us love nuclear power. You will find people here [in DG-XII] that live for nuclear power or for big machines: they find them beautiful. Technology can have that fetish aspect."[37] The problem, however, was not just one of fetishism. The fixation of DG-XII on advanced technological research could lead to neglect of the different ways in which technologies may be used, and a neglect too of the more mundane but perhaps more critical role of technical standards and regulations to the European political project.[38] Although the European Community was committed to harmonization, its research programs were not necessarily oriented to the pursuit of this objective, or, if they were, it was sometimes in an inappropriate way.[39] In effect, there was a disjuncture between the technological project of European integration—which had, as we have seen, come to involve the harmonization of a whole series of mundane and technical instruments (such as procedures and devices for assessing the safety of toys or the quality of river water)—and the direction of research policy—which had been geared toward the development of the most prestigious and most "advanced" technologies.[40]

In this context part of the problem confronting those in favor of change was the problem of changing the culture of commitment inside the commission to such absolutist technological solutions—whether based on nuclear power or on more recent information and environmental technologies—"for the mainstream in DG-XII believes that research on the environment should be restricted to its technological aspects."[41] In short, many Commission intellectuals and social researchers saw themselves opposed to the dominant view of officials working for DG-XII. Although they worked on quite specific research projects—such as examining the current state of biotechnology research in Europe—they had a broader agenda, one that was simultaneously political and intellectual. In theoretical terms this was expressed as an opposition to the linear model of innovation: the idea that commercially successful new products resulted from innovative technology, which in turn resulted from advanced scientific research. One framed the critique of the reductionism of the linear model by reference to the work of evolutionary economists, such as Christopher Freeman and Luc Soete: "So now we come to a more complex view of research where there are a lot of mediations through which research can influence economic and social welfare. So it makes us more modest, if you want and it leads us to look more at the use of technology; the way that technology is incorporated into the organizational framework of companies and public institutions."[42] Not Big Science but modest science.

The need for more attention to complexity could be further justified by a consideration of Europe's diversity. The notion of unity in diversity had always been, as we have noted, a key feature of the rhetoric of European integration but one that was not implemented in the development of policy. But an attention to the complexity of technology suggested a way to rework the notion of diversity in a more productive way. On the one hand, the idea of a common European policy failed to recognize that research programs, industrial policies, and technical standards simply do not have the same implications in different places. The ideal of a common policy was not sufficiently sensitive to the fact that policies and instruments have to be adjusted, to take account of the diversity of different regions and actors, and their autonomy, and to value it. It was a "paradigm shift to go from European integration despite our diversity to European integration because of our diversity."[43] There was a clear connection to be made here for one researcher between a sociology of local actors and a reformulation of economic policy in terms of regional networks and local actions. He commented, "If you look at internalization and globalization and so on then the autonomy [of different actors] is very limited. . . . I turn this round and say I'm not interested in globalization and so on. Of course [such forces] influence price levels, technology and so on. . . . But what's interesting is how local actors or regions manage their actions within these frames. I'm Mister Bottom Up."[44]

Indeed the diversity of Europe was one of the conditions for the emergence of the idea of the network and the new concern to bring social questions into the development of technology. Above all, it was the work of members of the commission on the diversity of Europe that acted as a stimulus for the community to come to realize the need "to develop technology to meet diverse sociocultural needs."[45] In developing this new way of thinking, the work of DG-XIIA on socioeconomics of technology was no doubt important, but it was but one input of many. Experience may have been just as important as expertise. One member of the Cellule de Prospective reckoned that the notion of the network and the concern with the importance of diversity derived as much from the experience of the Commission in regional and social policy, and in particular the work of a person in DG-V (Employment and Social Affairs) monitoring Commission programs in relation to the issues of poverty and the family.[46] It seems that the notion of the network had simply become too pervasive in the Commission to be owned by anyone, or tied down to any one particular sense or point of reference, or to have simply one point of origin. For the European commissioner responsible for research and development, Antonio Ruberti, the idea of networking had become the principle underlying all Community activities.

On the other hand, there was the issue of scale. Europe has always been thought to be bigger than any of its individual constituent member states—a supranational political entity, a federal political system, a superstate. Increasing the scale of Europe was an ambition, even if at the same time it generated hostility and anxiety from those who viewed this enterprise as a threat to local cultural differences. The concept of subsidiarity set down in the Maastricht Treaty on European Union stipulated that the European institutions should only do things that could not be carried out effectively by the member states acting on their own.[47] Without doubt the principle could be interpreted in different ways, implying different accounts of the relation between the functions of the Community and the functions of the member states. It could suggest, for some, that nation-state should be, and would remain, at the center of the European political system.[48] Europe was, in this view, a space marked and divided territorially.

But when seen in terms of networks, this vision could be radically changed. For a network could both cut across national borders (and hence be "European") yet, in containing only a few elements, be much more localized than any nation-state.[49] Space could be collapsed and reworked. Indeed, for the intellectuals of FAST and the Cellule the notion of the network offered a more profound account of subsidiarity than the one entertained by the heads of the member states at Maastricht. For it implied that the European Union could, in some circumstances, operate at a lower level than the national governments.[50] In comparison to the European networks identified through socioeconomic research, individual nation states could be both bigger and less well integrated. They were geographically extended but not necessarily internally well connected. Research on the sociology of local industrial networks suggested there was sometimes a greater connectedness across national borders than within the territorial boundaries of nation-states. The structural analyses of systems theory suggested a similar view, if for different reasons. A senior figure in FAST put it thus: "We have to get away from the linear and hierarchical model of the infranational, subnational, national and international and so on. To my mind there are now five major spatial and temporal systems [the city, the region, the national, the regional-continental, and the global] which are not in a linear-hierarchical top-down or bottom-up relation to each other—they are overlapping using different temporal scales and different systems and connections."[51]

Despite the remarkable attention paid to socioeconomic accounts of technology in DG-XIIA and the Cellule, it would be misleading to suggest that they had a straightforward impact on technology policy. After all, the documents coming from the research units and think tanks were only a small fraction of those that came across the desks of those officials given a responsibility for drafting or editing. All too often the interventions of the intellectuals came too late or in an inappropriate form or language to influence debate at critical points. Or they were pitched at an extraordinarily abstract and general level. At a FAST conference held in Wiesbaden in 1993 a remarkable attempt was made, involving a hundred researchers over the space of three days to condense the results of a vast body of research on the complexity of the global technological and economic system into five short points that could be presented to the Commission later that summer in an effort to influence policy. The notion was that only if arguments about the complexity of technoeconomic systems were put in a simplified form would they have any chance of convincing senior political figures. This particular effort failed.

Some people were clearly more successful or more skilled than others in developing the informal personal connections within the bureaucracy necessary for their work to have any chance of being translated elsewhere.[52] One university economist who had carried out contract research for DG-XII thought that his work on technology was influential because, through his father's acquaintance with Jacques Delors, he had managed to get the Commission president to sign a short preface (which the economist had himself written) to the book deriving from his work. He reckoned that my concern with political rationality and technology was naive in failing to address the importance of familial and social connections, a reflection of the (British) belief in the real existence of disinterested bureaucratic administration.[53] I had to agree. In any case, whatever their success in being heard or read, the degree to which officials' and researchers' projects could be turned into action was necessarily limited given the strength of earlier commitments and other alliances made by the Commission: "With time you have obviously many more people who have a vested interest in the ongoing actions and it's much more difficult to change the system."[54]

POLITICAL COMPLEXITY

So far the lines of the debate seem clear. On the one hand, the dominant culture of the European Commission seemed to favor purely technological solutions to political and economic problems. Witness the enthusiasm for nuclear power and aerospace technologies in the 1950s and 1960s and for advanced information, communication, and biotechnologies today—a movement which has parallels with a similar shift in thinking in the United States during the same period. But within the European institutions there were also many officials and intellectuals who were critical of such reliance on the intrinsic value of technology. They questioned the idea that advanced technologies did have necessarily beneficial effects. And they articulated their opposition not just in conventional "political" terms but in terms of the complexity of science and technology. Is the political debate about complexity therefore fairly straightforward—a contest between those in favor of complexity and those who do not recognize its importance? Between a dominant culture and a few influential marginals? Not quite. For if the intellectuals of DG-XII and the Cellule suggested a number of ways to rethink the activities of the European

Community, their suggestions were not the only ones. Another was formulated in terms of the need for evaluation and value for money. For the British government, in particular, the European Union's problem was, in part, a problem of evaluation. Not surprisingly. For if the new liberal forms of governance that developed in Britain in the 1980s promoted the idea of the free market as a panacea, they were equally associated with an emphasis on the importance of audit and evaluation. As Michael Power has argued, audit has become a central technique in the reinvention of liberal government.[55] Trust in the performance of professionals and institutions has been displaced by a concern to monitor professional and institutional performance. This desire to monitor and to evaluate applied to Brussels as much, if not more, than anywhere else; for there was, in the view of the British government, little systematic attempt to assess European programs, whether in terms of their effectiveness, their value for money, their justification, or their "added-value" to the U.K. In the British view, "European" programs were marked by inefficiency, and, as such, they needed effective evaluation.[56] There was little rigor or control over the mechanisms of control. Brussels was, in effect, considered a bastion of the continental ancient regime. It displayed all its worst features: big government, corruption and patronage, and a dependency culture that simply provided state subsidies to those research institutions that were not sufficiently productive to gain funding from the private sector. The concern with audit had to be exported to Brussels in the interests of good government. Evaluation was the mechanism through which any illusions of sovereignty on the part of the European Commission were to be curtailed.

What was the relation between this political project and the kind of work promoted by the intellectuals of DG-XII? Could talk of actor-networks and regional industrial networks be translated across the Channel, from Brussels to London? Could the particular form of British concern with evaluation be translated to Brussels? And in what way, with what intersections and effects? The situation was less clear than one might imagine. To be sure, the Commission intellectuals themselves had little enthusiasm for the kind of conservative interest in "value-for-money" all too often promoted by the British government. And the kinds of quantitative indicators that might be developed by those interested in the complexity of sociotechnical networks would be quite different from the kinds of crude input and output indicators sometimes used to measure the value for money of research expenditure in Britain.[57] But their work, in suggesting the possibility of a form of social and economic assessment of scientific research independent of the kinds of assessment made by scientists themselves, could be aligned with the British demand for more rigorous methods of evaluation. A network, SPEAR (Support Programme for Evaluation Activities of Research), had been established to disseminate and develop best practice in research evaluation across Europe: from the northern countries (U.K., the Netherlands, France, Germany), where it was considered well developed in comparison to southern Europe.[58] For scientists, such a dissemination could represent a threat to their autonomy. Why? "There is a fear in DG-XII that traditional basic scientific research not only will be given less money but if social science is introduced then some part of the freedom of research will be lost."[59] This fear of the intrusion of the social into the assessment of the importance of scientific work was reckoned to be deeply embedded. In an effort to promote more debate about the character of scientific culture in Europe, the Commission sponsored carrefours in different member states. At the British meeting a French Commission official had this experience of what he believed was the conservatism of the scientific establishment: "I remember in Oxford University the President of the British Academy of Science [the Royal Society], Sir . . . I can't remember his name . . . being strongly opposed to Prigogine's view."[60]

Negotiations over whether and how the European Commission should develop more rigorous forms of monitoring and evaluation and value for money had gone on for some time. They continued. The Commission had shown a "complete abuse of the evaluation process," according to one senior British official, and had failed in the proper task of evaluation: "Any evaluation must not just focus on success in meeting objectives. . . . It must evaluate objectives [to see if] they were the right ones."[61] Evaluation must, in the British view, be exhaustive and continuous.[62] But even if the British were to insist that the Commission move in this direction, those working for the Commission knew that the evaluation unit could and would resist this. The head of the unit in charge of evaluation was at best ambivalent about the idea that social scientists should be engaged in evaluating the work of engineers. And his unit played a key role in determining who would conduct evaluation, how the results were edited prior to publication, and when and to whom evaluation reports were circulated. He knew that there was a difference between the formal requirement for evaluation and its political effects. After all, the time and space within which documents circulate is always of significance to the ways they are read and the effects they have on the conduct of others. But in this case this was particularly so. Would more evaluation per se open up European research to a more rigorous scrutiny? Certainly, large numbers of evaluation reports were printed as public documents, but most lay unread in the evaluation unit store cupboard. Few were seen by members of the European Parliament who had the formal responsibility of representing the public interest. Evaluation was carried out systematically, but its effects were uncertain, and the political space within which it occurred was highly circumscribed. Those concerned with the complexity of science and technology and those concerned with the rigorous evaluation of scientific and technological programs had a similar ambition: to translate texts into practices. But the extent to which this had happened was difficult, even for those involved, to observe.

THE MIDDLE

I returned to London after a number of visits to Brussels over a period of a year. At a small meeting held to publicize the results of the research program that funded my own work, I spoke about the interest in networks and networking that had emerged in certain places in the Commission. There was some interest from academics present, but the paper also attracted the interest of a senior official at the U.K. Treasury, an institution that had been at the forefront of demands for more rigorous forms of evaluation and the need for value for money, an institution apparently at the center of the British culture of audit. I wondered why he was interested: was my research going to be of use to the Treasury in developing more effective ways of controlling expenditure in Europe? On going to the Treasury offices in Whitehall several weeks later I found that the reality was different. The official wanted to talk to me as much about my political analysis of the Commission as he did about my contribution to the evaluation of European research programs. Yes, he said. You're right. The Commission is, in the best sense, a Machiavellian organization. It is small and needs allies, and it's not surprising that it should think of its own place in Europe in terms of the mobilization of other actors. He put forward his own theory: that the enthusiasm of certain elements of the Commission, both for the instrument and the metaphor of the network, is a reflection of their place in the European political system. In the middle, but not at the center.

IRREDUCTIONS

The issue of complexity arises in government as well as in science. For through the deployment of expertise, part of the ambition of government has been to reduce complexity and, in this way, to form a unified political order. In the tradition of social and political thought that runs from Nietzsche and Weber to Adorno and Foucault there is at best an ambivalence toward this reductive project. In the face of the historical development of modern government, the problem for social and political thought was to develop a form of thinking that revealed a sense of the irreducibility of the social and the individual to any model or order. In particular, the reductive notions of the state, conceived of as a unified source of political power, and the individual, conceived of as a nucleus of rational action, had to be interrogated. In this way some sense of the complexity of social life could be both maintained and valued.

But why should this long-standing sociological and philosophical concern with the complexity of the social and political order need to be brought together with an attention to the complexity of the natural and the material? Why should a concern with irreducibility be generalized, as it has been in recent years, in the history and anthropology of science and in actor-network theory? Why is it necessary not just to think about the complexity of the material and the social independently from one another but also the complexity of sociotechnical arrangements? How, in short, is it possible to understand the conditions of existence of the interest in the complexity of science and technology today? There is no single answer to these questions, nor are the answers to them of purely an intellectual order. Certainly one can point to the ways in which the boundaries between what is human and what is not human may be reordered through the process of contemporary scientific research, thus challenging reductive accounts of science. And one can investigate how nonhuman devices have become increasingly important to the conduct of government, whether for the public authorities or for individual subjects in their everyday life. But one can also point to a different, although connected, set of issues that relate to reductive formulations of a more conventionally political order: the equation of government with the state; the equation of value with market value; the set of rigid hierarchical divisions between the local, the national, the international, and the global. The story here is an account of a resistance to some of these formulations, albeit one that occurs largely inside a bureaucracy: in the middle of a network. Here is an attempt to introduce some thinking about the complexity of science and technology into the deliberations of the public authorities. But the story should be of more than local interest. For it can be read as an account of how, today, a consideration of the complexity of science of technology is important not just to specialists in science and technology studies but to all those concerned with the complexity of the problem of government.

NOTES

My thanks to the U.K. Economic and Social Research Council for funding the research on which this essay is based and to Dick Holdsworth and Gordon Lake of the Office of Scientific and Technological Options Assessment of the European Parliament for their support in Brussels. My thanks also to Georgie Born, Steve Brown, John Law, and Annemarie Mol for their comments on an earlier draft of this essay.
1. On the ethical formation of the bureaucrat, see Osborne (1994).

2. See, for example, Louis Althusser's account in his essay on ideological state apparatuses (1971). For a critical account of the idea of the state, see Rose and Miller (1992).

3. On this point see, in particular, Latour and Coutouzis (1993).

4. On this point see, for example, Mann (1996). For an account of the weakness of European "cultural policy," see Shore (1993). According to Shore, many European officials working in the field of cultural policy conceived of Europe in relation to an idea of a "functional, harmonious and unproblematic integration through hierarchical levels of belonging" (784).

5. For a general account of the importance of regulation to the operation of the European Union see Majone (1996).

6. In the technical sense of arrangement suggested by the work of Deleuze (1996). See also Akrich and Latour (1992) and Law (1994). Callon and Latour (1981) develop the idea of the thinking of "the state" as a heterogeneous arrangement of human and nonhuman elements.

7. There have been some efforts in the European Parliament to improve this situation

through the formation of the Office of Scientific and Technological Options Assessment (STOA).

8. Since their inception in the middle of the nineteenth century, the majority of international organizations have been concerned with "technical" matters. The United Nations is a notable exception. Today, for example, important international organizations include the International Telecommunications Union (ITU) and the World Intellectual Property Organisation (WIPO).

9. See, for example, Collins (1981).

10. On the importance of thinking about ordering rather than order, see Law (1994).

11. Here I use the term *government* in Foucault's sense, not to refer to an institution but to a form of regulating action. See Foucault (1991).

12. One could say that this work is inscribed in a political situation. But this does not mean that it is reducible to this situation, for that which is political is precisely, as Geoffrey Bennington reminds us, that which is irreducible. See Bennington (1994, 3).

13. On striation, see Deleuze and Guattari (1987). As Alan Milward has convincingly argued, it would be wrong to think that the development of Europe has led to a reduction in the strength of national institutions anyway. On the contrary. The European Community, particularly in its early years, provided a space within which national institutions could be rescued and reconstructed. See Milward (1992).

14. On the "new approach" adopted to harmonization, see Pelkmans (1987). My account here draws from an earlier paper, Barry (1993).

15. See Latour and Coutouzis (1993).

16. See Barry (1997).

17. The second law of thermodynamics states that entropy (a measure of disorder) always increases so that any attempt to increase order is marked by an increase in disorder elsewhere. The third law states that it is impossible to reach absolute zero—where there is no disorder.

18. See McDonald (1996, 47).

19. On enterprise culture, see Law (1994); Rose (1994); and Strathern (1992).

20. This observation, no doubt, underpins Foucault's interest in liberalism and neoliberalism in his work on governmentality. For Foucault liberalism and neoliberalism are interesting precisely because they articulate an idea of government that does not revolve around the functions of the state but instead relies on dispersed techniques of government and the multiple perspectives that they generate. See Foucault (1991). Maryon McDonald has suggested to me that Foucault's notion of *gouvernmentalite* is sometimes used by Commission officials (personal communication).

21. For an excellent account of the critical importance of regulation to the operation of the European Community, see Majone (1995).

22. See Commission of the European Communities (1993).

23. The ways European networks are formed, their degree of coordination, and their effects have been extremely variable. As we shall see later, there have been surprisingly few good critical studies of the operation in practice. Given the diverse forms that they took, it would not be possible to provide any simple characterization of such networks or the implications that they had for those who participated in them.

24. "Synonymy, metonymy, metaphor are not forms of thought that add a second sense to a primary, constitutive literality of social relations; instead, they are part of the primary terrain itself in which the social is constituted" (Laclau and Mouffe [1985, 110]).

25. The Commission was divided into twenty-three directorate generals, each with responsibility for specific policy areas such as industrial affairs (DG-III), Information (DG-X), and Fisheries (DG-XIV).

26. Interview with Richard Escritt, Brussels. In 1993 DG-XIIA organized a program of research in "the field of strategic analysis, forecasting and evaluation in matters of research and technology (MONITOR)." *Official Journal of the European Communities,* 89/C 144/04.

27. One could equally say that technical quality is something that is produced through assessments made by scientists and engineers.

28. Interview, Brussels. In all interviews with Commission officials I agreed to keep the identity of those interviewed anonymous. All interviews were carried out between June 1993 and June 1994 and were tape recorded and transcribed.

29. Interview, Brussels. The reference is to Ilya Prigogine, coauthor of *La Nouvelle Alliance.* See Prigogine and Stengers (1984).

30. The connections between the work of the various Commission services (or directorate generals) is generally reckoned to be very poor. As far as I know, however, there has been no in-depth study of this (see, however, McDonald 1996).

31. Interview, Brussels (1994).

32. See Rose and Miller (1992, 177).

33. See Latour (1993, 8–9).

34. Following one discussion Jean gave me a copy of a paper by Michel Callon.

35. Cf. Law and Mol (1996).

36. With the rundown of the European Commission's own nuclear research program its own laboratories diversified into other areas. Some of the staff at the commission's ISPRA laboratory, north of Milan, formed a new unit called PROMPT, which also dealt with the assessment of science and technology. Unlike the intellectuals of DG-XIIA, however, the PROMPT researchers considered their work apolitical.

37. Interview, Brussels (1994).

38. Interview, Brussels. See also R. M. O'Conner (1991).

39. Witness the failure of European attempts to establish a European technical stan-

dard in high-definition television (HDTV) in the face of American and Japanese competition.

40. There is some considerable debate as to whether the most "advanced" technologies (from the point of view of engineers) would emerge from Commission-supported research as companies would be unlikely to want to share the results of their most commercially viable products. Of course, the debate between the sociologists and economists of DG-XIIA and others was, in part, a debate about whether what was "advanced" should be judged by specialists alone.

41. Interview, Brussels (1994).

42. Interview, Brussels (1994).

43. Interview, Brussels (1994).

44. Interview, Brussels (1994).

45. Interview, Brussels (1994).

46. The distinction between the intellectual labor of DG-XIIA and the experience of DG-V mapped onto a gender distinction. In DG-XIIA all research was carried out by men, and the only women employed in the offices were secretaries. The experience of DG-V was that of a woman official.

47. "In areas which do not fall within its exclusive competence, the Community shall take action, in accordance with the principle of subsidiarity, only if and in so far as the objectives of the proposed action cannot be sufficiently achieved by the Member States and can therefore, by reason of the scale or effects of the proposed action, be better achieved by the Community" (Article 3b, Treaty on European Union).

48. According to Jacques Delors, "subsidiarity, because it assumes that society is organized into groups and not broken into individuals, rests strictly speaking on a dialectic relationship: the smaller unit's right to act is operative to the extent and only to the extent (this is forgotten very quickly) that it alone can act better than a large unit achieving the aims being pursued." Delors (1991, 9).

49. The point is made by Marilyn Strathern: "Networks can take any scale—have the power to cross different organisational levels—precisely because each relation invokes a field of embodied [social] knowledge about relationships." Strathern (1995, 27–28). For a discussion of different configurations of space, see Mol and Law (1994).

50. Interview, Brussels (1994).

51. Interview, Brussels (1994).

52. This is an old story in the anthropology of science. In the communication of science and technology persons are important. Rarely do written accounts suffice, however simplified.

53. Interview, Rome (1994).

54. Interview, Brussels (1994).

55. See Power (1994, 17). See also Power (1997).

56. The British were certainly not the only ones concerned with evaluation. But in some other European countries the problem was less likely to be formulated in terms of a notion of value for money.

57. Interview, Paris (1994).

58. For an account of SPEAR, see Commission of the European Communities (1993).

59. Interview, Brussels (1994).

60. Interview, Brussels (1994).

61. Interview, London (February 1994).

62. See also Law (1994); Strathern (1995).

REFERENCES

Akrich, M., and B. Latour. 1992. "A Summary of a Convenient Vocabulary for the Semiotics of Human and Nonhuman Assemblies." In W. Bijker and J. Law, eds., *Shaping Technology/Building Society: Studies in Sociotechnical Change.* Cambridge, Mass.: MIT Press.

Althusser, L. 1971. "Ideology and Ideological State Apparatuses." In *Lenin and Philosophy and Other Essays.* Trans. Ben Brewster. London: New Left Books.

Barry, A. 1993. "The European Community and European Government: Harmonisation, Mobility, and Space." *Economy and Society* 22, no. 3.

———. 2001. *Political Machines: Governing a Technological Society.* London: Athlone.

Bennington, G. 1994. *Legislations: The Politics of Deconstruction.* London: Verso.

Callon, M., and B. Latour. 1981. "Unscrewing the Big Leviathan, or How Actors Macrostructure Reality and How Sociologists Help Them Do So." In K. Knorr-Cetina and A. Cicourel, eds., *Advances in Social Theory and Methodology: Toward an Integration of Micro and Macro Sociologies.* London: Routledge and Kegan Paul.

Collins, H. M. 1981. "Stages in the Empirical Programme of Relativism." *Social Studies of Science* 11: 3–10.

Commission of the European Communities. 1993. *Growth, Competitiveness and Employment.* Luxembourg: Office for Official Publications of the European Communities.

Deleuze, G. 1996. *Negotiations.* Trans. M. Joughin. New York: Columbia University Press.

Deleuze, G., and F. Guattari. 1987. *A Thousand Plateaus: Capitalism and Schizophrenia.* Trans. Brian Massumi. Minneapolis: University of Minnesota Press.

Delors, J. 1991. "The Principle of Subsidiarity: Contribution to the Debate." In *Subsidiarity—Guiding Principle for Future EC Policy Responsibility: Proceedings of the Jacques Delors Colloquium.* Maastricht: European Institute of Public Administration, March 21–22.

Foucault, M. 1991. "Governmentality." In G. Burchell, C. Gordon, and P. Miller, eds., *The Foucault Effect.* Hemel Hempstead: Harvester Wheatsheaf.

Laclau, E., and C. Mouffe. 1985. *Hegemony and Socialist Strategy.* London: Verso.

Latour, B. 1993. *We Have Never Been Modern*. Hemel Hempstead: Harvester Wheatsheaf.

Latour, B., and M. Coutouzis. 1993. "Eurometrics: Should We Have Taken the Measure of Europe?" In J. Durant and J. Gregory, eds., *Science and Culture in Europe*. London: Science Museum.

Law, J. 1994. *Organizing Modernity*. Oxford: Blackwell.

Law, J,, and A. Mol. 1996. "Decision(s)." Unpublished paper.

Majone, G. 1996. *Regulating Europe*. London: Routledge.

Mann, M. 1996. "Nation-States in Europe and Other Continents: Diversifying, Developing, Not Dying." In G. Balakrishnan and B. Anderson, eds., *Mapping the Nation*. London: Verso.

McDonald, M. 1996. "Unity in Diversities: Some Tensions in the Construction of Europe." *Social Anthropology* 4, no. 1: 47–60.

Milward, A. 1992. *The European Rescue of the Nation-State*. London: Routledge.

Mol, A., and J. Law. 1994. "Regions, Networks, and Fluids: Anaemia and Social Topology." *Social Studies of Science* 24: 641–71.

O'Conner, R. M. 1991. "Standards, Regulations, and Quality Assurance." SAST Report 2. Brussels: Commission of the European Communities.

Osborne, T. 1994. "Bureaucracy as a Vocation: Governmentality and Administration in Nineteenth-Century Britain." *Journal of the Historical Society* 73: 289–313.

Pelkmans, J. 1987. "The New Approach to Technical Harmonization and Standardization." *Journal of Common Market Studies* 25, no. 3: 249–69.

Power, M. 1994. *The Audit Explosion*. London: Demos.

——. 1997. *The Audit Society*. Oxford: Oxford University Press.

Prigogine, I., and I. Stengers. 1984. *Order Out of Chaos*. London: William Heinemann.

Rose, N. 1994. "Governing the Enterprising Self." In P. Heelas and P. Morris, eds., *The Values of the Enterprise Culture: The Moral Debate*, 141–64. London: Routledge.

Rose, N., and P. Miller. 1992. "Political Power beyond the State: Problematics of Government." *British Journal of Sociology* 43, no. 2: 173–205.

Shore, C. 1993. "Inventing the 'People's Europe': Critical Approaches to European Community 'Cultural Policy.'" *Man*, n.s., 28, no. 4: 779–800.

Strathern, M. 1992. *Reproducing the Future*. Manchester: Manchester University Press.

——. 1995. *The Relation*. Cambridge: Prickly Pear Press.

CHARIS THOMPSON

When Elephants Stand for
Competing Philosophies of Nature:
Amboseli National Park, Kenya

African elephants are a classic endangered species. Their huge size, primordial-looking trunks, and baggy skin give them the appearance of relic species serendipitously surviving into modern times. When this morphological uniqueness is combined with elephants' high intelligence and complex sociality, their conservation-worthy credentials seem impeccable. Even when there is broad consensus that a species such as the African elephant is *worth* conserving, however, the idea that a species should be "saved" is not nearly as transparent as it first appears. Always lurking just—or not quite—below the surface are such questions as what the species is to be saved from, by whom it is to be saved, how and where it is to be saved, and how and by whom conservation gains and setbacks will subsequently be assessed. With African elephants, as for most other real-life conservation examples, these questions have very different answers for different groups of people. Because of their size, elephants are unusually demanding on their habitats. Each adult elephant is reputed to consume some two hundred kilograms of biomass per day and to require upward of a square kilometer of habitat, depending on the quality of the forage.[1] Given the amount of contiguous land with appropriate vegetative cover that is necessary to house sizable elephant herds, elephant range states face greatly intensified versions of the land-use conflicts that commonly beset conservation. Land use in the postcolonial African range states is about independence, development, and emerging democracy, so conserving elephants is also about all these things. Add to this mix the fact that wildlife tourism is a major foreign exchange earner in many of the range states, and that the illegal ivory trade has been at various times an important underground economy, and it is apparent that the stakes are high and the stakeholders numerous.

In this essay I show that the African elephant tags competing philosophies of nature and that these different philosophies are in turn metonymic for key disputes in science and epistemology, in distributive justice, and in governance. I explore these metonymic relations among knowledge, justice, and legitimacy by discussing in detail a scientific workshop on elephants that was convened in southern Kenya in 1995 and by considering some of the events that have since unfolded around those populations of elephants. I argue that long-term conservation strategies, if they are to produce durable and widely agreed-on conservation gains, need to be pluralist in a way that the notion of complexity helps to elucidate. They also need to be responsive to and expressed within the existing political potentialities, however, or they will be highly vulnerable to political instability.

AMBOSELI NATIONAL PARK, WOODLAND LOSS, AND ELEPHANT COMPRESSION

The scientific meeting described here aimed to air a number of competing theories as to the role of elephants in the Amboseli ecosystem and to allocate funds and initiate programs to promote elephant conservation in the area. The competing theories were framed by the putative problem of elephant compression (too many elephants in too small an area) within Amboseli National Park. During the meeting "the elephant problem" was staged and argued through rival scientific views of the significance of elephants. But, as always in environmental science, the scope of the differences in views was much greater than that. Each group had different moral, political, legal, economic, disciplinary, and normative commitments informing and informed by their model of science. My analysis tracks the rival positions and the allegiances among differing positions that emerged. In so doing I demarcate the strategies that decided which groups triumphed at the meeting. I have tried to show what was involved in achieving consensus where it was achieved and just what was rendered incommensurable where conflicts were not resolved.

The body of the case study is divided into four parts, the first of which gives the background to the workshop, describing how elephant compression came to be proxy for so many other elements at stake in bio-diversity conservation in Kenya. The second section describes the work-shop itself, showing how the different scientific arguments were made. I then analyze the models of science and end by showing how each model of science indexed specific views across a wide range of conservation-relevant disciplines. I pay particular attention to the question of who manages to collaborate and agree with whom, and what kinds of schisms seem at this moment unbridgeable, because these are among the pres-sure points toward which environmental advocates need to be directing conflict-resolution resources.[2]

Amboseli is a national park in southern Kenya, on the border with Tanzania, at the northern base of Mount Kilimanjaro. The park is 388 square kilometers at the center of an ecosystem of approximately twenty times that size. The ecosystem is inhabited primarily by Maasai, who are still partially nomadic pastoralists but who also farm small *shambas*. Amboseli's hyperdiverse savanna ecology is accounted for by its varied geology and soils, a strong gradient across the basin, and the hydrological influence of Kilimanjaro, which creates swamp oases in the middle of the desert. Before extensive settlement and before the creation of the park, Maasai, livestock, and wildlife moved together in migrations into the central swamp area in the dry season and out again in the rains.

In 1970–71 the worldwide price of ivory jumped tenfold, intensifying incentives to poach. According to elephant counts, organized gangs of poachers armed with automatic weapons reduced the number of ele-phants in the Amboseli ecosystem by about half, to under five hundred.[3] The poaching and settlement in the migration areas around Amboseli led the remaining elephants to concentrate in the park, where they were safe. The combination of the concentration of the elephants in the park, the cessation of migrations, and the increase in the elephant population led to a fivefold increase in elephant densities in the park during the 1980s. During this time the vegetation and consequent drainage patterns of Amboseli started to change rapidly. In particular, the rate of tree loss increased dramatically, and the hydrology was disrupted during the rains, flooding roads and tourist lodges.

In the late 1970s a Kenyan ecologist and conservationist named David Western and a number of Maasai researchers, including David Maitumo, began a series of experiments to tease out the reasons for the accelerated rate of woodland loss. They fenced off different plots of land within and outside the park using electric fences at different heights, selectively restricting wildlife access. This enabled them to separate the effects of salt, elephants, invertebrate browsers, and plant competitors on restraining woodland regeneration. The simplicity of this experimental setup was striking: it used nothing other than fence posts and single-electric-wire barriers at different heights to differentiate experimental conditions. An earlier explanation for loss of tree cover in Amboseli had been that varying amounts of salt in the surface soil, owing to natural variations in the level of the Kilimanjaro-influenced water table, were responsible. In this setup salt effects would be constant throughout the plots, and any other differences in vegetation would be a product of what types of animals could get into the area and what types were kept out. The experiment had the great advantage that the different experimental conditions and the results were eminently visualizable.[4] By the late 1980s these plots showed differential rates of woodland regeneration, suggesting that elephants were responsible for about 85 percent of the loss of woodland.

David Western and his colleagues were already significant in the international rise of conservation biology. They were putting in place through their work in Amboseli and elsewhere the move toward "the conservation of biodiversity" and somewhat away from the older notion of "the management of wildlife." In the process of simultaneously furthering and benefiting from the international expansion of the concept of biodiversity, Western was able to establish key epistemological, scientific, moral, legal, and political alliances.[5] What these researchers drew out was a relation between biodiversity and elephant concentration.[6] Where elephant densities were too low (outside the park), there was a loss of biodiversity, and where they were too high (inside the park), there was also a loss of biodiversity. Somewhere along the elephant density gradient, biodiversity was at its highest, suggesting the possibility that elephants were a "keystone species," indicative of biological diversity wellbeing across vast areas of Africa. This increased the stakes of resolving the enigma of the effect of elephants on biodiversity.

In the late 1980s Western asked Daniel Sindiyo, then head of the wildlife department, to convene a seminar to discuss elephant density and woodland and associated biodiversity (and tourist appeal) decline. Before the seminar could be convened, Sindiyo had been replaced by Perez

Olindo, another prominent Kenyan conservationist. Olindo tried in turn to organize the seminar, but acrimonious opposition from elephant researchers in the park caused the event to be scrapped. The wildlife department became the Kenya Wildlife Service (KWS) with the adoption by parliament in 1989 of the Wildlife (Conservation and Management) (Amendment) Act, and Olindo was replaced by Richard Leakey, son of paleoanthropologists Louis and Mary Leakey. Leakey made a trip early in his tenure to Amboseli to review the woodland experiments and called for immediate action to reduce the elephant numbers by culling.

The opposition to Western's woodland experiments and the view that elephants were indicative of the well-being of the ecosystem generally came mainly from a number of elephant behavior researchers in Amboseli. An American, Cynthia Moss, had earned a considerable reputation for her studies of elephant social behavior and aligned herself with a more typically North American/European view of the rights of animals, individually naming the elephants and referring to them in the international press as "her" elephants.[7] Over many years she urged caution in concluding that elephants were responsible for the loss of woodland and biodiversity in the Amboseli ecosystem, pointing out that accepting the importance of woodland and the role of elephants in woodland loss could be dangerous because it could lead to endorsing the killing of elephants.

Aggie Kiss, senior ecologist for the multidonor program providing the bulk of the external funding for Kenya's wildlife conservation efforts, became an important ally of Moss's Amboseli elephant research group in the 1990s. Kiss was skeptical about the conservation biologists' alliance with local people and the implicit trust- and knowledge-based model of conflict resolution on which it rested. Kiss credited Moss's group with having discussed with her a potential solution to elephant compression in Amboseli. The solution was to enlarge the park by leasing land from local landowners and then helping the sedentarized landowners to diversify economically. Kiss admitted that this approach would be expensive and would be management intensive, requiring continued efforts to separate people and wildlife and mitigate conflict from the always imperfect separation. But it was, she believed, the only sure way to protect the elephants.

For the elephant behaviorists and their allies, those pursuing the woodland experiments were using their science to sanction one of two solutions to elephant compression within the park, both of which would lead inexorably to sanctioned killings of individual elephants. It seemed they either had to endorse Leakey's earlier suggestion of the "Zimbabwean solution," that is, the culling (management killing) of elephants to reduce numbers and density within the park and thus encourage woodland regeneration, or they had to tempt elephants back onto old migration routes outside the park, where local people would be likely to kill individual elephants that inflicted crop or property damage or bodily injury. Along with this latter view went the sentiment on the part of the animal behaviorists that involving the local community in conservation is suspect because it relies on one form or other of utilitarian attitude toward wildlife. Any form of utilitarian attitude toward wildlife threatened to undermine a major reason in their view for these elephants' protection, namely, that each elephant had intrinsic rights stemming from its complex social and mental life that Cynthia Moss and her coworkers had documented.

The conservation biologists doing the woodland experiments insisted that they did not endorse culling, which left open the second option of getting elephants back onto migrations. Like the elephant behaviorists, the conservationists wanted the elephants alive but for slightly different reasons. They didn't want elephants killed or culled because of their endangered status but equally because elephant presence outside of parks for such things as seed dispersal and brush removal was necessary, in their view, to assure the processes reproducing the shifting mosaic of habitats characteristic of savanna habitats. David Western was careful to pose the argument about keeping space open for wildlife outside of protected areas as a proxy for more intensive management inside parks. If wildlife were allowed enough space, the processes that promote and regulate biodiversity would come into play without very costly park management (such as culling, seeding, and so on). For a developing country and its donor constituents, this "ecological, hands-off" solution to management had clear attractions. Western attempted to shift focus from inside parks to outside parks without ceding park management to those who wanted solutions to the elephant problem that were park-based.

The option of getting elephants onto migrations provided the link to the local Maasai, who would need to tolerate elephants on their land for that to be a possibility. In conjunction with representatives of local

Table 1. Elephant Compression

	Inside-Park Solutions		Outside-Park Solutions	
	Culling	Expanding Park	Resume Migrations	Use Incentives
Leakey (prior to ivory burn)	X			
Cynthia Moss and allies		X		
David Western and allies			X	
Koikai Oloitiptip and other Maasai				X

Note: Table shows proponents of proposed solutions for the problem of elephant compression, from the most "fortress," park-based view to the most community-based view, left to right.

Maasai group ranches, years of work began on means of making it worth local landowners' while to tolerate elephants on their land.[8] The Maasai, long disenfranchised by the creation of parks and the placing of wildlife ownership in the hands of the national government, were cautiously enthusiastic about the potential to regain some control over land use and wildlife.[9] However, they did not, and do not, speak with one voice, and intergenerational conflict about the appropriateness and means of taking an entrepreneurial attitude to wildlife continue to divide Maasai residing in the Kajiado District. Likewise, Maasai women are only slowly beginning to participate in conservation politics and did not speak in public at the workshop described here.[10] The "local community" did not come any more prepackaged and unconstructed than any of the other constituents, but, being composed of local voters and landowners, it had local political clout that could be exercised in favor of, and benefit from, any relocalization of wildlife resources. The development of wildlife utilization schemes and use incentives in exchange for Maasai custodianship of wildlife was a general strategy for the partial relocalization of wildlife resources.[11]

In early 1990 Richard Leakey had capitalized on the already almost complete negotiations of the international ivory ban by staging an internationally televised burn of several tons of confiscated and stockpiled ivory in Nairobi. The ivory burn drew a lot of attention to Kenya as a country determined to stamp out poaching, and it also reinforced the international perception of Kenya as against hunting and all forms of consumptive utilization (unlike the other African countries where wildlife tourism is also a significant part of the economy, such as Tanzania, Zimbabwe, and South Africa, all of which cull and hunt according to supposedly sustainable yields and all of which took reservations of the CITES appendix 1 listing of elephants).[12] Leakey became a protector of the endangered elephants in the eyes of the all-important donor countries and consequently lost interest in the culling solution and indeed ignored the evidence of the destructive effect of elephants on biodiversity so as not to be seen as endorsing the killing of elephants. By early 1994, however, Leakey had been ousted from the helm of the Kenya Wildlife Service,[13] and David Western (the same person who did the woodland experiments) had been appointed by President Moi as his successor.[14] The workshop was finally convened, and the competing interpretations of the Amboseli elephants came face to face.

THE AMBOSELI ELEPHANT/BIODIVERSITY WORKSHOP

On April 4, 1995, approximately fifty people including local Maasai, ecologists, lodge owners, tour operators, donor representatives, elephant watchers, Amboseli's warden and other officials from the Kenya Wildlife Service, and representatives of the local press and local government assembled in the Serena Lodge Conference Room, Amboseli National Park, for the start of a two-day workshop on the fate of elephants in the Amboseli ecosystem. The workshop was convened by the Kenya Wildlife Service. Its aim was to present the scientific evidence about the impact of elephants on the area's flora and fauna and to decide on the basis of the evidence how the elephants should be managed. All the participants with a stake in the fate of the elephants were asked to present their results, which I summarize here in the order in which they were presented.

As the director of KWS, David Western spoke first. He showed aerial photographs and elephant counts and correlated woodland decline with elephant density. He described a biodiversity gradient from too many elephants through to optimum densities, to too few, as one moves from the center of the park to the areas outside the park, and he concluded by examining the possible ways of reducing the impact of elephants. Fertility control would be management intensive and take a long time to have an impact. Culling, to get the Amboseli elephant densities low enough to allow woodland regeneration, would require killing 80 percent of the animals. The only alternative, Western argued, was to get the elephants back outside the park and onto their migration routes, but this alternative required Maasai agreement to house the elephants.

Cynthia Moss interpreted the question about the fate of the elephants in a different way, arguing not for their management as a proxy for ecosystem biodiversity but for their importance as a scientific population. She argued, quite plausibly, that the Amboseli elephant population had been very well studied and that our understanding of elephants owed more to the Amboseli work than to any other work done in Africa and that each year of further study would be a bonus to science. The findings on elephant behavior she had produced were to be valued in and of themselves, and the elephant population was to be protected because of the intrinsic rights of complex social animals and for its value to science. Value to science meant the ability of the population, with her and her colleagues as its amanuenses, to continue yielding new knowledge; the elephant population should be viewed as a scientific gold mine. Her conclusion on the fate of the elephants was that elephant protection should be paramount.

Elephant researchers Joyce Poole and Kadzo Kangwana both acknowledged the loss of woodland in their presentations and the desirability of getting elephants back onto some kind of protected migrations. Poole's interest in increasing the land available for the elephants was to protect the elephant social structures that were starting to regenerate now that the ivory ban was allowing elephant bulls to live longer. Kangwana's talk focused on the distance elephants maintain between themselves and human settlement, means by which elephants could be enticed back out of the park, and the prospects for their security if they ventured outside. Moss, Poole, and Kangwana all conceived of the conservation issues as being about the protection of this particular elephant population.

John Waithaka, elephant programme coordinator at the Kenya Wildlife Service, described the country-wide effects of elephants on biodiversity, ranging from very dry areas like Tsavo to very wet areas like Aberdares and Mount Kenya. He argued that elephants are a keystone species: too few elephants is bad for biodiversity, and so is too many. He illustrated this with data from two ranches in Laikipia, one of which encourages elephants and has ideal grazing conditions for livestock, and one of which fences out elephants and has become overgrown with thickets and trees that the livestock cannot penetrate. In terms of the fate of elephants, he emphasized that it is not just a question of regulating elephant numbers but that the mosaic of savanna and wetland and forest habitats that underpins Kenya's biodiversity requires the appropriate movement of elephants through space in relation to other wildlife, human activity, and livestock.

Koikai Oloitiptip, the Maasai director of the local wildlife association, used a flip chart to describe the changing swamps and woodlands and the role of elephants in the change.[15] He pointed out that the solutions being proposed for the fate of the elephant and biodiversity by both the elephant researchers and the conservation biologists relied on Maasai tolerance of wildlife on their land but that it was the Maasai who suffered damage from wildlife, especially from elephants. James Mboi and other Maasai Group Ranch members explained that the ecologists' findings supported their common knowledge that "cattle create trees and elephants create grass." They pointed out the irony of expelling the Maasai from the park in the early days on the grounds that they were destroying the woodlands. Their coexistence with elephants had been undermined by the shift of elephants into the parks, and by the Maasai protection from poachers that the elephants had received, because the elephants had subsequently lost their fear of people. Now that the elephants had depleted almost all their food resources in the park, they were beginning to move outside the park and to inflict serious crop damage.

THE MODELS OF SCIENCE AND THE CONTEST

The dispute over the convening of the workshop can be understood as a conflict of interests between one group of scientists allied with local community members (conservation biologists in active conjunction with members of the Maasai who saw the potential to regain control of local natural resources) based in Amboseli against another group of Amboseli scientists (elephant researchers) and their Maasai project employees. Which voice has been heard at different points of the controversy has depended in part on which group has managed to garner credibility through aligning its interests with the relevant government bodies, but this process is two-way: the interests, composition, and policies of the relevant government bodies have depended on the prevalence and success of the views of the actors on different sides of this argument.

During the years in which Cynthia Moss maintained that Western's woodland experiments did not show the role of elephants in woodland loss, Moss evinced considerable hostility to Western's increasingly frequent practice of bringing people down to Amboseli to walk around the experiments and "see for themselves." Moss told Western, in defense of her resistance to holding a workshop on elephant compression and woodland loss, that if Western and the Maasai had real data, they should publish them in peer-reviewed, and preferably international, journals. She argued that there was no reason for others to believe or act on the experiments if the experiments had not stood the test of academic peer review. Moss also requested that Western not invite the press to attend the Amboseli workshop, arguing that it would not be disinterested science if the press was there.

David Western used a series of arguments that had long informed, and to some extent been informed by, the science and technology studies writings of Bruno Latour, with which he was familiar as a result of the long-term collaboration between Western's wife, primatologist Shirley Strum, and Latour. Western countered that conservation science had priorities that were not possessed by the academic science for which peer review and the ideal of disinterestedness had been developed. He argued that all science serves constituencies and that peer review is a means of serving the interests of academic science, where uniformity of opinions throughout a disciplinary community is a principle aim of the process. The constituents of relevance in Amboseli, he maintained, were necessarily local, as well as national, and only secondarily international. Appropriate field science should be developed that would reflect the local context and that would be verifiable by local constituencies. He also pointed out that conservation science needed to be linked to planning and management. The lag between peer-reviewed publication and the trickle down of scientific knowledge to park managers was simply too long and too vague to meet the imperatives of rapidly changing, heterogeneous, and locally specific ecosystems. If peer review worked by removing the links between the locally specific production and application of scientific knowledge and the knowledge itself, this was a separation not appropriate for conservation science. University-based or centralized peer review should thus not be considered a means of establishing the reliability of the science appropriate in Amboseli. Western suggested that accountability should be built into conservation science at other stages than at peer review, such as in allowing interested people to "see for themselves."

David Western put his model of science to the test at the Amboseli workshop, staging a dramatic event of "seeing for themselves," to which all participants, press and hoteliers and tour operators included, were invited. Western's notes report that Moss "buried her head in her arms" when he announced that the whole group would be taken to see the experiments. The group traveled along a transept from Olodare in the center of the park, where there are no trees of any size left at all, out to Namelok, a Maasai village outside the park where the trees are dense. Having shown everyone the gradient according to elephant density, Western then announced that the density of trees outside the park could be recreated in the center of the park just by excluding elephants. The whole group then drove to the woodland experiments back in the center of the park and were able to witness for themselves fenced areas of differential tree densities. They were now witnesses primed to interpret tree cover as good, and as an index of elephant density, and were well convinced by what they saw with their own eyes.[16] The field trip had made them rational citizens, able to "see" the reality of the elephant compression problem; elephants stood in for ecosystem well-being and thus for tourist revenue, local community prosperity, and, ultimately, national security. Elephant watchers Moss, Poole, and Kangwana refused to accompany the rest of the workshop participants to view the woodland experiments, abandoning the group after Namelok, in what Western referred to as a "trail of denial."

James Mboi, Koikai Oloitiptip, and other Maasai Association members gave broad agreement to Western's and Waithaka's results and produced their own data on the changing ecology and prevalence of predators. But they also insisted that science was a first step in a political process. It turned the knowledge they already had into political currency. That currency then required spending to ensure gains for the people who were implicated in the scientific findings. If conservation science showed that the Maasai were important to savanna habitats, then that science was the means by which the Maasai interests in land tenure, wildlife conflict mitigation, and wildlife use should be pursued. Something the state needed—a thriving wildlife industry—could be shown to be in their hands, and that was equivalent to gaining a political voice. Arguments about the disinterestedness of science did not ring true.

The press picked up on the antagonisms but were themselves impressed by the evidence they had seen on the field trip. A member of an East African conservation nongovernmental organization (NGO) reported that the elephant research groups spent until 11 P.M. trying to persuade the Maasai against Western's views. The attempt to co-opt the Maasai failed largely because these particular communities were already working with Western's program in a number of concrete ways, stretching back over many years. First, Western had been living with and learning from these Maasai since the 1960s, and their ecological expertise and nonoppositional ontology between humans and ecology lay at the heart of his community-based approach to conservation. Most important, many of the Maasai had been involved in the science and the politics of the woodland experiments and so were not a neutral persuadable lay populace in any ordinary sense.

As described, the Maasai had their own views of both the value and purpose of science in Amboseli and of the problems of the loss of biodiversity. Western's view and the Maasai view of science were compatible because both groups had done the work to keep making political connections by sharing knowledge over many years. The conservationists' model of science, which involved local witnessing and local stakeholders, as opposed to the centralized elephant watcher's model of science, had local consensus building and open local access as ideals. These were the principles invoked to guarantee the truth of their science, and they were also the ways in which the local communities and Western and the other conservationists had worked together politically. Probably the elephant watchers could only have had their model of science triumph at this meeting if their political relations, based on maintaining the concerns of the Maasai separate from the intrinsic scientific and moral value of the elephants, and so separate from the framing of the elephant problem, had also triumphed. As long as the meeting was held locally and the event of witnessing was going to take place, the elephant watchers were already defeated.

The workshop just described focused the dispute around the different models of science and different sets of values and understandings of conservation of two groups, broadly understood by those who want park integrity above all else, and those for whom the fiftieth anniversary national parks slogan, "Beyond Parks," is the key to biodiversity conservation. What is immediately apparent is that other aspects of conservation—legal issues, land-use disputes, economic and moral concerns, and so on—did not disappear but were all easily recoverable within the scientific dispute itself. The scientific dispute was a way of packaging and then managing the much more unwieldy set of conflicting views. The different conglomerates of views indexed by the scientific dispute can be unpacked analytically so as to make the dimensions of difference much clearer. Table 2 compares the "inside parks" position with the "beyond parks" position on a number of dimensions.[17]

The clusters of beliefs and values that distinguish the two approaches to elephant compression make it clear that the meaning, means, and goals of elephant conservation vary between the two groups. Of critical importance to anyone concerned with conservation is how to recognize and measure conservation gains and setbacks. Not surprisingly, but to the great chagrin of policy makers, managers and those required to monitor and assess different approaches, conservation success and failure are no more independently given or self-evident than any other part of the story. Success, depending on which camp were to prevail, would be constituted by very different scenarios.

If the elephant watchers followed through with their scientific agenda from the meeting, one could anticipate a growing and aging population of Amboseli elephants, and a growing stock of human knowledge about elephants, which would bring with it additional reasons and resources to care for these magnificent animals. It is likely, too, that the future of national parks could be more or less guaranteed through the focus on jurisdiction and containment within parks. This would secure the heart of the country's wildlife and tourist industries. It would be less likely, though, to yield solutions to the woodland loss or to the conflict between the separated humans and elephants. Insofar as elephant conservation

Table 2. Comparison of "Inside Parks" and "Outside Parks" Positions

	Inside Parks	Outside Parks
SCIENCE		
Disciplinary base	animal behavior, zoology	conservation biology, ecology
Status of elephant	scientific gold mine, intrinsic rights	keystone species, ecological role
What is to be conserved	wildlife	processes that maintain biodiversity
Livestock and parks	livestock should be kept out of parks	livestock should be allowed into permanent water sources during drought
Management strategy	within park	beyond park
POLITICS		
Attitude to local people	locals are in competition with wildlife conservation	locals are principal stakeholders and are custodians of wildlife
Attitude to modernity/ development	development means expanding population plus urbanization/sedentarization and new industrial and agricultural land use, so is opposed to conservation (antipastoralist/rural)	development includes turning conservation into a profitable form of land use for the landowner and incorporating it in national land-use planning (propastoralist/rural)
Local/national/global connections	national wildlife resources supported by international (animal-loving) donor constituency in colonial format	globally understood notion of biodiversity maintained at local level to provide long-term national natural resource conservation
LEGAL		
Local people	should have legal protections and compensation; should be arrested for revenge killings	should have legal standing and responsibilities; should have wildlife-use rights
Elephants	should have rights represented by their scientific spokespeople	should be "stakeholders" by virtue of their action in maintaining the ecosystem

Table 2. Comparison of "Inside Parks" and "Outside Parks" Positions (cont'd)

	Inside Parks	Outside Parks
Optimal land tenure and settlement in area surrounding park	sedentarization with leasing out of buffer zone for elephant movement	nomadic pastoralism with group land title; possible park entry rights in droughts

ECONOMIC

	Inside Parks	Outside Parks
Wildlife ownership	should be state owned, with international endangerment status ratified domestically	should be state owned, but with the possibility of the delegation of revocable use rights in exchange for conservation gains
Distribution of park revenue	revenues should be managed centrally and a proportion of gate receipts distributed to local communities as goodwill or in compensation for wildlife-inflicted damage	revenues should be managed locally within regions, and locals should be paid direct costs based on animal counts and numbers of wildlife housed
Nonconsumptive utilization	park-based tourism	park- and community-based tourism
Consumptive utilization	no hunting except for management culls and limited problem-animal control	limited hunting to benefit locals, based on sustainable offtake and delegation of culling and problem-animal control

VALUES

	Inside Parks	Outside Parks
Wildlife-human conflict recognition and mitigation	animals have rights; people and animals should be kept separate	people have rights and responsibilities; animals and people should coexist
Emotions	sentimental, anthropomorphic	compassionate, anthropocentric
Underlying model of humans in conflict resolution	human parties are basically untrustworthy, so there is no link between beliefs and behavior	human parties are basically trustworthy, so behavioral changes will follow from changes in ideas
Other reasons and means for valuing nature	monist and "separatist," aiming to prevail over other views, including those of conservationists	pluralist and "federalist," aiming to incorporate without assimilating other views, including those of elephant watchers

was considered, it would be more about protecting an individual population of an endangered species than about promoting the processes underlying biodiversity. The long-term protection of elephants by the people who live side by side with them would not necessarily be encouraged, so Kenya would risk being locked into a long-term commitment to separating elephants and humans, managing both exogenously and expensively to mitigate conflict, and even valuing the rights of elephants over the rights of humans.[18] Those whose interests would immediately be served would be the scientists who are expatriating the knowledge and gaining the rewards of international science, this population of elephants, those who are privileged enough to learn about and perhaps come to care for the individual destinies of these animals through the scientific findings, and other conservation efforts funded by the interest generated by these elephants. These expatriate scientific and donor constituencies are the conventional, and still powerful and wealthy, patrons of wildlife conservation.

The great strength of this approach is that the retreat to securing parks is robust under conditions of high political and social instability. The political unrest, elections, drought, floods, and disease outbreaks of 1997–98 put great pressure on attempts to enact devolutionary and democratic reform in wildlife management because of the short-term loss of social order. The elephant watchers' model of wildlife management—maintaining wildlife and the associated foreign exchange earning potential inside parks and under central state control with the backing of wealthy overseas conservation-minded donors and international science—became politically powerful again in this period. Domestically, wildlife management, in the form of the leadership of the Kenya Wildlife Service, became a political prize, eventually rewarded to Richard Leakey after David Western's firing in September 1998.

If the views of the Maasai at the elephant meeting and the Amboseli ecologists followed through with their scientific and conservation agenda, what would be the best that could be expected? Optimally, one could anticipate a partial resumption of the elephant migrations, which would contribute to a more processual and comprehensive understanding of biodiversity and conservation, which would facilitate park woodland regeneration. By putting management and benefits from wildlife into local hands, one could hope for simultaneous gains in social justice and reductions in central costs of elephant containment and management. The constituencies who are the prime targets of this conservation agenda are, for the most part, less powerful and less wealthy than the large interest groups successfully captured by the elephant watchers. The Maasai's and conservation biologists' position exchanges the strengths of the elephant watchers for two other sources of strength. First, a new kind of strength comes from the increased (but not fixed) numbers of both human and nonhuman stakeholders.[19] Second, there is a strength in the projected longevity of conservation solutions based on space and local custodianship. The weakness of this position is that, by espousing applied science, it is effectively espousing a scientific methodology (albeit one with fewer abstract standards than is familiar within academic science in the West) for political issues of land tenure, control over foreign exchange, tribal relations, and so on. In times of relative political stability, bringing wildlife management under this kind of regime could stand as a model of transparency in governance for other sectors. In Kenya the absence of a tradition of institutional transparency and accountability in government, however, means that this approach is politically vulnerable under conditions of high political and social unrest. The high numbers of stakeholders and the flexibility and longevity of this model's interconnections have meant that despite its recent vulnerability to political excision from government bodies, this policy approach is displaying resilience on the ground. Some local landowners and wildlife associations have continued to build on their institutional and legal gains won during Western's time at the head of KWS, and some are dealing directly with overseas donors and the tourist industry. Community-based conservation, because it is "bottom up," can to some extent go on despite central wildlife policy directions if the two diverge.

COMPLEX, BUT NOT COMPLICATED OR DIFFICULT

This book is an exploration of the complexity that seems so to characterize our times and of the complex connections between politics and science found in applied environmental science like that debated at the Amboseli workshop. It is perhaps obvious that the narrative here is complex. First, the conflict over the elephants was framed at the meeting as a scientific dispute, and several points of view were argued, which presented the stakes in different and sometimes incompatible ways. Second, one of the principal protagonists, David Western, had read and, indeed, informed the writing of many of the theoretical texts on which I, the analyst, drew in my account. Thus, the story fails to present neat or simple distinctions between the analyst and the analyzed, between local and international knowledges, between knowledge flowing from the north or from the south, or between interested actors in the site and disinterested analyst. The story is thus complex because it is multiple, and it is complex as a piece of writing in science and technology studies. Although I have attempted to explain both the motivations and moral universe of the elephant watchers, as well as those of the conservation biologists, a strictly "symmetrical" account, where each "side" is treated in the same way, is not available to me. I am in the site, and an entwined partisan, and to attempt to write that out of the story would be ethnographically unwarranted. But there is a much more interesting notion of *complex* involved in this story that suggests a more generalizable model after which one should strive when approaching contemporary environmental disputes. I turn now to this notion of complexity, which I simply call "complexity," but distinguish from difficulty and complicatedness.

One of the strongest motivations behind giving complex, multivalent accounts is that all episodes of technoscientific practice link, in mostly surprising ways, many kinds of things. There is a frugality, however, to following selective, reductionist narrative trails through an episode and resisting multivocality. This frugality often has aesthetic, cultural, and, in the case of scientific stories, stunning instrumental value, even if occasional veering from established trails is a venerated strategy for creativity. There is a corresponding self-indulgence, or romanticism, to insisting that all elements—content and context, little and big—are too important to be lost from the story.[20] Both the reductionist and the romantic holist strategies have an associated notion of complexity that is not fitting for the story just told above. The first case, modernist frugality and reductionism, goes with *difficulty.* A pure or hard science gives explanations that are understood as complex in the sense that they are too hard for those who are not members of the relevant and relatively closed epistemic communities to understand. Antimodern romantic or nostalgic holism goes with *complicatedness.* Simplicity and reductions are resisted and connectivity, detail, and emergent properties valorized. Only those most intimately conscious of and immersed in the entire situation can make sense of it. The Amboseli case was not difficult, nor complicated, but complex nonetheless.[21]

In describing the Amboseli elephants, I tried to reveal links among different orders and scales of things: science, politics, law, economics, culture; individuals, elephants, the whole of biodiversity, nations, parks, and the global environmental community. But the story is not without order; ordering devices, such as the concept of a park boundary, or the fences that selectively reduced access to grazing, or the local wildlife associations, or the elephant counts done on behalf of the CITES secretariat, or the density of trees, or the collaboration of elephant watchers and transnational NGOs, proliferated, in fact.[22] The theoretically and normatively interesting complexity of this case stems from the connecting of different orders and scales of things, without reductionism or holism. The science did not derive its validity from its political backers, for the keystone species theory as applied to Amboseli's elephants was based on island biogeography and the rainfall gradient, not on who was or was not in power. Yet the keystone species theory as applied to Amboseli's elephants successfully tagged one set of answers to political order and not others. Whether the elephant was a keystone species or a complex creature with intrinsic rights went with such things as whether the elephant should be a stakeholder or should be spoken for, whether it should sometimes be or never be a commodity. The alliance between the science and the politics it went with was successful insofar as the science was not compromised by the politics (if seen as sui generis, with its own standards of truth and efficacy) yet was conceived over land, time scales, and forms of economic activity to which those with political clout at that time could be convinced to aspire as integral to their vision of the nation.

The conservation biologists stressed the need to form links such as getting legal standing for Maasai wildlife groups, resolutely pursuing the science as apolitical knowledge, developing community tourist capacity, and so on. The elephant watchers, on the other hand, retrenched into park integrity and security, both literally and ecologically. The David Western/Maasai alliance was victorious at the meeting because they had the power at the time to run the meeting such that their epistemology of on-the-ground witnessing was the one that got staged and subsequently reported. It was their space and land and actors—and so their science and polity—that were validated. The political compromises and alliances, however, did not get reduced to the truths of science or vice versa, so the case was not complex in the difficult sense. Neither did the political and scientific aspects of the case coalesce into a holistic frame of reference; indeed, the separation of the politics and science was what kept the linkages strong, so the case was not complex in the sense of holism. In a broad conservation debate that is very far from over, this was the more robust solution in the times of relative calm that surrounded this meeting. To have further cemented the community-based approach that triumphed at the meeting, it would have been necessary somehow to protect it from, or incorporate it in, the centralized politics of influence and charisma that are Kenya's hallmarks. If one is to draw a lesson from this case for the politics and science of conservation, it must be that successful complexity lies precisely in assiduously tending linkages while avoiding either reductionism or holism.

Conservation and environmental debates are often marked by strong emotions lined up on different "sides." Conflict resolution is, from one way of looking at things, the central element of conservation. How can one move beyond adversarial deadlock, where entire "moral universes" face off, neither side even being able to engage the other? The debate over the Amboseli elephant compression problem had many phases that were best described by that kind of adversarial dynamic, and I presented the debate as being between two sides in the case study. But the model instituted by David Western and the Maasai triumphed when they managed to connect, but not completely convert or align, more stakeholders to their "side" of the scientific dispute. Critical to this success was the creation of enough space to engage without running roughshod over other moral universes. This is a form of relentless pluralism that is, I think, a key aspect of the complexity of the conservationists' side of the Amboseli story. The question inevitably arises as to whether the elephant watchers could be connected to the conservationists' program in a similar nonreductionist and nonholistic way. On my reading, the opening left for the policy within parks could have made room for, and legitimated, the powerful "animal loving" emotions of the animal behaviorists. It is the moral brokerage that is possible in this kind of complexity that I think carries the greatest hope of this case study. The reversibility of this pluralism, the fact that the potentialities always remain for disintegration back into opposing sides and opposing moral universes, is the cautionary tale of the case.

NOTES

1. Figures relayed to me by Dr. John Waithaka, elephant specialist, based on his Ph.D. fieldwork in the Aberdares and Mount Kenya region. I traveled with Dr. Waithaka at the end of 1994 to witness the relations between biodiversity, land use, land tenure, fencing, and elephant density.

2. My sources include the workshop minutes, David Western's diary notes, interviews with some of the participants and/or their close allies, related academic literature, and press accounts. I did policy work for the Kenya Wildlife Service during 1995 and 1996 and carried out my own fieldwork in Kenya in 1994, 1995, and 1997. I stayed in Amboseli National Park in 1994 and 1997. I attended the follow-up meeting to this one in February 1997 and interviewed several more people during that trip.

3. D. Western, interview by author, May 1995; Western (1994).

4. The experiments could not have been better designed to match the "civil epistemology of seeing" (Ezrahi 1995) advanced by David Western at the workshop.

5. The canonical account of the international expansion of the concept of biodiversity (and consequent global standardization of biodiversity as a conservation-worthy commodity) is given in E. O. Wilson's editor's foreword (Wilson 1988). See also Takacs (1996).

6. They measured biodiversity as a combination of species richness and species diversity. D. Western, interview by author, summer 1993.

7. The Amboseli elephants have appeared in *National Geographic,* on *Sixty Minutes,* in a BBC film series, and elsewhere and have been referred to by Moss's names. The question of naming animals is complex: it arose as a means to establish identities for individual animals, and it also helped ensure interobserver identification reliability among researchers. This allowed the gathering of long-term data and the compilation of life histories. The gains in understanding animals afforded by long-term life history data, and the consequent willingness of researchers and the public generally to attribute complex social and mental life to studied species, should not be underplayed in its significance for conservation. On the other hand, when the status of the animals is contested, as in the case of the Amboseli elephants, naming is quickly coded as anthropomorphizing and privatizing of the elephants and colonizing of the claims of other people to speak for and about the elephants. See Moss (1988, 1992). The trope of white Western women in the bush who care more for the animals they watch than for the local people reached its nemesis in primatologist Dian Fossey (Fossey was one of Louis Leakey's so-called trimates, along with Jane Goodall and Birute Galdikas).

8. One kind of land tenure in Kenya involves group title to communal land, which

carries with it for the group ranch members similar jurisdiction over the land and freedom from state intervention to that accorded private landowners. There are four group ranches around Amboseli that have been involved in community-based conservation initiatives: Ogulului, Kimana, Mbirikani, and Selengei.

9. The national parks are sometimes referred to in Swahili as *shamba la bibi,* or "gardens belonging to the Queen of England."

10. Maasai culture is notorious in popular representations in the West for the extent to which its women are privatized. As for all group stereotypes, there are some who dispute this. For all its startling diversity for a scientific field meeting, the latter is notable for the absence of women. By the 1997 follow-up meetings a Maasai women's group, "The Women Forum," was there, emboldened by the "gender equity" clauses in many overseas conservation and community development aid packages.

11. Utilization includes consumptive and nonconsumptive, and the former includes subsistence and sport hunting, live-animal sales, trade in wildlife products, trophies, and meat, as well as killing for any of these purposes as a means of problem-animal control or cropping for management purposes. Nonconsumptive utilization includes a spectrum of tourism enterprises. Because wildlife is owned by the state in Kenya and because of the extant bans on hunting, live animal exports, and wildlife trophy sales, the local people who live alongside wildlife and who have to suffer from crop and property damage and human deaths and injuries do not have the right to benefit from the wildlife that comes on their land. The current review of the national wildlife laws seeks to devolve user rights to local landowners as a means of assuring access to migration routes and dispersal areas for wildlife.

12. The status of CITES, and the listing of elephants under its terms, continues to be a battleground for differing visions of conservation policy. In June 1997 the question of whether elephants should be downlisted was debated again. See Cussins (forthcoming).

13. Despite his tenure as chairman of the East African Wildlife Society and his stint as head of the Kenya National Museums, where he was credited with opening up a bastion of white power to black Africans, Leakey battled charges of racism and elitism from top ministers and local communities while he was director of KWS. He spent long periods abroad, paid expatriate "consultants" large salaries, overspent KWS's budget on such things as a plush new headquarters in Nairobi, and was accused of building up a formidable private wildlife security force to carry out the shoot-to-kill antipoaching policy (in the Wildlife [Conservation and Management] [Amendment] Act of 1989). All of these things left him vulnerable to political sacrifice. See Hammer (1994). His reinstatement in 1998 as director after the second firing of David Western illustrates the reversibility of politics.

14. President Moi issued a statement to the press declaring that antipoaching patrols would remain under KWS control, despite previous threats to Leakey to consign anti-

poaching activity to the national army. He also guaranteed D. Western freedom from excessive oversight by government departments (exemption from many of the laws governing state corporations).

15. Koikai is also one of many of the sons of Stanley Oloitiptip, former area MP and assistant minister of health, who was very influential in the first community-based development plans for Amboseli in the 1970s.

16. Cf. Steven Shapin's and Simon Schaffer's (1989, 225–26) notion of the virtual witnessing offered by literary technology. Western's literal witnessing can be thought of as an epistemic challenge to the appropriateness of centralized virtual witnessing as a means of guaranteeing truth about the natural world. Western is peeling back, as it were, three hundred years of supposedly transparent chains of witnessing and saying that for sciences that must stay in the field, like conservation science, virtual witnessing is not a way to generate normative standards.

17. These headings should not be taken to imply discrete realms; I return to the relations between different kinds of issues and expertise below, where I consider what is complex about this case study.

18. This is one of the things complained about in the report of the independent wildlife review commissioned by KWS and conducted nationwide in local meetings during 1994. See Kenya Wildlife Service (1994). Members of the review group were Mr. Idwasi (chair), former district commissioner; Mr. Rotich, KWS and EAWS; Mr. Somoire, Group Ranchers Education Programme; Mrs. Kathurima, Tropical Nature and Cultural Safaris; Mrs. Oduor-Noah, environment officer and Task Force for the Review of Laws Relating to Women; Mr. Taiti, reporter. This report is the rhetorical and empirical bridge between the local landowners and the conservation biologists, spearheaded by Western. Consider the following quote: "Wildlife-human conflicts are not just a litany of specific problems but a whole unacknowledged perspective on reality. Their solution requires a concept of sustainable wildlife management by and for people on their land, not in spite of them" (26).

19. By *nonhuman* here I mean such things as elephants, grass, trees, water, soil, and so on—anything that becomes an object of care (and conservation) and, simultaneously, an agent in crafting the environment. Under a diffuse and processual understanding of biodiversity, stakeholders in this sense can range widely through the nonhuman world. See discussion below.

20. There is a humility and awe that also characterizes romanticism about nature, having to do with feeling wonder across different scales of things and with the recognition of forces beyond human control, and often expresses itself in holistic philosophies of nature. *Toticonnectivity* is the word used by Bruno Latour to criticize such philosophies of nature as "deep ecology" and "the Gaia hypothesis" for their holistic, transcendent, and totalizing view of nature, which he links in turn to Edenic portrayals of

nature as "pure," especially in North America. For criticisms of the coherence of environmental nostalgia for human-free nature, see also, e.g., Cronon (1995), Guha (1989), Mitman (1996).

21. Harman and Shapiro (1992).

22. Cf. Law (1994, 104–12).

REFERENCES

Cronon, W. 1995. "The Trouble with Wilderness; or, Getting Back to the Wrong Nature." In William Cronon, ed., *Uncommon Ground: Toward Reinventing Nature*. New York: Norton.

Cussins, C. Forthcoming. *Conservation Philosophies on Trial: Realigning Science, Identity, and Politics to Save CITES and the African Elephant*.

Ezrahi, Y. 1995. "Technology and the Civil Epistemology of Democracy." In A. Feenberg and A. Hannay, eds., *Technology and the Politics of Knowledge*, 159–71. Bloomington: Indiana University Press.

Guha, R., 1989. "Radical Environmentalism and Wilderness Preservation: A Third World Critique." *Environmental Ethics* 11.

Hammer, J. 1994. "Richard Leakey's Fall from Grace." *Outside*, June, 66–74, 172–77.

Harman, P. M., and A. E. Shapiro, eds. 1992. *The Investigation of Difficult Things: Essays on Newton and the History of the Exact Sciences in Honour of D. T. Whiteside*. New York: Cambridge University Press.

Kenya Wildlife Service. 1994. *Wildlife-Human Conflicts in Kenya: Report of the Five-Person Review Group*. December.

Law, J. 1994. *Organizing Modernity*. Oxford: Blackwell.

Mitman, G., 1996. "When Nature *Is* the Zoo: Vision and Power in the Art and Science of Natural History." *Osiris* 11: 117–43.

Moss, C. 1988. *Elephant Memories: Thirteen Years in the Life of an Elephant Family*. New York: W. Morrow.

———. 1992. *Echo of the Elephants: The Story of an Elephant Family*. New York: W. Morrow.

Shapin, S., and S. Schaffer. 1989. *Leviathan and the Air Pump: Hobbes, Boyle, and the Experimental Life*. Princeton: Princeton University Press.

Takacs, D. 1996. *The Idea of Biodiversity: Philosophies of Paradise*. Baltimore: Johns Hopkins University Press.

Western, D. 1994. "Ecosystem Conservation and Rural Development: The Case of Amboseli." In D. Western, R. Michael Wright, and S. Strum, eds., *Natural Connections: Perspectives in Community-Based Conservation*, 15–52. Washington, D.C.: Island Press.

Wilson, E. O., ed. 1988. *Biodiversity*. Washington, D.C.: National Academy Press.

MICHEL CALLON

Writing and (Re)writing Devices as Tools for Managing Complexity

Although collective and organized action has been the subject of numerous theoretical and empirical analyses, these studies have paradoxically paid very little attention to the tools used by actors as they organize themselves.[1] Indeed, until recently management science, adopting a normative approach, was more interested in developing such tools than studying how they work. There are signs that this shortcoming is now being remedied. Recent studies in economic anthropology show the importance of management tools for the emergence of rational agents capable of calculating and making decisions (Callon, ed. 1998; Law 1994; Meyer 1994). And management science has started to reflect this: without tools for collecting, constructing, processing, and calculating information, agents would be unable to plan, decide, or control. In short, organized action would be impossible (Moisdon 1997).[2]

The importance of management tools becomes even more obvious as organizations and their environments evolve (Moisdon 1997). The intensification of competitive constraints, the accelerated rate at which goods and services have to adapt, the rapid growth of the economy of variety in which categories of products are multiplied, the spread of service relationships that are replacing classical market transactions yet are more difficult to formalize (Callon et al. 1997; Gadrey 1996), the increasing number and heterogeneity of actors involved in the design (Henderson 1998; Hennion 1995; Jeantet 1998), the production and distribution of goods, and the proliferation of performance criteria (including, for example, environmental protection or health and safety standards [Miller 1998]—all these add to the *complexity* of the calculations facing economic agents. At the same time they enhance the strategic importance of the necessary tools. If we add the explosion of computer technology and information processing, we see that to understand the functioning of organizations, we have no choice but to explore the role and the effects of the varied and evolving organizational instruments.

This evolution is most obvious in the service sector.[3] This is because coordination becomes most difficult when the service is the result of long-standing cooperation between several actors involved in its design and realization and when customers pay not for a specific material good but for the organization of a complex system of action that enables them both to progressively become aware of what they want and to express and fulfill this wish.

Under these circumstances firms are faced with a tension between greater complexity and simplification. On the one hand, to survive, the firm has to allow complexity to proliferate. If demand is to emerge and be satisfied, the firm needs to encourage the exchange of information among increasing numbers of actors, to facilitate negotiations that lead to compromises, and to allow the possibility of mobilizing novel resources. This is the basis of innovation, and it is how firms obtain a competitive advantage. On the other hand, this growing complexity also has to be controlled if the firm is to maintain a hold over the process and to profit from innovation. Greater complexity is needed for innovation and to harness any demands that are coproduced. However, to be managed and controlled, this complexity has constantly to be reduced and simplified.

Thus, instead of talking of complexity (which might characterize, for example, advanced societies or modern economies as opposed to simpler traditional societies), it is better to talk of a dual process of "complexification" (Mol and Law 1994; Strathern 1991) and "simplification" (Callon 1986). For it is at the heart of this process that management tools are to be found. And the specification of these tools is particularly demanding because they have to encourage a profusion of actors and initiatives while also securing aggregation and ensuring that the actors can be supervised and controlled.

There is of course a wide variety of such tools, and an inventory would be useful. However, my intention here is more limited. I would like to explore the role of a category of recently developed management tools important to the service economy. I will call these *writing and rewriting devices.* They are important in establishing and transforming systems of collective action because they work by a method of *successive adjustment.*

They also make possible the progressive expression of demands that are partially undetermined and the definition of actions needed to respond to such demands. Finally, they make the complexity of systems of action manageable and controllable without eliminating it.

The material I will discuss was collected during two field studies made in 1995 and 1996. The first was of a company (BC) that organizes cruises on the Seine (ranging from simple pleasure trips to dinner with a variety show). The second was of a company (CR) developing meal vouchers ("chéque-restaurant") to be bought by firms for their employees (and to be used in a restaurant of the employee's choice).

This essay comprises five sections. In the first I briefly present the writing devices used by these two firms. These devices, highly complex and rich, objectify the services offered together with the system of action behind their delivery. The compulsion to write observed in the two organizations is striking: actors constantly write down everything they do and have to do and describe the content of the services they buy and sell. I then attempt to show that these writing devices eliminate the conventional dichotomy between collective and individual action. In the third section I focus on the act of writing itself, highlighting the collective, negotiated, and distributed nature of the work through which the actors participate in the formulation of their own behavior. In the fourth section I suggest that writing helps to reproduce and enhance the asymmetry of the incomplete contract, binding the firm to its employees and customers. Finally, the fifth section explores the role of these devices in the coproduction of supply and demand.

A final preliminary note: methodologically I have chosen to show how these tools were put in place by the management of the firms. This makes it easier to show the asymmetries that they produce and the effects of domination. The process of complexification and the multiplication of narratives is at least partly a strategy of power that cannot be fully understood without exploring the mechanisms of simplification on which it depends.

WRITING DEVICES

In the two years before my visit, the two firms in question had established and developed management tools intended to better define demand and develop customer loyalty. The concern was with quality—and in one case to obtain a "quality label." In many of these new tools writing was crucial. Some sought to objectify the service, others to monitor customers from first contact up to provision of service, and others to put the sequences of actions making up the service into words. In the following section I describe some of these tools.

Putting Service Provision into Words

The first category of texts is what one of the firms (BC) calls "product-files." Because the product does not exist in a tangible, directly observable and transferable form, it has to be put into writing in the form of a file that is then copied and widely circulated. An extract from an interview with one of the managers of the company gives an idea of the content of this file:

> There on my shelf is the file containing the exact description of all the products we offer our customers.
> [He opens the file.]
> Here, the presentation of "Menu des Isles," with all the possible options: the pillars of the boat are transformed into palm trees, the maîtres d'hôtel wear white gloves, plants are rented for the decor. For the sound system [showing me another page] you have all the kinds of microphone we offer, all the video techniques available. Here we provide all the technical details on the boats.
> [Then:]
> There are twelve copies of this file. We update them periodically as our services evolve. With that our sales people can go anywhere; it's a great selling tool. Anything that can be sold, that's already been sold, can be sold by them without them having to consult us. As long as the form has been signed by the sales manager and the catering manager.[4]

Note that there are as many material elements mobilized in this service as in any other economic activity. Files filling entire shelves describe the product in words and make it transportable from one place to another within and outside the organization. And if one acknowledges the "slight shift" in a so-called intangible service when the latter is made to correspond to a series of files that describe it in detail, then the dramatic scope of the objectification involved becomes clear.

In the case of CR it is the "Quality Charter"—a document given to the customer describing the mutual commitments of firm and customer—that contributes toward the process of objectification. It can be read as a series of statements describing the content of the service. For instance, article 2 describes how the date and place of delivery of checks suggested by the customer are guaranteed, how specific orders are dealt with without any change in the schedule, and how a contact person is constantly available to the customer. By contrast in article 3 the customer has to specify the date of issue of its order. What the charter describes is the content of the service. Its role as a tool for objectification depends on the way it defines a series of actions to be completed.

Putting the Customer into Words
If the first device objectifies the service, a second form of writing contributes toward formulating demand. This takes the form of computerized customer cards or forms called *fiches-diffusion*. These record all contact with customers and contain numerous details about prices and customer requirements. As negotiations and discussions with the customer progress, the relevant card is updated and circulated within the firm. In this way the customer exists, inscribed on these cards, and is transformed as the cards are updated and completed: "All contacts, events, requests and answers are recorded. Information is gathered, customer by customer. Everything is written down, presented in the form of a document called 'diffusion' received by each sales person and manager" (a manager).

In this way information is built up and disseminated, replacing a multiplicity of contacts often based on implicit understandings. Accordingly, it is quick and easy to learn anywhere, at any time, of all the commitments undertaken, from the contents of the menu to the type of aperitif glasses and the music, together with customer details. Initially elusive customers thus become objectified, tangible, and manipulable. To categorize the different steps in this process of objectification, marketing specialists have invented an eloquent system of classification. Before contact has been made with customers they are called "suspect." Once the contact has been made they become prospects that may be either "cold" or "hot." As they "warm up" and enter into negotiations with the firm on the content of the service to be supplied, they develop a progressively clearer idea of what they want and are thus able to define better the demand they will eventually submit to the firm. So it is on these cards that we witness the first appearance of the customer, whose identity takes shape as it is written down in the series of documents concerning her or him.

Whereas this device puts *demand* into words, the questionnaire given by BC to its customers is intended to put *customers' relationships* with the service into words. During the cruise a questionnaire is handed to all passengers, and those who wish to do so fill it in and hand it back at the end of the trip. This form consists of about sixty items that describe the content of the service and possible attitudes by the passengers as precisely as possible. The authors of the questionnaire want to define the main components of the service, together with the influence these may have on the guest or customer: quality of the commentary, temperature of the food, sound level, courtesy of the staff, all these and many more are included. Gradually, through the questions, the outline of the service emerges, then its substance, and finally its component parts. Each item is an element in the profile of the service, one of the elementary interactions that, when brought together, constitute what is called a cruise.

When the results are processed, indicators are created. These show, for example, that 55 percent of the guests thought the sound was too loud or that 95 percent of them enjoyed the commentary but that 23 percent thought the toilets were not clean enough. This quantification is one way of objectifying the relationship that is established when the service is delivered. The company uses the questionnaire to objectify its service further and so to build up a more stable relationship with its customers that otherwise would remain evanescent and undefinable.

The CR company also uses a questionnaire to test customers' opinions. The problem with the meal voucher is that "the voucher is simply a bit of paper; only the color changes from one firm to the next. Users don't even know the name of the firm from which they buy the vouchers!" (a manager).

A voucher that goes from hand to hand—that is transformed into a subsidy from employer to employee, then into a meal, and finally into hard cash—has a predictable but convoluted trajectory. And that trajectory says very little about what it really offers the customer or how the customer uses it, even when this is monitored and the transactions involved are recorded. The firm therefore cannot assess the quality of the service it provides; it cannot play on price (to test demand elasticity); nor can it interpret disloyalty given that customers have hitherto been amazingly loyal. The only way to obtain a representation of demand—one could say the only voice—is the questionnaire. So about thirty customers of the four main firms offering meal vouchers were interviewed, and this questionnaire was followed up with a series of telephone calls. The results of this inquiry undermined a number of preconceived ideas: "We noticed that a good delivery period was 72 and not 24 hours, and that the supplementary services we offered such as discounts at certain suppliers were totally irrelevant, nobody gave a damn, whereas we'd based our entire marketing strategy on them!" (a marketing manager).

The inquiry replaced a vague and unverified sense of customer expectations with one that was clear and defensible. The passengers or meal voucher users who filled in questionnaires thus participated, through their answers and reactions, in the construction of the service. Consumers were invited to enter into a process of writing that, after being processed, guaranteed their presence at the heart of the firm.

At BC most of the results of the questionnaires given to passengers are made public. All the managers receive a copy and the most significant results are circulated:

> In our monthly news flash there's a section on quality: waiting time on the telephone (measured automatically: number of calls, percentage of unanswered calls, percentage of customers who waited for more than 30 seconds, more than 10 seconds) and an analysis of 100 questionnaires. All the management staff in the firm, that is to say about ten people, receive the flash. In addition, we present the results at a management meeting. (a sales manager)

What the customer thinks and says, as ascertained by the questionnaire, is distributed throughout the firm. The questionnaires are thus part of the construction of a widely shared representation of the service.

The results of the CR customer survey are also widely disseminated. Moreover, the "Quality Charter," which solemnly reflects the main conclusions, is a document held by all salespeople: "I had meetings with the agencies; I organized a debate and a seminar with the sales assistants" (a manager).

Paradoxically, in these service companies, where the service becomes

objectifiable only after a long process, the customers with their preferences and expectations are ubiquitous, whereas in firms producing material goods they are often kept at a distance.

Putting into Words the Sequence of Actions Making Up the Service
There are further texts that actors call "handbooks" and "bibles." For
instance, here are extracts from the (fifty-page) stewards' handbook given
to each steward at the beginning of the season by the cruise firm:

> Guide the first passengers to the exit by clearly showing them the
> way out. Adjust the ropes to make the way out clear. You should
> constantly remain present while the passengers are disembarking and
> say "Good-bye" to them as they leave the boat.
> [And:]
> You must give the hostess enough time to welcome the passengers
> and to distribute souvenir pamphlets. You can then start selling, in
> other words around the Pont de l'Alma.

Making the service explicit in this way—a procedure repeated for each
category of employee—gives it content by describing each person's role.
The normative tone ("you must," "it is necessary") should not hide the
fact that it is a way of both defining the appropriate sequence of actions
and of making it known that they have to be accomplished. It is a script
for the service, a scenario in which the role of each player is specified,
encompassing interactions with machines and objects. Some of the actions described refer to an environment or, more precisely, to material
devices that serve as guides and references for the action. For example, for
opening the roof: "Lever to the left: 'Bays mobile.' Forwards/backwards.
Watch out for the passengers' arms!"

The bibles used in the catering service are equally detailed. On page 11,
entitled "The service, action by action," we find the following:

> Take the order by saying: "may I have your order . . . ; would you
> like details on any of the dishes?"; in taking the order distinguish the
> choice of each guest by means of a letter, so as not to disturb them
> when serving their food.
> [And further on:]
> When serving a customer, warn her/him that the plate is hot. After

clearing away the plates, give each person cutlery and a plate for the cheese (always served *à l'anglaise*); don't forget to fill the bread basket before serving the cheese; the customer doesn't have to have the cheese platter under her/his nose; etc.

The bible contains pages and pages of descriptions of the sequences of actions to be followed by the maîtres d'hôtel, stewards, supervisors, and other actors. Everything is broken down and listed in detail. But, most important, this is a process that puts actions into words without being a mere statement of what happens: writing down the sequences of elementary actions *defines* the content of the service. The service is no more and no less than a system of actions, and its construction depends on describing the sequences of actions involved—so that these may be prescribed.

THE WRITING DEVICE AS MEDIATION BETWEEN INDIVIDUAL AND COLLECTIVE ACTION

So writing devices play a crucial role in constructing and objectifying services, their consumers, and, more broadly, the collective actions that make it possible to deliver services. The documents all contribute toward the presentation of an organization in action—called by some an *actigramme*—in which the different operations and the sequences to which they belong are described.

Writing devices—and this is my second point—thus mediate between different actors on the one hand and the collective (the *organization* and its customers or partners) on the other. This suggests a novel definition of actors because these, whether stewards, maîtres d'hôtel, or passengers, are set into a *narrative* in which they become one of the protagonists. The argument, then, is that stewards, maîtres d'hôtel, and Japanese tourists are *constructed in and by* writing devices. In a sense actors do not really exist outside texts and the sequences of actions these suggest. These texts do not describe an existing reality. Instead, they format it. Just as we know since Austin that the statement "I declare the session open" is an act that opens the session, so too the charters, bibles, and other handbooks or customer cards *perform* the service they describe. They cannot be dissociated from the various relevant actions. Insofar as they accomplish the written actions, the steward and maître d'hôtel, together with the consumer with whom they interact, are all in the narrative created by the different writing devices and nowhere else. They are the subjects of a narrative, of a story into which they fit, in and through which they act, which they cause to progress, and through which they progress.

The extraordinary effectiveness of writing devices derives from the fact that they solve a theoretical question—in practice. However, the question is theoretical only when it is asked by observers so far removed from practice that they do not grant actors competence. "What is the relationship between individual and collective action?" asks the sociologist who first carefully distinguishes between two levels of reality and then finds it hard to describe how they are related. Answer: the link is woven by the plot produced by writing devices. Like any narrative this resolves the tension between the viewpoints and actions of individual agents (which may themselves be collective), on the one hand, and the constantly renewed unit of the narrative on the other. Could one say of Aurèlien d'Aragon that he is "acted" by the narrative when the stray bullet hit Bèrènice, with whom, he realized, no common future was possible? Of course not. The stray bullet surprises Aurèlien as much as it does the reader. At that moment Aurèlien is hardly the outcome of the preceding chapters, and his behavior is scarcely predictable for the reader. He is not the master of the narrative. The unexpected German armored car, and its equally unexpected meeting with a car without headlights on a lonely road, sends the story off in another direction, allowing characters to act but in novel circumstances. *The narrative is the mediator that makes actions and their unity compatible.* It is a mediator in the sense intended by Antoine Hennion (1993). It is not merely a passive intermediary linking two distinct and preexisting levels of reality (individual action with the story). Narrative mediation is situated *in-between*; it *reveals* both realities, individual and collective; and it does so by organizing the unexpected overflowing that, by renewing the action, reveals the existence of a story-already-there, which might have been concluded but which the actor opens and sets off again in an unexpected direction.[5]

Consequently, the fact both of being an actor and of being "plunged" into a collective is not contradictory, just as it is not contradictory for a character in a novel to be shaped by the novel and yet to cause it to progress. This tension between framing and overflowing is at the heart of all the writing devices described above. Talking of the actors' room for maneuver or even, as in Giddens's sociology, of constraints that the actor transforms into resources, leads us away from the practical solution devised by the two service companies that write narratives to organize action that is *both* framed *and* open.

Writing is action. Writing devices are both results and starting points. They prompt the observer to question their creation and transformation. Who writes? How is writing solicited, framed, and distributed? How are these texts produced, and how are they transformed? These questions lead me to three empirical observations.

Writing by Several Hands Involves Tough Negotiations
Writing the different documents presented above involves the employees at various stages and in various ways. They are asked to give their opinions, formulate rules, and draw up texts that will be binding on them. The quality handbooks presenting what has to be done and how to do it for each category of employee are the result of writing by several hands:

> It is a collective task with the people already concerned: the head skipper, the head hostess and the assistant operations manager. But in the future I'll include even more people in the consultations and participation. (a manager)
> [Or:]
> We worked hard on the Bible. For the past two years we've written down everything we possibly can. Putting everything into writing: what one says on the phone, what we say to the customer when s/he leaves, how to ask a customer to pay, how a cleaner sweeps. It needed two years of observation, and a further year's work. We took each post. For example, we said to the head chief: 'how do you organize your chaps, what do they have to do?' Like that we can give it to each new recruit. The maître d'hôtel's bible is thirty pages long. Mine's 300 pages. (a manager)
> [Or:]
> We took a maître d'hôtel. We told him to write: "I arrive at 9 o'clock, I divide my team into two, 2 on the setting up and 2 on the

preparation; I give them half an hour and then I check." We then took another maître d'hôtel, we compared and we got them together. We got them talking. Then we set it all out. (a supervisor)

The fact that the tasks to be carried out by each employee are put into the form of a written document, that this document is drawn up with those concerned, that it is then circulated among the employees, and that it is incorporated into a single document combining all these texts (the bibles become a comprehensive "Bible") ensures the coherence of the document and the transparency of the organization to itself. It also ensures that all employees know what their roles are and how each employee contributes toward achieving corporate goals. The legitimacy of this process of putting things into words depends both on the fact that it attempts to satisfy the customer and enhance the quality of service and on the fact that it is applied to everybody without distinction of rank or seniority. The Bible is a constraint but one that is defined jointly by all concerned.

The value analysis at BC was also collectively motivated:

> We carried it out with the reception and hall staff. We analyzed all the operations. We wanted to draw conclusions, to identify the things that were unacceptable for customers. There were, for example, five problems to sort out immediately: wobbly tables, the temperature of the food, tired supervisors, dirty carpets and glasses, and the sound level. At reception there were seventeen points which irritated customers. They found a solution or the best way of dealing with them. (a manager)

A CR the most striking example of this collective work was the construction of a matrix of points of contact with customers. After the questionnaire on customers' perceptions mentioned above, staff meetings were organized to list all customer contacts. These were grouped into several broad categories: written communication, commercial contact, taking orders, managing disputes, delivery, refunds, customer requests for information, customer relations, lost or expired, VIP club. During a series of meetings over a four-month period each form of contact with customers was systematically studied. These included analyzing needs, actions for planning and implementing those needs, the results of actions, necessary follow-up. This involved almost all the members of the firm, requiring them to define their own commitments for achieving the objectives identified through the customer survey.

In all this collective writing there was debate and conflict. In the meetings we attended viewpoints diverged, and, depending on the subject under discussion, alliances and oppositions changed. Debate about written communication with prospects and customers was particularly heated. Differences revolved around how to subdivide these groups, defining an important (real or potential) customer being particularly difficult. Some related it to turnover, others to growth rate, others to the nature of the sector of activity, and so on. Once agreement had been (painfully) reached, it was necessary to precisely define the content of communication at each moment. And the "Quality Charter" itself was the product of writing that mobilized senior management, as well as customers, and served, through successive compromises, to determine corporate doctrine.

Deleting and Rewriting

I am arguing that writing devices that put organization-in-action into words are the product of a *collective* effort that involves conflict and leads to intense negotiation; and such collective work is *never concluded,* for writing leads to endless rewriting. For instance the "Quality Charter" went through eight successive versions. I had access to the different versions and was struck by the way the nature and content of the charter changed along the way. Initially conceived of as a legal contract—a "notarial act," as one of our respondents put it—it gradually turned into a moral commitment. The first page of one of the early versions reads as follows: "The present QUALITY CHARTER is made BETWEEN the Company C.R. represented by . . . with authority to . . . AND the Company . . . represented by . . . with authority to . . . , hereinafter referred to as 'the Beneficiary.' " The second page continues in the same legal style: "The parties first noticed that . . . ; in witness whereof they recognised the advantages of concluding the present QUALITY CHARTER."

In the first version the notion of quality appears in the title but only occasionally in the text itself. The overall tone is legal.

In one of the later versions this is quite different: "The present Quality Charter is concluded between the company C.R. and . . ." The second page opens with: "QUALITY: THE LEGITIMATE ANSWER TO YOUR EXPECTA-

TIONS" in capitals and continues with a long reminder of the results of the customer survey, underscoring the four points that define quality, as perceived by users of the vouchers. Article 1 leaves no room for ambiguity. Entitled "SPIRIT OF THE CHARTER," it stipulates, "This charter must be perceived as an ethical commitment by the parties concerned," after confirming that "the present charter is conceived entirely in a spirit of partnership with the common wish to find the appropriate technical and human means to develop this quality relationship."

Here there has been a total metamorphosis. It is like reading a text in political economy. The contractual commitments, in which each party emphasizes its interests, are followed by a description of trusting cooperation, of a partnership in which each party has its place. Over and above the words and especially the insoluble question of their sincerity, that is to say, their real ability to shape practices, what should be noted are the efforts of the authors. Between the first version and the last they themselves underwent a metamorphosis. This shift from a legal to a moral style, a sort of collective maieutics, would have been impossible without the project of writing the "Quality Charter." The rewriting—the deletions, erasures, and insertions—changed the nature of relations between the agents; pure market cooperation was progressively replaced by cooperation based on relations of trust. Collective and individual actors and relations were transformed in rewriting. This is where the full significance of these devices and their successive metamorphoses lies. To redefine their identity, agents do not have to resist or try to break free from the framing or formatting imposed on them. Instead, they participate in their own reconfiguration in the process of writing. It is not that there are actors on the one hand and a writing device for accounting for them and shaping them on the other. In rewriting, both collective and individual actors are reconfigured.

A similar process can be observed at BC, which makes their Bible a somewhat strange document. Whereas initially it took the form of a bound volume with a set text, it is currently a large file of loose sheets. The initial device that fixed the rules for once and for all was unrealistic. As philosophers insist and actors understand, it is continuous rewriting that is realistic. This writing is not prescriptive but performative, for by the tenth rewriting the collective had changed. Indeed, one of the interviewees suggested that rewriting the Bible was like compiling the dictionary at the Académie Française. Discussions on the meaning of a contract or the precise definition of a maître d'hôtel might last for hours, and this collective effort might define the state of the collective and its actions for quite a while.

Distributed Writing

Who writes and on behalf of whom? That is the question we now have to consider.

Take the case of the stewards' handbook. It is not written by the stewards themselves for an apparently simple and convincing reason. The steward's post is seasonal and is generally filled by inexperienced students. Once they have gained experience, they leave. The same is often true for hostesses. This is why prescribed behavior is written down in detail—a need compounded by the fact that in service businesses the contact between customer and firm tends to depend most on the least qualified, the least stable, and very often the least committed employees. Hence, the crucial role of the handbook and of writing down the rules. Because stewards have no reason to smile at passengers and because it is essential that they do so, given that they represent the firm, they are reminded that they should "smile while saying hello." They are also told "to be well groomed at all times, to have tidy hair, not to wear heavy make-up (in the case of women), to be clean shaven, not to wear dark glasses near the customers although tinted lenses through which the person's eyes can be seen are acceptable, etc."

Who can write all this? Not the new recruit, who is, of course, totally unfamiliar with the job and who basically couldn't care two hoots about what the customer thinks of him or of the firm and its service. The writing is therefore delegated to the stewards' superiors, which means that it is distributed selectively and asymmetrically. Just as spokespersons exist, so do "wrote(s)-persons" or, more simply, scribes.[6] And more broadly, during the meetings held to draw up the different documents, there is a separation between those who are questioned, instructed to talk, and those responsible for writing up the information thus provided. There are few scribes, and their role is crucial: who writes these documents is an important subject in its own right. Indeed, putting customers into words through administering and analyzing questionnaires involves three parties: first, those who prepare the questionnaire, formulate the questions, and make suggestions; second, customers who answer the questions; and, third, analysts who process the statistics, interpret the tables and correlations, and make observations, comments, and suggestions.

THE QUESTION OF THE AUTHOR

Everything that semiotic analysis tells us about texts and their three distinct roles or functions of reader, actor, and author applies to the writing devices presented here.

The *reader's* function is clear for the case of the steward. As soon as he arrives in the firm, he is given the handbook and videos. These documents, together with informal verbal comments, form a set of prescriptions or formal rules that, in a sense, give content to the work contract. The participation of stewards in the writing, as authors, is indirect: the stewards' scenario is written by an intermediary who observes, notes, analyzes, and gathers testimonies and comments. Elsewhere the writing is more direct, although always, as we have noted, the outcome of a collective process.

So who is the author? The answer is that this is undefined. In a fine and classic (although somewhat obscure) text that has received little attention in France despite numerous foreign commentaries, Michel Foucault suggests a number of possible responses (Foucault 1969).

First, he rules out the tempting solution of treating the author as the *result of a process of attribution.* This facile sociological solution breaks the process of writing down into two distinct phases. In the first everyone acts—that is to say, writes. In the second phase there is attribution—necessarily arbitrary—of the paternity of action and thus of authority, to a particular actor. But although it is convenient, this does not work. Even if they had the power to do so, managing directors would not dare to claim authorship of all the written documents. This is because the force of the writing device rests precisely on the fact that the viewpoint of each person is carefully recorded and that the plurality of contributions is emphasized: yes, consumers write, and it is precisely *because* they write that their answers can be taken into account. This is quite different from a process of attribution.

A second solution, also dismissed by Foucault, is no better. This identifies the author as a *scribe,* as the one who writes, who holds the pen. But how can one assume that the person who writes is really the source of the text? In our case not only are there many scribes, but each writes by delegating, translating, and transforming the discourses of those they represent and for whom they speak. How can one talk of an author when there are as many authors as there are scribes and—at one remove—agents consulted? As we have seen, the writing is dispersed.

A third possibility is to emphasize *ownership.* As Foucault notes, an author may be identified on the basis of property rights—a legal device into which the writer fits and which establishes her or him as the author of her or his works. This works for the case of the firm, even when the texts are not written directly by the managing director. The figure of the author has no meaning outside this legal device.

But this suggests a fourth possibility, which takes us beyond Foucault. This is that what documents put into writing is *a contract that binds three types of actor together:* the firm, its employees, and its customers. As we have seen, this contract is never complete, but in the service sector, where the content and organization of activities are constantly being adapted, it is nevertheless a device for coordinating different actors. It is not based on a simple and stable division of tasks, as in bureaucracy, and neither does it correspond to the written contract, which links two parties in a classical market transaction. Instead, it may be understood as the writing and negotiated adjustments of an incomplete contract in which employees and customers are linked to the firm.

Two observations about this. First, what we are witnessing is a way of linking individual contracts to the writing of collective contracts. Standard economics, which treats organization as a set of bilateral contracts, underestimates the capacity of the actors to produce revisable commitments involving both collective and individual agents. But the writing device grants autonomy and efficacy to collective action, avoiding the dualisms that oppose individualism and holism. This practical solution created by the actors integrates collective and individual learning in the same movement, a point to which I shall return in my conclusion. Second, the asymmetry created by property rights leads to another asymmetry: the fact that all the writings are brought together in a single place—the general manager's office. This has a series of important consequences.

In particular, it makes it possible to correlate results and sequences of actions. Look, for instance, at the following, which comes from an overview document that lands on the general manager's desk in early November every year (the excerpt quoted concludes a long and detailed statistical analysis): "It therefore appears that xyz [the initials of the new boat launched by the firm during that year] has an influence on the items of satisfaction directly related to the attributes of the boat (seats, toilets, etc.), but there is no significant correlation with other items independent of the attributes of the boat (e.g., pace of the commentary or the quality of the sound). We therefore cannot talk of a positive effect of xyz on the service as a whole. Thus, it is a matter of presentation only and the customer isn't fooled."

Here the manager is saying that a particular sequence of actions described in a specific document produced a particular type of result, such as customer or passenger dissatisfaction. The implication is that there is a *position* in the firm where planned and scheduled action becomes possible (Latour 1987), where sequences of action may be correlated with observable and measurable results. And the correlations are so precise that, by skillful cross-referencing, they can be used to calculate a steward's bonus from passenger satisfaction or more precisely from his compliance with the rules that he helped—directly or otherwise—to define.[7]

This asymmetry—generated by the writing device and how the texts are compared and analyzed—gives substance to the notion of an author. An actor, corporate management, may treat the entire process as its own work and may remodel or reconfigure it. This is something that none of the other scribes can do, not because they are intrinsically incapable of strategies or foresight but simply because they do not see the entire set of documents that alone can provide an overview. But the manager, who sees all these papers in her or his office, can plan her or his action as if it were intentional, guided by objectives and culminating in observable and measurable results, just as novelists in the position of "author" obviously see their writing as their own work and endow themselves with the capacity to change its course.

In short, firms may be conceived as voluntary, collective, and simplified actions that can be attributed to a function and managed by the person in charge of that function, if we treat them as effects of writing devices.

When a consumer says "I want a trip and a meal on the Seine," what does this mean? *Who* wants the cruise on the Seine? What does *want* mean? What *is* a "cruise on the Seine"? Given the ambiguities, we need to explore the way the request is expressed, but we also need to avoid two pitfalls.

First, we must avoid thinking that the consumer is being manipulated. We must avoid assuming that the desire being expressed cannot be imputed at all to the consumer, that instead it passes through the consumer because he or she is a member of a certain social class or victim of commercial manipulation. Second, however, we also have to avoid making the assumption that the consumer knows exactly what he or she wants and is the sole author of his or her demand.

The data I have presented are not consistent with these alternatives. Customers' expectations only become clear in the collaborative process of writing and rewriting. It is only at the end—when customers' satisfaction is measured—that firm and customers discover the precise nature of supply and demand. Consumers are "grasped" by a writing device in a process of *joint elaboration,* which generates that demand.

But there is more, for not only does the customer not know precisely what he or she wants, but the category of "customer" itself is vague. It may be singular or collective (*this* customer or the customer *in general*?) and in any case is ambiguous and difficult to define. In the BC case a significant part of the firm's efforts aimed at creating customers with whom it could interact and negotiate. But how does this work? I will explore this by looking at customers on simple cruises and show how the firm simultaneously performs their identities, their existing demands, and their future expectations—thus determining what may be still shaped.

On simple cruises passengers are often casual customers who will never be seen again. Getting them to write is not particularly difficult, but why bother if they are unlikely to return? The answer is *segmentation.* What BC is trying to do is to determine regularities, starting with the idea—common in marketing and social science—that there are *populations* of mutually substitutable customers. This means that when it collects the comments of one customer, BC is in fact consulting the entire population to which that person belongs and is helping to determine the expectations of future customers who will, in turn, be questioned. In this way isolated casual customers are being replaced by a chain in which each writes for the next.

We are so used to the idea that society is made of homogeneous categories that the idea of grouping customers together seems obvious. But it is an assumption that needs constant verification. What BC is doing as it puts on its sociologist's hat is to continuously identify relevant subpopulations, to refine the criteria used to characterize them, and to monitor the ways in which they change. With such "typological analyses" (the expression used by BC managers) the firm links actual customers, usually seen once only, with the abstract, representative, and differentiated customers that make up its *clientele*.

One implication of this is that a "preexisting" demand cannot be determined outside these techniques. For although demand is formatted in advance, *knowledge* of this formatting is revealed only in the particular test of the cruise and the questionnaire. Indeed, the word *revealed* is not quite right. It would be better to say that demand and expectations that are *both* real *and* constructed are articulated when the cruise is "turned into questions" (Desrosières 1995). They are *real* because they are relatively stable and robust—BC can safely rely on the results when devising strategies or innovations. But they are *constructed* because they cannot be dissociated from the way they are produced: the cruise itself, but also the questionnaire and the statistical tools of analysis, with their limits, hypotheses, and biases.[8]

The process combines regularities and singularities: other tests with other tools would have produced other results that were equally real—and equally constructed. We might say that the cruise-in-practice preforms and performs a demand that is both structured and emergent, set in regularities and open to singularities. For instance, this is how the firm's multifactorial correspondence analysis reveals the importance of geographical origin. It turns out that how customers judge the reception, the sale of drinks, and the length of the cruise all depend on whether they live in or near Paris. Class membership is barely significant. In this way we discover the unexpected existence of a population from the Parisian region with its own expectations and preferences. These customers are mostly employees, they have been on cruises before, they take their families with them, and they do not visit the Eiffel Tower—all of which is also tested in focus groups. What sociological theory would ever have dreamed up such a population?

These typologies are used to reorganize or invent new cruises—changes that are like life-size experiments for validating or slightly modifying the typologies. Adapting services to presumed subpopulations makes it possible to confirm, invalidate, or slightly modify their reality (for example, by organizing jazz cruises for some foreign customers or special cruises for primary-school children from the Parisian region). These "new" services serve, in turn, as frames for new tests that will lead to further segmentation, comments, and services. Distinguishing between what is prestructured and what can be shaped depends entirely on this process of consultation and experimentation. A cruise is a trial, a full-sized experiment to determine what must be taken as given and what may be redefined.

The notion of coproduction is therefore complex: identifying preformatted consumers and their expectations and transforming those consumers and expectations take place together in the process of testing. And writing devices are crucial in this double investigation and experimentation. By handing out questionnaires, filling in customer cards, and organizing meetings with representatives of customer segments, BC transforms itself into a specialist in social science. The similarities between techniques used in marketing and in sociology cannot be overemphasized. However, BC has a life-size experimental device that sociology cannot afford, which is why it is able to produce practical, albeit temporary, answers to questions about the malleability of expectations and demands. This suggests that the social sciences do not so much need to find answers about how much demand is prestructured—participants are much better placed to do this—but to explore the mechanisms by which participants perform this demand (Callon 1987).

CONCLUSION

BC's and CR's writing devices are used to interrelate a whole series of heterogeneous requirements and to make them compatible. In particular they adjust supply in terms of demand and ensure compatibility between collective and individual learning;[9] define the sequences of actions that make up the service, establishing measurable correlations between behavior and performance; make it possible to capitalize on actions and their outcomes at a single point, while allowing some decentralization; and allow for a form of participation by employees in the formulation of prescriptions that they undertake to follow. These results suggest that writing devices lie at the heart of the organization in action and that without them the organization would not exist, as it does, in a location between knowing and acting.

Compared with the more traditional instruments of accounting or management control, such writing devices are highly effective. They make it possible to integrate a large number of actors and variables into decision making. And these devices can be multiplied as need be. They respond to the dynamics of increasingly complex systems of action, but they also make it possible to coordinate different points of view, expectations, and behaviors. This is done by constant analysis, interpretation, and rewriting. These are tools that make it possible to deal with the tension between complexification and simplification, between decentralized initiatives and centralized control.

However, these tools are more than mere rules or conventions, for although they help to produce rules and prescriptions, they also evaluate and transform these.[10] That is, they both structure behavior and allow for restructuring. In particular, they leave the question of identity open instead of facilitating the identification of the groups needed to allow coordination.

Furthermore, these instruments also endow agents—at least some of them—with the ability to calculate. They render decisions calculable and locate the maximum power to calculate a single point in the managing director's office. This means that they play a decisive part in competition. For instance, BC is engaged in a veritable naval battle for the control of cruises on the Seine. And since it set up these new management tools, the growth of its market share has been spectacular. Although this development needs further investigation, the questionnaires appear to have contributed substantially to winning over and developing the loyalty of customers. The ability to continuously rewrite the contract between the firm, its employees, and its customers provides BC with a substantial competitive advantage, and BC controls that most strategic of resources: the coproduction of a demand that can be partially shaped.

The emphasis on writing devices should not allow us to forget all the other devices with which they overlap. We have already stressed the importance of technical artifacts (Akrich 1992): boats, for example, play a key part in the organization of the cruise as a trial. Again, adjustments to talk (which enable a steward, for example, to improvise a response to unexpected customer demands) are not inscribed in lasting texts but also play an important role. In the cases studies however, coordinating a large number of actors and the management of complexity would be far trickier without writing devices, and that is what makes the devices interesting. If action is successful, it is because it is constantly narrated and commented on.

Yet despite the structuring and stabilizing of technical devices and rewritten texts there is always the possibility of overflow (Callon 1998). Textual organization is never completely successful. Take the case of the stewards. Why do they conform to the texts that describe and prescribe their behavior? The answer comes in four parts.

First, the handbooks, bibles, and other documents are constantly rewritten, year after year, building on experience as it occurs. Thus, the precision and relevance of these texts is continually increasing because the performance they suggest is measured and serves as an instrument of control.

Second, this relevance is all the greater because stewards are always recruited from the same population of students who want holiday jobs and treat the job in a purely instrumental way. The collective stability of their predispositions (stability that is confirmed in the experience of BC) guarantees their suitability for the positions prescribed for them. The firm is aware of this and seeks the same kinds of recruits year after year.

Third, the sequences of actions described in the texts include material markers that limit ambiguities and possible leeway. The shape of the boat and its equipment frame the action in a highly restrictive way and limit overflowing.

Finally, performance incentives (bonuses) are used to reward standard behavior, which is observed and measured, indirectly, as indicated, through the daily statistical processing of questionnaires given to passengers and guests.

These four mechanisms do not altogether prevent unexpected behavior, but they make it possible to identify and control it. The failing student employee might be interviewed and given further instruction or even dismissed. And it is here that the asymmetry of these constantly reworked writing devices becomes important.

Here, then, collective action is rooted in devices that both give it its materiality and define its tyranny and asymmetry. Written and rewritten documents frame the action and render it asymmetrical. At the same time they define and locate overflowing actions that may be seen either as acts of creation that enhance strategic capacity or as deviant acts that reveal once more the arbitrary nature of domination. This means that we must not forget that collective action is always tyranny. It is a tyranny of the past acting on the present and the future and a tyranny of those who write acting on those who are permanently excluded from writing. This is the other side of the management of complexity: the domination of those who have access to the tools without which management would not be possible.[11]

NOTES

Special thanks to Jean Gadrey and my colleagues at CSI for their suggestions on this text.

1. On this subject, as on others, Max Weber is an exception. His classical analysis of bureaucracy pays ample attention to files and their management.

2. The specific nature of organized action, according to Moisdon—who thus summarizes over ten years of research by the CGS (Centre de Gestion Scientifique, Ecole des mines de Paris) and CRG (Centre de Recherche en Gestion, Ecole Polytechnique)— "stems from the need to instrumentalize all the activities concerned" (22). This point of view leads, in particular, to a radical critique of the paradigm of bounded rationality. However, although such a critique emphasizes, and rightly so, that human agents are endowed with limited capacities for calculation, it does not go so far as to make these capacities depend on the tools and instruments at the agents' disposal. Contrary to the assertions of methodological individualism, the agent who makes decisions is not the human being but the human being equipped with tools. Admittedly, on this point the ambiguity in Herbert Simon's work has proved fertile. By underscoring the role of routines, Simon opened the way to analyses—notably evolutionary—that see rules and procedures as cognitive tools in their own right. Yet very few empirical and theoretical studies consider these routines as instruments enabling actors to make calculated decisions.

3. And among the service activities, those for whom the archetype of market transaction between two strangers who, at a precise time, exchange ownership rights to a material good is less relevant.

4. The interviews were undertaken by Michel Callon between September 1995 and February 1996. Most were from two to three hours long. They were not tape-recorded, but reconstructed from notes taken during the course of each interview.

5. This is an example of a general property of the double process of framing and overflowing in which calculative and strategic agencies are formatted (Callon 1998). Each attempt at framing preexisting or expected overflowing mobilizes materials (here narratives and writings) that in turn provide grounds for new unexpected overflowing. As I've shown elsewhere, overflowing can be expressed in all kinds of modalities, ranging from mute disobedience to protest movements aiming at creating new compromises or to the proliferation of new independent narratives. Here what needs to be recalled is this double property of narratives and writings that both frame action (establishing boundaries) and let actors prolong it in their own and unpredictable manner.

6. The production planning department in the classical manufacturing firm has a similar role. In neither of the companies studied is there a service specialized in writing. The "scribes" are spread throughout the different departments and are therefore close to those on whose behalf they write.

7. The tripartite contract discussed above is therefore not unrelated to the work contract linking an employee to her or his employer. The writing device provides, at least partially, the constantly revised explication of this contract by establishing a link between the steward's performance and his bonus.

8. For a similar argument about the performative role of marketing see Cochoy (1998).

9. For similar analyses see Berg (1997) and Hutchins (1995).

10. They produce rules but cannot be reduced to rules because, engaging actors in an uninterrupted process of rewriting, they constantly are open to redefinition and to new expressions as a function of actors' interpretations and critical comments.

11. My approach bears some resemblance to the analyses that describe organizations as knowledge systems having to manage a fourfold tension between: (i) tacit and explicit knowledge (Nonaka and Takeuchi 1995); (ii) individual and collective action (Spender 1996); (iii) routine and creativity (Stacey 1996); and (iv) centralization and decentralization (Tsoukas 1996). But only in focusing on the tools of management themselves, and more specifically on the writing devices, can we come to understand how organizations can practically resolve these tensions.

REFERENCES

Akrich, M. 1992. "The De-scription of Technical Objects." In J. Law and W. Bijker, eds., *Shaping Technology/Building Society*. Cambridge, Mass.: MIT Press.

Berg, M. 1997. *Rationalizing Medical Work: Decision Support Techniques and Medical Practices*. Cambridge, Mass.: MIT Press.

Callon, M. 1986. "The Sociology of an Actor-Network." In M. Callon, J. Law, and A. Rip, eds., *Mapping the Dynamics of Science and Technology*. London: Macmillan.

——. 1987. "Society in the Making: The Study of Technology as a Tool for Sociological Analysis." In W. Bijker, T. Hughes, and T. Pinch, eds., *New Directions in the Social Studies of Technology*, 83–106. Cambridge, Mass.: MIT Press.

——. 1998. "An Essay on Framing and Overflowing: Economic Externalities Revisited by Sociology." In M. Callon, ed., *The Laws of the Markets*. London: Blackwell.

Callon, M., P. Larédo, and V. Rabeharisoa. 1997. "Que signifie innover dans les services?" *La Recherche* 295: 34–37.

Cochoy, F. 1998. "Another Discipline for the Market Economy: Marketing as a Performative Knowledge and Know-How for Capitalism." In M. Callon, ed., *The Laws of the Markets*. London: Blackwell.

Desrosières, A. 1995. *La politique des grands nombres*. Paris: La Découverte.

Foucault, M. 1969. "Qu'est-ce qu'un auteur?" *Bulletin de la Société Française de Philosophie* 69, no. 3.

Gadrey, J. 1996. *Services: La productivité en question*. Paris: Desclée de Brouwer.

Henderson, K. 1998. "The Role of Material Objects in the Design Process: A Comparison of Two Design Cultures and How They Contend with Automation." *Science, Technology, and Human Values* 23, no. 2: 139–74.

Hennion, A. 1993. *La passion musicale*. Paris: Métailié.

Hennion, A., and S. Dubuisson. 1995. "Le design, entre création, technique et marché." *Sociologie de l'art* 8: 9–30.

Hutchins, E. 1995. *Cognition in the Wild*. Cambridge, Mass.: MIT Press.

Jeantet, A. 1998. "Les objets intermédiaires dans la conception: Eléments pour une sociologie du processus de conception." *Sociologie du Travail* 3: 291–316.

Latour, B. 1987. *Science in Action: How to Follow Scientists and Engineers through Society*. Cambridge, Mass.: Harvard University Press.

Law, J. 1994. *Organizing Modernity*. Oxford: Blackwell.

Law, J., and A. Mol. 2000. "What Is Social Context? A Note on Boundaries, Fractals, and Technologies." Working paper, Sociology Department, Lancaster University, UK.

Meyer, M. W. 1994. "Measuring Performance in Economic Organizations." In N. J. Smelser and R. Swedberg, eds., *The Handbook of Economic Sociology*. Princeton: Princeton University Press.

Miller, P. 1998. "The Margins of Accounting." In M. Callon, ed., *The Laws of the Markets*. Oxford: Blackwell.

Moisdon, J. C. ed. 1997. *Du mode d'existence des outils de gestion*. Paris: Seli Arslan.

Mol, A., and J. Law. 1994. "Regions, Networks, and Fluids: Anemia and Social Topology." *Social Studies of Science* 24: 641–71.

Nonaka, I., and H. Takeuchi. 1995. *The Knowledge Creating Company*. New York: Oxford University Press.

Spender, J.-C. 1996. "The Science of Complexity: An Alternative Perspective for Strategic Change Processes." *Strategic Management Journal* 16, no. 6: 477–95.

Stacey, R. 1996. *Complexity and Creativity in Organizations.* San Francisco: Berret-Koehler.

Strathern, M. 1991. *Partial Connections.* Savage, Md.: Rowman and Littlefield.

Tsoukas, H. 1996. "The Firm as Distributed Knowledge System: A Constructionist Approach." *Strategic Management Journal* 17 (winter, special issue): 11–25.

ANNEMARIE MOL

Cutting Surgeons, Walking Patients:
Some Complexities Involved in Comparing

In health care most facts come as comparative facts. Few conditions or treatments are ever treated as simply good or bad—as if there were absolute standards. Rather they are better or worse: than they were, than their alternatives, than an agreed threshold, than might be expected. Thus assessments involve comparisons. This means that they raise questions about what is similar and different between different situations. When analyzed in detail, similarity and difference are complex rather than simple matters. Comparing is by no means a straightforward activity. In this essay I explore some of the complexities involved in comparing treatments and the conditions of patients before and after treatment.

This is what lies behind my inquiry. Making comparisons implies simplification. But there is not just one kind of possible simplification: quite different things may be skipped, bracketed, smothered, or left out. There are simplifications that flatten the world and others that do not. And depending on the site where and the moment when comparisons are made, the effects of making them show variety as well.

I will explore these broad issues by looking at a single (simple?) case. This is a comparison of *walking therapy* and *operation* as treatments for arterial disease in what medicine calls "the lower limbs." The material for this study was gathered primarily from two university hospitals in the Netherlands, hospital Z and hospital G. There my research assistant Jeannette Pols and I spoke with medical professionals, technicians, and patients and observed practices of diagnosis and treatment. We also read relevant medical literature and spoke with general practitioners, physical therapists, and patients working or treated elsewhere in the Netherlands.[1]

A patient information leaflet in use in hospital Z:

> A vascular obstruction or an occlusion has been found in one or more of the arteries of your leg. . . . Due to these obstructions or occlusions less blood flows through your leg. This may cause pain in your leg when you walk which disappears again after a short rest. Even though not everybody in a comparable situation has to have an operation, in your case it may be the only way to relieve you of your symptoms.

An operation "may be the only way to relieve you of your symptoms" if you get pain in your legs when you walk. It may take such pain away. But operations are done for other reasons too. The same leaflet:

> It may also be that so little blood flows through your leg that you have pain even when you are resting or at night in bed. There may be ulcers that do not heal or a toe may have died off. In such cases an operation is necessary to improve blood flow through your leg. Without an operation it is often not possible to avoid an amputation of the leg concerned.

Thus an operation may be done when wounds ulcerate and don't heal. This is because if gangrene were to set in, survival would require amputation: gangrene is deadly.

The patient information leaflet in hospital G doesn't speak of ulceration and gangrene. It only suggests walking therapy for people whose legs hurt when they are walking:

> You have been in the hospital for an investigation of your blood vessels. In the arteries of your legs one or more obstructions have been found. You have been advised to start to do walking therapy. . . . Because of the obstruction in the arteries of your legs, the latter start to hurt after you have walked a certain distance. In the end this makes you stop. The pain can be in various places in the leg: the hips, upper

legs, calves or feet. The medical name for this problem is intermittent claudication. Walking therapy is a treatment for claudication which gives good results. The treatment aims to increase the distance that you are able to walk without pain.

These, then, are the two treatments that are being compared in this study: operation and walking therapy. In the information leaflets they are not presented as treating the same problems, but neither do they treat different problems. Their indications overlap. Both may be used if your legs start to hurt as you walk and stop hurting if you rest.[2]

REASONS FOR TREATMENT

The question, then, is how much one's legs should hurt, and how little one should be able to walk, before either treatment is considered. Patients are responsible for the first step in dealing with this question. It is only if patients consider their own situation bothersome or worrying that they go and see a doctor.

As one general practitioner observed: "There are always old people who say, well, it's old age. I can't walk all that well any more, but what should I expect? And then they never even come to see me, or any doctor, with complaints about pain when they are walking."[3]

Some people whom the general practitioner talks about as "patients" never even become patients. But others do: they come to see a doctor with their questions and their stories. These are not all taken into account by the consulting doctor. The consultation is a filter. Here, distinctions are made. People who describe pain that only occurs when they are sitting are not classified as having vascular disease or intermittent claudication. And if they do have pain when they walk, then the question of how much pain is not explored. It is too hard to handle: people express and may even feel pain in different ways.[4] Instead, what doctors want their patients to talk about is something simpler: the distance they can walk before their legs start hurting, their so-called pain-free walking distance. This is easier to communicate than an inexpressible amount of pain. For ideally it comes in standard numerical form. If we want to talk about distance we have the meter, which was especially designed to facilitate comparison between sites and situations.[5]

However, one doesn't need to talk to medical practitioners for very long before they start to tell stories about the way in which the intricacies of practice defy the ideal of numerical standardization.

> Angiologist (internist specializing in vascular problems) in an interview: "How far are you able to walk? In America they express this in blocks. That's a fairly standard measure. We don't have that. I ask: how far can you walk? 'Yes, a good 100 meters, doctor.' 'At a reasonable pace?' 'Oh, yes, sure.' And then, if you walk along with them, such answers appear not to be correlated at all with the actual walking distance you find."

People do not live their daily lives in meters but think of the distance they can walk as "too little" or "from our house to the corner." In the translation from such experiences to a medical assessment of "pain-free walking distance" things may get lost. Once numbers are scribbled in the patient's file, they come to have an independent existence as "indicators," and possible errors of translation are no longer retrievable. Nor is the tone of voice (confident, hesitant, pleading). Thus some complexities are left out; but something is also gained, for numbers are easy to handle. The numbers that belong to any specific patient are comparable to those of other patients and to agreed thresholds (above or below which further investigation is indicated).

Numbers may be mapped on a linear scale: individual metricated walking distances may be plotted on a graph. In research and clinical trials there are overviews of this kind of many patients and the way their conditions did or did not change (without or after treatment). In clinical practice, however, linear scaling is not usually the way of handling the numbers that express pain-free walking distance. For here there is little distinction between fifty and sixty meters: both are pretty bad. And to clinicians the difference between fifty meters and one hundred meters is far more "impressive" than the difference between 300 and 350 meters. In practice often a potentially numerical linear scale is dissolved into a few classes. Sometimes there are two of these, as in "normal" versus "pathological." Sometimes there are more: three or four (six would be too complicated). Thus various walking distances may end up being distributed between something like "normal," "acceptable," "slightly disturbed," and "seriously troubled."

In the clinical interview the complexities of a person's daily experiences with pain are transformed into a metricated value, the pain-free walking distance. This value is written in the patient's file (and may be counted at a later stage, for instance if the patient's fate becomes a topic of clinical epidemiological research). And the same number accompanies the patient during his or her trajectory as a vascular patient. Next to the words clinical findings *(abbreviated to* clin.*) on future forms and letters, an indexed number will appear: 100 m or 250 m. But it may well be that decisions about treatment translate this value into something like "severe" or "too short."*

In the outpatient clinic pain-free walking distance is not the only parameter for assessing the severity of intermittent claudication. Surgeons also consider whether a patient's condition is *lifestyle limiting*. Finding an answer to this question takes them beyond metrication to a group of more or less heterogeneous elements. The old man who lives in a home and still makes it to his cigar shop is not necessarily limited all that much, even if his legs start to hurt after eighty meters.[6] But that spry woman who talks in such a lively way about Brussels, Rome, her old friends, and the grandchildren she likes to visit is hampered a lot even if her pain only starts after 150 meters. This is because her lifestyle includes—included—traveling, and with all this pain she's severely limited in that.

> Another patient in an interview: "So, yes, sometimes you've got to climb the scaffolding. And if, so to speak, you've got to go up ten, twelve meters, then I couldn't get there. And then, if you were up there, if you had to use some strength, then it became too much. Sometimes. And I couldn't walk well. We always had to walk a lot, and then I took a bicycle, but in the end that was no longer a solution either, for if there was wind and strength was required, I had none."

While pain-free walking distance is a numerical variable based on a single measurement, lifestyle limitation is composite. The elements fused together in composing it are interdependent but in a nonlinear way.

Together they form what our surgeon informants take to be possible reasons for operating even if there is no immediate risk of developing gangrene. They work on the assumption that measurements of bodily characteristics aren't enough to decide whether to operate.

> Vascular surgeon in an interview: "A short walking distance. Bad pressures, a bad angiography. Fine, fine, but I can't operate on such data alone. You see: there's always a risk, especially with these patients, they have bad arteries, after all. Bad cardiac vessels too, more likely than not. So they may not survive the operation. Can I make someone run a risk like that? Not if they have nothing to gain. So if they're not bothered, if they're fine, however bad their vessels are, I'm not going to operate on them."

Establishing when lifestyle limitations are bad enough to make the risk worthwhile requires a complex cultural assessment. In the clinic this tends to result in a binary conclusion: a patient's condition is lifestyle limiting, or it is not. This then becomes a transportable fact again. Whereas scaffolding, cigars, Rome, and the grandchildren do not fit into most forms or files, the verdict *lifestyle limiting*, in which they may come to be included, does.

There are various ways of taming the complexities of living-as-a-patient in such a way that a manageable assessment of the patient's condition is generated.[7] Presenting just two of these, pain-free walking distance *and the notion of* lifestyle limiting, *is enough to see that one simplification is not quite like the other. One gives a value that may be plotted on a graph and counted, a number that may be validated by walking in the corridor together with the patient. The other is a composite cultural assessment that assumes that numbers alone are empty: their true value depends on a specific person's particular circumstances.*

Instead of deploring the way medicine reduces patients' lived reality, while having little alternative in practice but to accept the truth of medical facts and the efficacy of its techniques, social scientists and other analysts might consider doing something different.[8] They might ask how *a patient's condition is turned into a problem that medicine takes itself to be capable of handling, or* how *a patient's condition is turned into a problem-to-deal-with at any particular site or situation, to then shed light on what are, locally, the actually existing alternatives. This is relevant because within medicine a patient's situation can be understood in various ways. And it is important to point to this variety, which tends to disappear in the format of the clinical verdict, which, in the end, says of patients with intermittent claudication that they are amenable to treatment. Or not.*

THE PROBLEM TREATED

For patients with intermittent claudication whose walking distances are too short and/or whose lifestyle is limited, various kinds of treatment are possible. Here I will compare two of these: walking therapy and operation. One of the comparative questions to ask is what they each intervene in.

Operations intervene in arteries. The story goes that the pain that occurs when one is walking is a *symptom*, a surfacing sign of something that lies hidden deeper in the body, a stenosis or an occlusion in the arteries that are meant to carry blood carrying oxygen from the heart to the tissues. If there is not enough room for this blood to flow, if it faces too much resistance, not enough reaches the lower legs and feet. Blood pressure there falls. The muscles do not get enough oxygen to work. Surgeons, when operating, make room for the blood to flow again. They may scrape the debris that encloses the vessel lumen away or construct a bypass around the bad spot with a vein or an artificial tube.

> Patient in an interview: "Look, human beings have quite a lot of veins which they don't need. Quite a lot. They can be taken out of the arms as well, so to speak. In my case they took one out of the right leg. And the surgeon inserted it in the left leg, around the sick artery, you see. The sick bit isn't taken out, it stays right there, and the good bit is inserted next to it, here, down here. Good. And then it's all neatly sewed up again and a bandage is put round your leg."[9]

This is an intervention in how the blood flows to the lower leg and the foot that hurt so much before. The aim is to allow the patient to walk again afterward.

> Another patient: "You almost immediately notice the result, for your leg gets warm again, you see. Before, and that's a common characteris-

tic of these things, before you had a cold leg. It becomes warm again as soon as the insertions are made. And if there are no complications, you're allowed to get up again. Carefully at first. And then you're allowed to go home and they give you the message: walk, walk as much as you can. That's not easy, it takes a while. But those wounds heal pretty fast, after ten days the stitches are taken out. So you get the message 'don't smoke' and 'walk.' And all in all it takes about a month before you're reasonably well again."

Patients are encouraged to walk after their operation. Walking therapy also encourages them to walk but without operating on the arteries first. Arteries may still be mentioned in stories that help to explain to people what is happening in their bodies.

> Hospital G, a small consultation room: The trainer takes a picture of the vascular system out of a drawer. He shows it to the patient. "Here, you've got a vessel that is partly blocked here, at this point. Not enough blood is able to pass the obstruction. So when you use your muscles they don't have enough oxygen. That makes them produce lactic acid, which causes pain. That's the pain you feel."

Something is laid on the table: a picture of a vascular system. It is used to explain walking therapy. There is an obstruction in your arteries; *that* is why it hurts when you walk. But then again: walking therapy is not going to take this obstruction away. If it were measured now, if an angiography were made on which the vessel lumen were visible, then this lumen would be restricted. And if another angiography were made in a few months time, after the walking treatment, there would be no difference. It would still be restricted.

In studies that assess the results of walking therapy the arteries are not made visible on angiographic images (because angiographies require hospital admission and are a burden to the patient). Instead the pressure at the ankles is measured or the blood flow through the calves. Or the oxygen absorption in the (lower) legs is quantified. But often none of these parameters seems to have changed much as a result of walking treatment, even when there is significant *clinical improvement*. Consider the following case:

The clinical improvement was not, however, accompanied by any significant variation in the ankle/arm pressure ratio at rest or after exercise or in the results of the calf blood flow as evaluated by strain-gauge plethysmography. The levels of local oxygen as quantified by $TcPO_2$ basal values and the $TcPO_2$ half recovery times, which are today considered a valid index for oxygen delivery and tissue absorption, showed no significant improvement.[10]

Walking therapy does not intervene in vessels. Yet it may lead to *clinical improvement;* that is, it may increase a patient's pain-free walking distance. What is happening here? The most popular explanation given to patients is that walking therapy widens the collaterals of the stenotic artery (that is, the smaller adjacent arteries). However, if pressures and oxygen absorption do not increase, this is unlikely. Some other element in the complex physicalities involved must be undergoing alteration. Which one? The biochemistry of the muscles, maybe, or the pain threshold? So far, the studies we have found in the literature are not conclusive. But whatever the "mechanism," walking therapy does change the pain-free walking distance.[11]

So there is a simple image of disease: it talks about underlying structures that may go wrong and the symptoms that emerge and follow from this. This image assembles dispersed elements together into a single disease. The image suggests that intervening in the underlying structure (here the artery) alters the symptoms that emerge (here walking distance). It also suggests that not altering the underlying structure means that improvement is impossible. But in practice relations among the various elements linked up with any "one" disease are far more complex in character. This suggests that the disease is not a single object.

The two interventions being compared here treat different objects: one intervenes "directly" in a patient's ability to walk; the other intervenes in the arteries in the hope of thereby altering the ability to walk. And although the walking therapist at G explains the patient's pain as a problem caused by a blocked artery, this so-called cause is not the problem solved by walking. This is why the internist at G suggests that blocked arteries should not play such a central role in understanding what intermittent claudication is all about. Surgeons currently ask radiologists to make X-ray pictures, angiographies, of severely encroached arteries.

> Internist in an interview: "But if you look at their angiographies you see a pipe and it's clogged up. So the image itself suggests what should be done about it. Go ahead, unplug it. Or insert an extra pipe, if need be. It's plumber's work. Oh, sure, they may be good at it, it's difficult, I respect them for it. But no one would ever invent walking therapy by staring at angiographic pictures."

The invention of walking therapy depends on letting go of the idea that there is a single disease, arterial disease, situated inside the arteries, that emerges in the symptom of pain. It is only if we take the pain that occurs after walking to be a crucial and independent phenomenon, a problem important in its own right, that it becomes conceivable that training someone to walk further might be a good treatment.

Thus there also is a complex image of disease. This does not compose single diseases out of underlying structures and emerging symptoms, but neither does it fragment what were the various previous elements of the disease, its parameters, into ever so many independent beings, as if more than one disease necessarily meant many diseases. A clogged artery may be linked to pain, but pain may sometimes be treated without opening up the artery. Arterial disease, intermittent claudication, is more than one and less than many.[12]

AN INTERVENTION IN LIFE

Walking therapy is not an easy treatment. One of the conditions for its success is that the patient manages to turn walking twice daily into a routine, but even for patients who succeed in doing so, it takes a while before the results become apparent.

> Patient information leaflet of G: "The training implies that for six months you will exercise by walking daily. You can do so at a place you choose for yourself. You walk twice a day for half an hour, the same distance every time. The total distance is divided into sections. After every section you rest for a minute. In the hospital you establish with your trainer how long those sections will be and how often you have to

rest for a minute. The length of the sections is such that you can walk without pain. You have to include your twice daily walk in your time schedule."

If patients manage to include walking therapy in their lives twice daily, the pain in their legs may gradually diminish, or it may start after they have walked further. Including walking therapy in one's life, however, doesn't just increase pain-free walking distance. It also changes one's life.

> Trainer in an interview: "The average vascular patient who enters here is a miserable, down-hearted, socially invisible person. They literally don't follow what's going on around them any more, they don't keep pace with others. And then after a while, in the course of the training period, you see them crawl out of it. They become active, start to get involved in things again, know how to handle their problems. Often the idea that they can influence their own fate is very motivating for people."

Walking twice a day is a way of getting out of the house and into the world. People who do so get more outgoing. Walking, then, doesn't only alter a life that is separate from that walking: it becomes part of a new way of living. This new way of living involves more than walking alone: it implies general activity.[13]

One might thus come to think that the difference between the two forms of treatment is that whereas operations intervene in vessels, walking therapy intervenes in life. However, it is not that easy because being operated on, in its turn, is not something that only happens to vessels. It is part of a way of living, too. A different way.

> Patient in an interview: "For six hours I lay there. Six hours. And by accident I saw above my head, between those wide lamps, the operating lamps, there was something that reflected, and I saw my leg. What they were doing with it. And then you see those colours, the inside, the colours of the inside. And the blood. I saw my blood and what they did with my leg. All that contributed to it, of course. That in the end I felt unwell. I had local anesthesia. And I fainted."

Even though surgeons make cuts in a body and not in a life, lying for hours on an operating table is as much a part of life as walking twice a day. Or lying in a hospital bed for a few days and then slowly recovering for a month, at home, afterward.

In comparing treatments one may ask what these treatments do to a patient's life as if the treatments themselves were events external to that life. It all gets a lot more complex, however, once one starts to recognize that treatments themselves are a (more of less prominent) part of life. They imply a certain way of living.[14]

WHAT IT IS TO TREAT

Treatment implies activity, but whose activity is required for walking therapies and operations? At first sight this is an easy question: patients take it on themselves to walk, and professionals do the operation.

> The trainer in G sits across the desk from a new patient. He first explains where the pain comes from: the arteries that are encroached. Then he lays out the possibilities. A small balloon may be inflated inside the obstructed part of the vessel. Or it is possible to bypass the bad bit. "And then one may wonder: what can the patient do *himself*? Well, that's walking. A serious training program. We've seen good results with it."

Others will blow balloons inside your arteries; others are capable of making a bypass around an obstruction. By contrast, walking is something you, the patient, can do *yourself.* Or is it?

> Trainer in hospital G: "Well, this former professor of surgery we had, he didn't believe in walking therapy. For he said to people: walk! And then they came back after a while and they hadn't improved. But that doesn't surprise me. There are of course better ways of helping people than just saying 'walk!' I find out for them how far they must walk before they had better stop and rest for a bit. And then I have people come back here time and again and reporting back to me how well they are doing. That keeps them going."

If a professor of surgery tells a patient to walk, this is not necessarily effective, but if a trainer puts a lot of effort into it, walking therapy may work. Someone has to explain to patients that the pain in their legs doesn't mean that something in their bodies is being destroyed. Someone has to help them work out the number of steps that is best for them so that they may stop walking just before they start to feel pain and they start to lose their motivation (or, alternatively, in other variants of the treatment, to talk about how to keep going even when it hurts). It is a lot easier for patients to treat themselves if someone is willing and able to answer the questions that arise during all those hours of walking.[15]

> General practitioner: "Yes, surgeons tell patients to stop smoking and to walk. But how? People have trouble finding ways. In medicine it tends to be either, come here, we do it all for you; or: go home and do it yourself. There's little in between. Oh, I include myself in this. I don't know how to do it. There are very few techniques for supporting patients properly."

Surgeons tell their patients to walk (and to stop smoking), but to them this is not part of the therapy. It is something in addition to therapy, a matter of giving advice, providing information. In walking therapy, however, the talking cannot be separated from the intervention: talking *is* an intervention.

> Angiologist: "The power of this method is in the guidance. Simply taking it seriously. For if patients cannot figure out how to walk 200 meters, the risk is that they will get laughed at. But stick to taking them seriously. Talk about where they may take their minute's rest. Have them phone when they want, see them when they need it. It is a lot of work. It's a lot of work and it is not heroic."

One of the ironies is that the very people who do all this supportive work also help to hide it. This is not by chance: our informants even suggest that such hiding increases the effectiveness of the intervention. This is because the idea that the results of walking therapy are one's own achievement is a boost for a patient's self-confidence.

> Angiologist: "Sure, the patient expects a pill. A solution from the doctor. It is your problem, doctor, you've got to help me, that's what you're paid for. But no, that's not how it is. That's the nice thing about this treatment, of course. If people improve from walking I tell them:

'You've done that, you've done it yourself.' And indeed they are proud. Very proud. 'Look, what I've achieved!' "

A doctor who simply says, "Walk!" has little effect, but if all the nonheroic work of guiding and supporting is done well, the patient's self-assurance increases from having achieved improvement all alone.[16]

This is another complexity in the comparison between the treatments discussed here: for surgeons, talking is external to the "real" intervention, which is a matter of accurate cutting and neatly sewing up again. In walking therapy, however, the relational work is *the therapy, but hiding this work makes it more effective.*

Patients cannot do operations themselves. These are done by professionals and require the collaboration of an extensive medical team. Surgeons, angiologists, radiologists, anesthetists, technicians, nurses: for an operation to work, all of these have to cooperate and attune their activities to one another.

> In the operating theater a surgeon and a surgery resident are bent over the right leg of a patient. It is opened up. The skin that a nurse painted yellow with iodine is held aside with a scissors-like instrument. A short piece of artery is visible (to those able to differentiate it from the adjacent muscle and the connective tissue from which it has been loosely separated). The surgeon asks the nonsterile nurse (dressed in green but with no gloves on) for the instrument he needs to prevent the blood from flowing through the large artery that supplies the leg. She takes it out of a drawer, opens the plastic bag, carefully while avoiding touching the instrument. A sterile nurse, with gloves, takes it out and hands it to the doctor. He puts it on the artery, a little above the place where the bypass will be attached. And then he immediately addresses the anesthetist. "Be careful, Harry, he's got no right leg any more."

The nurses have to attune their movements to the doctor, sometimes on command but often before any words are spoken. The anesthetist has to keep blood pressure under control, even when the blood is no longer entering the right leg (the moment that, so far as circulation is concerned, the patient "has no right leg any more"). The points of contact and the need for mutual adjustment are many. In the middle of all this activity all a patient needs to do is to be patient. In the operating theater, well anesthetized, the patient is indeed capable of doing nothing more.[17]

However, the success of operations doesn't simply depend on the skills and the collaboration of professionals. For an operation to work, patients have to do a lot as well: they come to the hospital, stay sober, and answer questions, but being *patient* is hard work as well.[18]

> Patient in an interview: "So you have to lie flat. Oh, and first they give you nothing to eat or to drink. And then, for hours you lie there. Somehow everything was aching. My head was behind a screen, but I could *hear* them. And afterwards you're not allowed to move, that may take a while, too. Hours and hours without moving, that's hard. Did you ever do that?"

Once patients who have undergone an operation go home again, they are supposed to walk—without a therapist to support them. They must be careful when they sit in trains and airplanes or other places where they may get immobilized. And it is their duty to refrain from smoking.

> Surgeon in consulting room, talking to a patient on her first checkup after an operation: "So you still smoke, do you? Well. That's a pity. We'll see you again soon, then. For I'm sure your arteries won't need a lot of time to clog up again, if you can't stop smoking. It's fine with me, I earn my living operating." His voice is low but harsh. Almost ironic.

If a patient doesn't stop smoking, an operation may work in the short run, but it is of little value in the long run. The surgeon doesn't treat this as his own failure or that of the surgical team. Instead he treats it as a failure of the patient, who did not do what was needed to prevent further progress of the disease *after* treatment. Thus, smoking after an operation is seen as a wrong action by a failing patient, which leads to further deterioration and a reason for operating again. In the context of surgery smoking is not a *part* of a patient's problem but its *cause*.

The question of who does the treatment is related to the question of what counts as belonging to the treatment. Whereas in the case of walking therapy the activities of professionals are toned down, when it comes to operations the patient's activities are hidden. In the context of surgery, walking and quitting the habit of smoking are not treatments: they have to do with leading a so-called healthy life. They are not therapeutic tasks but part of a patient's civic duties. One is to blame if one behaves irresponsibly and fails to prevent the recurrence of a disease that the surgical team has so laboriously tackled.[19]

DOES IT WORK? THE STUDIES

The next important question in comparing walking therapy and surgery concerns how good these treatments are. This issue is investigated in clinical trials that are published in the research literature. Consider, for example, Mannarino's (1989) findings:

> The results of our study confirm the importance of physical exercise in the treatment of patients affected by intermittent claudication. Our physical training program did in fact significantly improve the walking capacity of the patients who followed it (group A). An average increase of 87% was registered in the pain-free walking time, while the total walking time was prolonged on average by 67%. On the other hand no noteworthy variations in walking times were observed in the control group B under placebo treatment. (9)

For someone with the necessary skills who spends an afternoon or two in the medical library, it is quite easy to find many articles proclaiming the effectiveness of either intervention. This still leaves open the typical question of a clinical epidemiologist, which is whether these articles indeed report good studies. Clinical epidemiologists tend to search for, and find, methodological flaws even in the published literature. The number of people involved is too low, control groups are inadequate, the statistics are not properly done, and so forth. Such methodological issues are important because they point to the inferences that have come to be accepted between what happens at a research site and what may be done analogously elsewhere. They point to the division between what is specific to a site and what may be extrapolated from that site as a valid fact.

Here I will not go into all the intricacies of method but will concentrate on only two questions. The first is, What is being counted in the process of producing facts? In the text above walking therapy is being assessed by measuring pain-free walking *time*. This differs slightly from the indicator we came across in hospitals Z and G, which was pain-free walking *distance*. Such small differences may or may not have consequences later on. It is important to pay attention to them, however, for the outcomes of evaluation studies depend on how the patients' conditions and the treatment's intervention are framed. I have shown that walking therapy and operations have a varied set of characteristics. This leads to the question, Which of these are taken into account and which are not in evaluation studies?

> Patient in an interview: "The disadvantage of walking therapy is that— well, you have to pause to rest. And if there are shops you can just stand in front of a shop window for a bit. But if you're somewhere where there's no reason to stop, people may think 'Heh, what's she doing there?' Like, if you come across someone you know, they may think 'What's she up to?' And I know there's no reason to be ashamed, but it's not written on your face that you have bad arteries."

This inconspicuous but significant experience is kept out of evaluation studies. The same goes for the suffering implied in lying for hours on an operating table or the fantasies one may have after having accidentally seen one's opened leg in the course of an operation under local anesthetic. That such details are left out is neither a matter of bad faith nor an error. Researchers may do their utmost to attend to the many elements involved in treatment, if not in concise clinical trials, where only a few parameters of success and failure are taken into account, then surely in broader evaluation studies. Where these tend to include monetary costs, many research groups also try to explore what they call the social costs of interventions. However, quantitative evaluation doesn't make this easy, for all it gives one, in the end, is a balance sheet on which numbers must be filed.

An example. For an operation a hospital stay is required: but how might one take into account *in an account* the fact that some people enjoy being taken care of by nurses for a few days, or to have their family and friends come for a visit, whereas others just loathe being all of a sudden dependent and part of hospital life?

> Researcher: "Sure, we know that it's something to stay in a hospital. We take it into account as best as we can." Question: "How?" "Hmm,

what did we do?" Shuffling through papers. "Here I've got it. We've subtracted 6 days from the life expectancy of someone who undergoes an operation, because that is the number of days they spend in the hospital."

This illustrates the difficulty of quantitative evaluation even more clearly than a story in which the effect of treatments on peoples' daily lives is simply forgotten. It is difficult not to flatten out the multidimensional complexities of treatments when they need to be turned into numbers. Such difficulties, moreover, don't only have to do with the intricacies of patients' daily life experiences. The very delineation of physical parameters is not all that easy either.

Surgeon in an interview: "It's always a problem. What have they been measuring if they report impressive successes? The number of patients going out of the hospital alive and with an open artery? The pain-free walking distance a few weeks later? It's rare, in clinical trials of surgery, as yet, that clinical parameters are used. What is more likely to be measured is whether the vessel is still open when evaluated with a duplex after three months, or a year, or something like that."[20]

The outcome of evaluation studies, then, depends on the initial design and the parameters delineated. Walking therapy, for instance, would never come out of a study as a successful intervention if the degree of lumen encroachment such as it is visible on an angiographic image were taken as a parameter of success. Nor would it seem an effective intervention if oxygen absorption or ankle blood pressures were measured. Walking therapy may emerge as successful only if the study's dominant parameter for success is a patient's ability to walk after a few months of training.

The point of asking what is being counted is not to argue that counting is doomed to do injustice to the complexity of life. This is certain. The point, instead, is to discover how and in what ways. For in that process something is foregrounded and something else turned into unimportant detail. Some changes are made irrelevant whereas others are celebrated as improvements or mourned as detrimental.

Success depends on the parameters of success. Evaluation studies do not show a treatment to be effective in a broad, unqualified way. What they may show is a link between an intervention and a few, very specific effects. The crucial question, then, is what effects to strive for. This question would be easy to answer if patients were always either simply diseased or simply healthy.²¹ However, in intermittent claudication, as well as in most other diseases for which patients nowadays visit their doctors, complete cure is out of the question, although many possible parameters might be substituted for improvement.

Evaluation studies hinge on the parameters they take into account. There is yet a second out of the many tricky elements of method that I want to point to here. Like the first, this is not a rule of calculation, and it also arises early in the process.

In order to be able to count, many variables—not just parameters— need to be fixed. Once this is done, they disappear from sight, but the findings of studies are widely disseminated. The findings get the attention, are taught, and are embedded in standards, protocols, and routine practice. The conditions under which these findings came into being, however, are hardly spoken about. Silently they are incorporated into the practices that emerge. The fact that these conditions might have been shaped differently only emerges again when they are challenged—which often they are not.

We're in a meeting where a thesis is being defended.²² The candidate, a young researcher who is also a trainee surgeon, has gone back into the files of almost two hundred patients in hospital Z who have had an endarterectomy: one (or sometimes two) of their leg arteries has (have) been stripped clean from the inside. Now he has to defend his thesis in front of an audience. One of the seven questions comes from a professor from university L, who asks: "Why is it that D found in the seventies in a clinical trial, properly done as far as I can tell, that endarterectomy isn't any good, while you find that it is?" The candidate explains that there may be various reasons. One is that endarterectomy is a difficult operation that is highly surgeon-dependent: if one is very good at it, it works; if one makes small mistakes, it doesn't. In hospital Z it has always been done a lot, and there is extensive training and careful supervision. Another reason has to do with the specific artery in which the endarterectomy is done. The poplitic artery has a lot of curves, and stripping it is hard. "But the superficial femoral artery is just like a highway, all straight." In the present study the results for the poplitic and the femoral artery have been separated. Stripping then proved a lot more successful for the second, straighter vessel.[23]

The success or failure of an operation may depend on a lot of specificities, such as who operates or on which artery the operation is done. When a study evaluates "endarterectomy in the leg vessels," it may prove this to be a poor treatment, but separating out "poplitic" and "femoral" arteries may show that the same treatment is effective for the latter.

A treatment is always done under specific—these, not those—conditions. Conditions that become fixed in the process of establishing the treatment through evaluation studies. This obscures the question of how they might have been—might be—shaped in a different way.

Fixing variables in order to compare and evaluate treatments is not simply to do with taming the complexities of clinical practice after the event. Engaging in evaluation studies also requires one to shape clinical practice in a quite specific way, that is, to standardize it. For "Rutherford stated that without uniformity in the standards for success and failure of interventional therapy for peripheral vascular disease, the results of different studies cannot adequately be compared."[24]

In order to evaluate a treatment, it has to be standardized. Treatment protocols are given or referred to in the studies, and for a study to take place, clinical practice has to be adapted to the protocol. Take walking therapy: this comes in a variety of forms. For instance, it is possible just to tell people that they should walk a lot, without further specification. It is also possible to ask people to walk until just before pain is likely to start. This is done in G: preventing actual pain is supposed to help people to stay motivated. Elsewhere, however, pain is supposed to lead the body to change the way it works and is therefore said to be the crucial factor in training.

The inclination of researchers is to either neglect such differences, going with one possibility, or to treat them as a reason for further comparative research. If walking therapy can be done in different ways, either one is opted for, or the question is asked: which is best? Clinicians have traditionally chosen another way to handle a diversity of possibilities: they tend to try to adjust the treatment they give to the individual patient who is being treated. This clinical way of working doesn't easily fit with comparative research methods.

> Walking therapist in the small hospital of D: "We adapt our training. We make an individual program for every patient. What we think they can handle, with their heart, their motivation, their social life. Some people we ask to walk quite a lot here, on the exercise belt we have here in the clinic. Others can do more by themselves, at home. Overall, it's very impressive. It works very well, even in people who'd been given up on, whose hearts are too bad for an operation. They're sent here as a last resort, and they don't heal, of course, but they improve. Our problem is that we can't prove anything. We've kept all these files, but we don't know how to do it. It's all individualized. We hoped that you, since you're from the university, that you might help us with that, with how to use our files for publications."

The creative adaptation of therapies to individuals that is developed by these physical therapists means that the clinical epidemiologists interested in physical therapy (to whom we suggested they should go and talk) will find it difficult to use their files "for publications": to use them as material to show the value of "walking therapy" in general. Their problem will be how, with all these variations, to phrase what's *general*. If there are too many variables, it is difficult to make outcomes transportable from this specific site and situation, this patient, this clinic, to other places, other people, elsewhere.

It is hard to adjust the complexity of good clinical work (directed at individuals) and the ordering devices of good studies (that measure populations) to one another. Doing so in one way (for example, by standardizing clinical work through protocols) forecloses the possibility of doing so in another (for example, radically adapting each intervention to singularly established individual characteristics).

There are widely accepted studies that suggest the effectiveness of walking therapy. The angiologist at hospital Z is convinced.

INTERVIEWER: What do you think about walking therapy?
ANGIOLOGIST AT Z: Yes, sure, walking therapy. The literature is impressive. It works. If you support people properly it works. But here in Z . . . there is no support for patients. The physical therapists work within a budget. They are not allowed to do more than their budget allows and they are overbooked already. So it wouldn't help to just ask them to do it. We all tell people to walk, of course, but it does not happen properly, with the support that makes it work. Just now there's nobody who can do it.

The strategy of setting up clinical trials to scrutinize different forms of treatment was based on the idea that there are too many treatments, all supported by eager professionals. Not all of these can be good, and surely not all of these can be the best one around. Thus clinical epidemiology took it upon itself to rule out therapies that do not prove to be as good as others. However, it doesn't work the other way around. Studies that show that a therapy *is* effective are not enough for this therapy to come into being. This is because therapies can only come into being somewhere: in a specific site and situation. If there is no site or situation where the institutional requirements for getting a therapy off the ground are in place or easy to put together, if there's nobody to do it, or just a few people against a set of rules and regulations, then it doesn't happen. Institutions have a life and logic of their own. The simple question of who and how they might be paid for taking on a new task may be tricky, and indeed stubborn.[25]

General practitioner in an interview: "I'd love to propose walking therapy to some of my patients. For I know it works, I've seen it does, in G. But if I tell people to walk, or even have them come back regularly, well, it often doesn't work. I'm not very good at it, I have no time, and a group might also be better, I don't know. Anyway: it's no option. None of the physical therapists around here offer walking therapy. They don't know the first thing about it. And if they did, they would have quite a job getting it off the ground, because as it is, it isn't covered as a separate activity by most insurance companies.

For this general practitioner, referring patients to a properly supervised walking therapy is no option. The specificities of the Dutch health care system have so far ruled it out.[26] This brings along that this doctor has no more options than quietly explaining to her patients all about walking and telling them about the advantages of keeping a notebook and of choosing a nice route. If for some of them this is not enough to get them to walk, there are no other resources in the town where she works. Walking therapy is offered as a separate treatment only in a few places, such as G, where an assistant in the hospital was specially trained to give walking therapy at the time the local angiologist wrote his thesis about it.

Thus in the clinic, the most urgent question need not be "Does it work?" It may as well turn out to be "Where is it done?" A treatment, after all, doesn't spread overnight if a few studies show it is effective, or cheap, or a boost to patients' self-confidence. It may well be that such arguments in favor of walking therapy would be enough if there were a single, central site where they could be addressed. That, however, is not how a health care system like the Dutch one works. It has no center from which it is directed. That does not turn it into a static system; there are shifts and changes all the time. Since we assembled the material for this study, for instance, properly supported walking therapy has come onto several Dutch research agendas. If given by physical therapists, it is even supported financially. Such developments do not depend on directives from a single center but on a multitude of discussions in a variety of sites. Discussions about costs, financial regulations, professional assignments, indication criteria, the desires and resistances of patients, and, no doubt, the effects of treatment: again and again. These are discussed long before *and* long after the publication of studies with a positive outcome.

Patient engaged in walking therapy: "And that doctor, he was so proud. He said to me 'Tell everyone.'" The patient's wife adds: "Yes, 'Tell everyone,' he said, 'because when *I* say that it works, they don't believe me.' And then I said, 'Doctor,' I said, 'he never stops going on about it. How much he's improved from all his walking.'"

If walking therapy works, this is not a self-evident consequence of a technique that has been shown to work. It is something to shout from the rooftops so that everybody hears the news. It is also a reason for pride. Our informants keep on stressing how much walking patients improve. Cutting surgeons never give rise to so much enthusiasm.

> Operation report: "Total anaesthesia. Cephalotine as a prophilactic antibiotic. Colleague R. starts in median side below the knee with the idea of trying to elongate the bypass that was still open last week. The bypass proves to be occluded and the popliteal artery and the tibio-peroneal trunk unfit for an anastomosis. . . . Tunneling of the varivas prosthesis subcutaneously along the lateral side of the knee and the upper leg. End to end anastomosis with a Propleen 6.0 on to the common femoral artery. When cuffs are loosened a good Doppler signal over the bypass. The foot regains colour well. . . . Post operatively an ankle/arm index measured on the dorsal pedal artery of 1.0."

The operation report describes what goes well and what doesn't "on the operating table." It was a successful operation, for even if last week's bypass was occluded, a new prosthesis has been successfully inserted. When the cuffs were finally loosened, the crucial indicators pointed in the right direction: there was a good Doppler signal, and the foot regained its color. After the operation the blood pressure in the ankle was as high as that in the arm. Blood flowed again where it hadn't properly before.

> Vascular surgeon: "But the problem is, of course, that if they have atherosclerosis in one site, usually their whole vascular system is bad. So you operate on their left leg, and then their right leg becomes the limiting factor: that starts to hurt. Or their heart gives problems. And you may tell patients to walk, but when they come back and you talk with them it appears they still don't get all that far. It's sometimes very disappointing for people. They go through all this, a hospital admission, a serious operation, recovery. And then they expect to be cured, but they've got a chronic disease. They're not going to get better. Not really. It's very difficult to explain."

It is striking. Whereas the proponents of walking therapy try to convince us, their interviewers, that it works, vascular surgeons tend to stress that however much effort they put into operating, in the long run they have no miracle cure to offer. They say that they keep on telling their patients so, trying to tone down their patient's excessive expectations.

> Patient talking about his history: "What you think is that you'll go to the hospital and have a new piece inserted. And that that's it. That that's how it normally goes. But in my case that wasn't how it went. And after every new operation I came out of the hospital in a good mood. But the last time I got a fever. And I'm sort of a stress sensitive person. I became homesick. What can I say?"

The institutional strength of the treatment is such that there is room for doubt without immediately undermining the possibility of continuing with it. For while the vascular surgeons of hospital Z do not hesitate to tell us, or their patients, about the limits of operative interventions, they nevertheless still keep on operating. That is what they have to offer. That is what they can do to help the patients who come to see them with often severe lifestyle-limiting intermittent claudication. That is what they're good at, and, even if they voice doubts about it, that, for sure, is what they get paid for.

Comparing is not simply a matter of producing transportable facts. It is as much a matter of getting walking therapy off the ground or of engaging in a difficult relation with operations that help some patients, even though this particular patient suffers, expects to be helped, might perhaps be helped, but may also be expecting too much. With bad luck this patient's situation may even get worse as a result of an operation.

COMPARISON SITUATED

Comparing treatments isn't usually done to illustrate the complexities involved. The aims tend to be more directly practical. Thus it may be a result of comparing treatments that one of them is designated as good whereas the other is seen as outdated. There are, however, also various possibilities for restricting the use of a specific therapy without ruling it out altogether. One of these is to split up the arteries targeted and to say, for instance, that endarterectomy is good for one kind of artery (the superficial femoral artery) and not for another (the popliteal artery). It also often happens that *indication criteria* are explored. These divide patients into groups: walking therapy is indicated for one group, operation for the other.

> We can see this happening in the current standard for general practitioners in the Netherlands, where patients with atherosclerosis in their lower legs are divided into four groups. These are said to be in a different stage of the disease.[27] People in stage 1 have atherosclerotic vessels but no complaints. This implies that they do not turn up at doctors' surgeries and will not necessarily be found through screening either. Patients in stage 2 of the disease come to their doctors with complaints about walking, and they should be treated "conservatively": the general practitioner must advise them to stop smoking and to regularly go for a daily walk. If a stage 2 patient's condition is deteriorating rapidly, however, it is wise to refer him or her to a vascular surgeon. And this is also indicated when people have reached stage 3 (pain that does not go away in rest) or 4 (persistent wounds, necrosis). For if patients have reached those stages, they no longer only have an intermittent claudication but something worse. Their legs are threatened.[28]

This, then, is the proposed division: patients who have the disease to a small extent get unheroic treatment: the advice to stop smoking and start walking. Patients who have the disease to a severe degree are sent to the surgeon for operation.[29]

This classification doesn't go uncontested. More strongly, dividing patients between these two forms of treatment by means of a system of classification doesn't go uncontested. The physical therapists of hospital D, for instance, tell about their success with patients in bad condition. Some had atherosclerosis too severely for operation (they had problems in various places in their leg arteries, and/or their cardiac vessels were in such poor condition that an operation would be too risky). In hospital D these people are sent to the physiotherapists for walking therapy as a last resort. Getting to walk often makes a considerable positive difference to them. This experience makes the physical therapists of D suggest that *all* patients with arterial disease should not merely be told to "get walking" but should be offered a properly supported walking therapy as a first option. The angiologist in hospital G suggests something similar: instead of dividing patients into two groups on the basis of *indication criteria,* the two therapies should be offered in *sequence.*

> INTERVIEWER: Isn't it strange that there is so little enthusiasm for walking therapy?
> ANGIOLOGIST IN HOSPITAL G: Like I said, it's not heroic. And a lot of work. Writing a prescription is much faster: medicine X, 300 milligrams, 3 times a day.
> INTERVIEWER: Could it also be because it isn't widely known that walking therapy has such good effects?
> ANGIOLOGIST, IN A SHARP VOICE: Look, that is, listen, it's absolutely harmless. You postpone a possible surgical intervention, that is still possible later on. And, well, once you insert a bypass, and it closes off, what's next? Another bypass. And the third one closes off as well. Within a year. And what can you do? Operate again? So there are a lot of arguments for trying walking therapy first. Always. For even if people end up having an operation, at least they'll be used to walking by then.

There are three ways, then, in which comparable treatments may come to relate: one of them may win and the other become obsolete; they may be distributed over different vessels or over different groups of patients by using indication criteria; or they may be put into a sequence: one treatment is tried first, and if it doesn't help, then the other is there as a backup.

What is similar in these three instances is the actor doing the comparing. After all, however different the relations between the therapies being proposed, the actor who compares them is each time a professional—a group of researchers, a set of standard makers, a single clinician, or a team of physical therapists. But in present-day medical practice yet another actor may also be engaged in comparing treatments: the patient.

> Patient in an interview: "And then this doctor said to me: we could operate on you. We could. But if you want to, you can try to do something yourself, first, you can try to walk. If you walk a lot—it is hard, for really it requires that you walk a lot, he said—you may postpone an operation. It may even no longer be necessary, in the end, if you train properly. And then he said that it was my decision."

This has become a common scene in Western health care: two alternative treatments are laid out before the patient in the consulting room. The doctor provides what is called the information, and it is up to the patient to compare them and make a decision. How does this situation, in which an individual patient is being asked to compare treatments using his or her own standards, relate to clinical trials and cost-effectiveness studies in which professional comparison occurs?

> A reception after a thesis defense. This is a good site for fieldwork—or is it discussion? I get to talk with a professor from hospital Z who is very actively involved in research, and I suggest: "There is a strange tension between the movement for evidence-based medicine and the call for autonomy of the patient. It seems to me as if there are two ways to go about making choices in medicine these days. Either you take it that making good decisions is a professional task and use all the effort, all the science, you can muster to find out what is, according to your standards, the best treatment. Or you do not engage in weighing and evaluating, but turn your data into 'information.' Thus you shift from a professional mode into a market mode and offer choices to your patients." Medical professor: "So you think of this as a tension, do you? Hmm. I thought they go together, evidence-based medicine and patient choice. We try our best to find evidence, and if we aren't able to, if our science falls short and we don't know what's best, then we shift our problems on to patients. And, in a very friendly way, we say to them that it is their own decision."

This is the question: how do professional modes of evaluating treatments and patient choice relate? It is a difficult question that I leave open here, delegating it to further study.[30] There are quite a few complexities involved.

Patients are assessed when treatments are compared professionally: their pain-free walking distance, lifestyle limitations, and ankle/arm index are established. They get to fill in questionnaires. Along the way simplifications may be made in one way or another. Yet what comes out of this process is called information. *Such information is presented as if it couldn't have been otherwise to patients who are requested, or allowed, to actively assess comparable treatments in their turn. They may, or must, decide what they deem the best treatment in their own case.*

As it is, in the Dutch context there is often as little choice for doctors as there is for patients. In most places the question of which is the "therapy-of-choice" is hardly a matter of listing and weighing decisive arguments but has to do with institutionalization. Therefore it may have been a clever move of the Dutch association for patients with arterial disease not to enter into professional discussions about effectiveness, indication criteria, or the possible sequential priority of walking treatment. Neither did the association demand that patients be granted the right to make their own decisions about this treatment. What it did, instead of arguing, was to support a *Working Group Walking,* which has produced a video:

> Working Group Walking. The walk video is finished! We are very pleased with the end result and on this occasion we want to thank our 3 actors, members of the Association, for their co-operation. Without their generous help the video could not have been made. At this moment funding is being sought to pay for the distribution of the video. Our final aim is that general practitioners and hospital specialists should give this video to patients with claudication who *have to do* walking training.[31]

Who they are, the patients "who *have to do* walking training," is modestly left as an open question. What is emphasized is the launching of a video to support them in it. The video isn't going to ask those who look at it every so often how things went during the last few weeks: whether they could cope, how they managed to do so, and what their troubles were. But at least it shows in practical detail, again and again, as often as need be, how to walk, rest, and carry on walking again. It also promises that if you keep on trying, then gradually the pain will set in after a longer walking distance.

COMPLEXITY

In unraveling what it is to compare treatments and patient conditions, I have presented a variety of complexities and simplifications.

First, there is the simplification that occurs when the intricacies of a patient's daily life and the problems experienced in and with this life are translated into a form in which it is possible to decide whether (and if so how) these problems might be amenable to treatment. Instead of following the criticism of the reductionism inherent in this move, I have tried to stress that different and coexisting reductions are possible. This means that it is worthwhile asking, locally and each time, what medicine is making *of a patient's problems as it opts for one reductive possibility rather than another. Asking a question of this kind goes against the idea that a disease is a single phenomenon hidden inside the body that surfaces in a variety of signs and symptoms. Instead it gives what used to be called "signs" or "symptoms" a relatively independent existence. They come to stand for various and related problems. A disease no longer remains a single entity.*

But this leads to a second kind of complexity: that of objects (diseases) that are not one *but that are* not many *either. For although intermittent claudication is not "really" an encroached vessel lumen inside the body, of which pain surfaces as a symptom when a person is walking, lumen width and pain are not entirely independent either. This relation of in/dependence that makes disease/s multiple is also a form of complexity, the complexity of being more than one and less than many.*

A third kind of complexity came into view when I asked who *in each treatment is engaged in the activity of treating. For answers to this question make it clear that the delineation of "treatment" isn't the same in the two cases. In the case of operations the events set apart from the rest of life and called "treatment" include physical action but not talking: talking is merely an external requirement for surgery. In the case of walking therapy, however, the "therapeutic act" is sometimes taken to be the actual walking, something patients do, and sometimes the supportive work, that encompasses talking, and that is done by professionals. However, if what falls under the category of "treatment" is not the same from one treatment to another, this generates an irreducible complexity if these treatments are compared.*

A fourth form of complexity surfaces when one asks which treatment is better. It doesn't do to ask which of them cures the largest number of patients, for no patients are cured at all. The old dichotomy normal/pathological is not adequate for making sense of what happens to people with chronic diseases. Different treatments may each bring a range of changes with them, and it is not immediately obvious which parameters to count. The simple question about whether an intervention is effective is greatly complexified as soon as it becomes clear that each intervention has a variety of effects, some good and some bad, effects that are difficult to balance.

A fifth complexity is linked to the social fact that the very act of comparing is not merely an intellectual task but also a part of health care practice. There is an ideal image about health care practices that wants them to change after the results of a good comparative study are published. However, reality is different. Some practices have already shifted before research has produced outcomes simply to make research possible in the first place. Clinical activities are standardized to allow (methodologically sound and not overcomplicated) comparison. Other practices do not change even when publications recommend this. Current practice, after all, is often solidified in existing materials, skills, routines, desires, institutions, and financial regulations. New ways of working may easily fit in with these—or not. And in all this, comparison may itself be an instrument of stabilization or of change. Establishing a fact about a treatment may, in any specific site or situation, be inseparable from establishing (or limiting, or continuing) a treatment.

A sixth complexity relates to the double involvement of patients in the comparison of treatments. On the one hand patients with intermittent claudication are the inhabitants of a diseased body and/or the central node in a lifestyle that is limited. The various possible parameters that may indicate "deterioration" or "improvement" in their condition involve different measurements of the patient-as-an-object. On the other hand patients are the clients of health care, which puts them in the position of a patient-subject, a person who may want, or need, to be the actor making a comparison between possible treatments to engage in and/or to undergo.

These various complexities are intellectually challenging, and they invite further study and reflection—indeed, a lot—for it is an urgent task to find ways of avoiding dreams of rationality and order, as well as equally pure dreams of holistic sensitivity or true messy wildness. It is important to escape from these dichotomies that, in the end, belong together like two sides of a coin.[32] As a part of this, it is important not to be in awe of, or in deference to, complexity but to find ways of analyzing it. To be sure, the socio-corporeo-technical realm of medicine lacks the magic of mathematics, where the complex fractal image appears as the product of a simple one-line equation. However, unraveling what at first sight seems too baroque to grasp may allow one to lay it out in a series of linear stories—as this text seeks to exemplify.[33]

In health care, however, handling complexities is not only an intellectual challenge but also an often urgent practical task, a task that may get squeezed in between others or dealt with implicitly. If I try to make complexities explicit here, this is not because I want to offer normative advice about how they should be handled in practice. It is, instead, an attempt to open them up for all involved to attend to, an attempt to open them up for discussion. Whether such a discussion might have practical implications depends on whether (some of) those involved in health care may be moved to shift (some of) their questions. Currently much effort is taken to give questions a factual format: research is set up that departs from the question "What is the case?" and answers are expected to result from proper counting. Here, however, those involved are invited to spend more time and effort to address questions that involve values: "What do we want?" Such questions should not be squeezed into the relatively short amount of time spent on the design of a quantitative study. The question whether, and if so what, to count deserves far more professional as well as public scrutiny.

Such a shift, however, can only be for the good if, and as long as, there is indeed a dispersed we in health care, who—were it to pay careful attention to all the simplifications it engages in, addressing the question what we want—is likely to come up with better alternatives than those implied in current practice.

Patient information leaflet of hospital G: "In this leaflet the procedure of the training has been described and some information about the calcification and obstruction of blood vessels has been presented. It is of course possible that you still have questions about these matters. Don't keep worrying about these questions but consult your general practitioner, your physician in hospital G, or your walking therapy trainer. The phone numbers you may want to reach in the hospital are printed in the front cover of this leaflet."

But who can we phone, you and I, if we still have questions?

Thanks to the patients and professionals who gave their time and shared their insights with us; Jeannette Pols for gathering so much material and for discussing walking therapy with me; Marc Berg for his work on rationalizing medicine; Ant Lettinga for her work on improving treatment; Dick Willems for his intellectual support; and John Law for taking complexity seriously.

1. Studying the relation between walking therapy and operations was part of a larger investigation into the diagnosis and treatment of arterial disease that was mostly done in Z alone. At a certain point it struck me that walking therapy was mentioned in the literature but did not (at that time) exist as a professionally supported therapy in Z. This seemed to me an important *absence*. That is why I asked Jeannette Pols in 1995 to go and look for it in other Dutch hospitals. She tracked down its existence in G and went there to study it. She also found patients in various places in the Netherlands willing to be interviewed about their experiences with walking therapy; Pols also found physical therapists engaged in it in hospital D. We jointly published this material in Dutch. See Mol and Pols (1996). An intriguing extra complexity is that while Jeannette was in G, a patient information leaflet about walking therapy had to be written. Jeannette, who had done her fieldwork on a short-term research assistant contract with my grant giver, was invited (as someone with writing skills who knew a lot about the therapy and who had some time to spend) to write the leaflet. She did (learning a lot in the process about what, in the hospital, does and doesn't count as "information"). Thus, if in this text I quote this leaflet, it is with a smile. We (modestly) mingled with our field while investigating it. We plan to write on this question in A. Mol and J. Pols, "How to Argue for Walking Therapy?"

2. Walking treatment and operation are not the only available treatments for this condition. Another important one is PTA, percutanuous transluminal angioplasty. In this treatment the vessel lumen is widened by inserting a thread into the vessel under X-ray monitoring and inflating a small balloon at the site of a stenosis. I leave PTA out here for the sake of simplicity. For the distribution of patients over operations, PTA, and conservative treatment in hospital Z, see Mol and Elsman (1996).

3. Almost all material quoted here is translated from the Dutch. I've taken some liberties in making these translations to achieve something that comes close to "natural" English. The health care situation in which events took place is also marked by its specific Dutchness. All people who are legally in the Netherlands have easy access to a neighborhood-based general practitioner (for people on low and moderate incomes free once their insurance is paid, which automatically happens when they have a job or live on social security money). Specialists are hospital based and can only be accessed through a referral. This implies that specialists only see patients preselected for them.

4. In the social sciences a lot has been written about differences in pain perception,

pain behavior, and the expression of pain among (groups of) people. In its cultural anthropological variants this work has been crucial in breaking down the notion of the natural, given body, replacing it with a notion of the body as a node in the enactment of culture. There are also psychological variants that differentiate between people who are more and people who are less "pain prone," thereby turning the sensitivity to pain into a potentially pathological condition. For some examples of an anthropology of pain, see DelVecchio Good et al. (1991). For a sociological study of (chronic) pain as a separate medical problem in its own right, in which various connections between physiological and psychological theories about pain are analyzed, see Baszanger (1995).

5. In the sociology of science and technology a lot of work has been done to show how generating numbers locally in such a way that they are comparable from one site to the other depends on large networks in which standards, techniques, objects, and references are shared and may be transported. In measuring we are, as Bruno Latour calls it, "tied in by a few metrological chains" (see Latour [1987]). For medicine, however, it is questionable whether travel depends on the transport of a metrological chain, with all the technology involved. This may well be the case for numerical measurement, but the transportation of other elements of clinical diagnosis (such as assessing "pallor" or "sickness") may well be a slightly different, *fluid* matter. See for this claim, illustrated with the example of diagnosing anemia in villages in Africa, Mol and Law (1994).

6. It is intriguing: patients with vascular disease are warned against smoking; it causes their condition to deteriorate. Yet the example of the cigar shop as a likely, attractive goal of an elderly man's walks comes out of an interview with a doctor. Many doctors have learned to appreciate what is important to their patients' daily lives and when talking in that register they may "forget" their other norms and be surprisingly non-moralistic. In medical sociology the moralizing effects of medicine have attracted so much critical attention that medical non-, un-, or antimoralizing, as well as handling the interferences among various norms, are understudied. For a good framework for engaging in such studies see Dodier (1993).

7. Note here that I do not focus on the *process* by which the problems with which patients enter a hospital are turned into problems amenable for treatment. Marc Berg has given a convincing (re)description of that process as one that is far more messy (or, one might say, more complex) than its rationalist reconstructions (in simplificatory mode) want it to be. The tale I tell here, however, focuses on *content* instead of process. It tries to articulate some possible outcomes of the "work-up" of vascular patients and how these "simplify" the complex problem patients have when they enter the hospital. These outcomes show a specific, analyzable pattern, however clean or messy the process of reaching there may be. See Berg (1997).

8. Deploring the way medicine reduces its patients' lived reality is widely practiced in the social sciences, as well as in the philosophy of medicine, and has been since the

early 1970s (for a recent overview and integration see Good [1994]). This has served the function of counterbalancing an excessive regard for what medicine is able to do but seems to have outlived its usefulness. Even in as far as it is true, repeating the message has lost a lot of its point. For the intriguing suggestion that patients, in their turn, may use their "objectification" by medicine in the process of establishing themselves as subject, see Cussins (1998).

9. The differentiation between *arteries* (that bring blood from heart to periphery) and *veins* (through which the blood flows back again) is crucial to understanding what happens here. Some veins may be missed and thus used as bypass material. The encroachment of arteries is the problem treated in operations. Veins may cause problems as well, not because they encroach but because sometimes their valves no longer function so that the blood has trouble flowing back to the heart again. This is the problem called varicose veins. Once one is literate in this domain, it is striking that most people are not. I encounter this when presenting talks to academic colleagues in the social sciences and philosophy. Many patients we interviewed say that they encounter this when trying to explain their problems to friends and relatives. And we also interviewed patients who had had an operation but had not been taught the language that comes with it extensively enough for their story about the operation to make sense, even to themselves. For a recent collection of essays about questions related to interpreting the body see Nettleton and Watson (1998).

10. Mannarino (1989).

11. The extent to which it does so varies among studies. Comparing the outcomes of different studies is made difficult by the fact that some give an average improvement (of, say, 60 percent or 80 percent walking distance or time), whereas others set a norm for what is to be called "improvement" and then say that, say, 60 percent or 80 percent or their patients are "significantly improved." For the disorder implied in ordering devices, such as outcome studies or, in his case, the protocols that allow for them, see Berg (1998).

12. This place between the single and the plural has been described before. See, e.g., Haraway (1991) and Strathern (1991).

13. For an analysis of the way a patient's subjectivity may be shaped during his or her daily dealings with a hampering body and bothersome or supportive material surroundings, see Moser and Law (1999).

14. Thus the effects of treatments on daily lives are not simply that they "normalize" it (as some earlier critiques of medicine assumed). They may, instead, differ strikingly from one treatment to another. Compare also the way diabetes treatment has entirely different effects on the lives of the people concerned depending on the standard for "normal glucose level" that they come to strive after. See Mol (1998).

15. The professional as a backup resource for when things don't go smoothly also turns

up in other self-treatment programs. In diabetes care, for example, there is often the possibility of calling a diabetes nurse or doctor at all hours in cases of doubt or crisis. In other sites and situations patient support groups may take such a task on themselves. See Rabeharisoa and Callon (1998).

16. Walking therapy may look old, but although people have of course walked forever, walking as a therapy for those whose legs hurt when they walk is rather new. There are research articles with positive results from the 1960s onward, but currently these are being received better, which may well be related to a more widespread trend in medicine, which is to shift responsibilities both for diagnosis and treatment to patients. For the professional/lay divides implicated, with the example of asthma, see Willems (1992).

17. For an excellent description of an operation that, in surgical mode, focuses on the bodies of the operating team, describing them as if their cooperation turned them into a single body, see Hirschauer (1991). The collaborations required, however, do not exclude tensions to be played out simultaneously. For an analysis of the tensions between anesthetists, who must take care of the patient's fitness, and surgeons, who make a patient's condition worse in order to make it better, see Fox (1994).

18. If overlooked by many scholars, a few have argued extensively that not just in specific diseases but in *all* of modern medicine an impressive if hidden part of the work is done by patients. See Strauss et al. (1985).

19. Here, then, surfaces the classical tension between framing people as citizens (who behave rationally or irrationally, properly or improperly, responsibly or irresponsibly) and framing people as fragile bio-psycho-social systems (who happen to be normal or disturbed, capable or incapable, together or broken apart). This tension has been mostly analyzed in the context of criminal justice (where disease categories are a way of escaping legal logic) and in the context of psychiatry (where, alternatively, civic rights are a way of escaping pathological logic). For the classical analysis, pointing at the tensions as well as the analogies between "irresponsibility" and "insanity," see Foucault (1975). This subject urgently requires further analysis.

20. In this quote *clinical* stands for the effects on daily life of a treatment such as it is reported by the patient and detectable in a physical examination. It is opposed to the outcomes of other, technological, diagnostic techniques. Interestingly enough, in the context of technological development these very diagnostic techniques are called *clinical* in their turn because they are actually used in the hospital, in opposition, this time, to techniques that are only relevant in research settings. See, for this tension, Reiser and Anbar (1984).

21. It has been argued that a clear separation between the two states "normal" and "pathological" was present in classical infectious diseases and that not only the clinical trial but the entire organization of the hospital still assumes that medicine was meant

to cure infections (as it was when these institutions were shaped). If this is right, then a lot of present-day problems arise from the friction between the infection-countering organization structure of health care and the fact that most present-day hospital patients have, in one way or another, chronic diseases. See Funck-Brentano (1990).

22. See Heijden (1992) and Heijden et al. (1992).

23. After this and other earlier clinical trials, endarterectomy was abandoned in most hospitals. It was rejected as "out of date." Had this been done rigorously, then the study reported here would never have been possible. But in Z, as is (or used to be?) often the case, the former professor of vascular surgery happened to believe fiercely in endarterectomies (not just because he believed that they work but also because they have fewer disadvantages for patients and are cheaper than bypass operations). Thus he kept the technique alive and taught it to those working with him. For the defense of this thesis that retrospectively investigates the department's patients, he had come all the way from Greece (where he was born and where he returned after his retirement). He was visibly moved and pleased to be turned (by the numbers) from an undisciplined maverick into a courageous and creative doctor.

24. See Heijden (1992, 9).

25. The specificities of such trickiness and stubbornness differ of course depending on the intricacies of health care organization and financing. The likelihood of change depends on such things as to what extent it is possible to influence organization and financing simultaneously; to what extent the costs that will be saved when an operation isn't necessary do or do not function as a possible push behind the institutionalization of walking therapy; and whether centers of calculation where such balancing takes place exist or are simply lacking. For the booming field of "organization and management of health care" it is important to take into account the fact that medical facts are not external to, but part of and dependent on, the organization of health care. For the argument that this follows from a historical shift, given that knowledge production is being inserted more and more in the institutions that use the knowledge, see Gibbons (1994).

26. Early in 1998 walking therapy was included in the list of physical therapy treatments that are financed with health insurance money in the Netherlands. But as the informant who told me this at the end of that year added: "Nobody seems to know yet." The time it took to spread the knowledge of the positive results of studies is even more impressive. As noted, we found publications of (positive) evaluation studies of walking therapy from the late 1960s onward.

27. In mobilizing the term *stage* the disease is given a historical dimension. It is assumed that it involves a gradually progressing deterioration of the condition of a person's vessel walls (even if this isn't what happens in every patient, for some may "never reach stage 3"). Talking about stages is part of the language of internal medicine

rather than of surgery (which tends to concentrate on current structure or performance). For a more extensive analysis of such differences in the case of atherosclerosis see Mol (2002).

28. This standard can be found in Nederlands Huisartsgenootschap (1990).

29. The standard shows what is the quintessence of the organization of the Dutch health care system: that general practitioners are supposed to treat "light" cases and send more difficult or rarer problems on to hospitals for specialist care. Meanwhile, however, the texts produced by the surgeons of hospital Z also begin by mentioning that people who have a "stable intermittent claudication" are not to be operated on but are to be treated "conservatively." Despite the fact that they *should not,* the surgeons obviously still get to see such patients. Despite the fact that they *should not,* surgeons also sometimes operate on patients with only intermittent claudication—and the question about how to draw a boundary between the cases in which there are "good reasons" for this and those cases in which there are not is one of the *objects* of the present study. It is also a shifting boundary: in 1998, when I was writing this text, a clinical trial investigating the effects of various walking treatment programs for patients with intermittent claudication was being started in Z.

30. See also the work on surgeons and decisions of Tiago Moreira (2001).

31. *News Vessel* (1996, 5).

32. It is not just that "order" and "messiness" are opposing but interdependent ideals. It is also the case that neither of these states can exist in a purified form: they each depend on their other. For this argument see Law and Mol (1998).

33. For the association between the complex and the baroque, see Chunglin Kwa (this volume).

REFERENCES

Baszanger, I. 1995. *Douleur et médecine, la fin d'un oubli.* Paris: Seuil.

Berg, M. 1997. *Rationalizing Medical Work: Decision-Support Techniques and Medical Practices.* Cambridge, Mass.: MIT Press.

———. 1998. "Order(s) and Disorder(s): Of Protocols and Medical Practices." In M. Berg and A. Mol, eds. *Differences in Medicine. Unraveling Practices, Techniques, and Bodies,* 220–46. Durham: Duke University Press.

Cussins, C. 1998. "Ontological Choreography: Agency for Women Patients in an Infertility Clinic." In M. Berg and A. Mol, eds., *Differences in Medicine: Unraveling Practices, Techniques, and Bodies,* 166–201. Durham: Duke University Press.

DelVecchio Good, M., et al., eds. 1991. *Pain as a Human Experience: Anthropological Perspectives.* Berkeley: University of California Press.

Dodier, N. 1993. *L'Expertise médicale. Essai de sociologie sur l'excercise du jugement.* Paris: Métaillé.

Foucault, M. 1975. *Surveiller et punir. Naissance de la Prison.* Paris: Éditions Gallimard.

Fox, N. 1994. "Anesthetists, the Discourse on Patient Fitness, and the Organization of Surgery." *Sociology of Health and Illness* 16: 1–18.

Funck-Brentano, J. L. 1990. *Le Grand Chambardement de la Médecine*. Paris: Éditions Odile Jacob.

Gibbons, M., et al. 1994. *The New Production of Knowledge: The Dynamics of Science and Research in Contemporary Societies*. London: Sage.

Good, B. 1994. *Medicine, Rationality, and Experience*. New York: Cambridge University Press.

Haraway, D. 1991. "Situated Knowledges: The Science Question in Feminism and the Privilege of Partial Perspective." In D. Haraway, *Simians, Cyborgs, and Women: The Reinvention of Nature*, 183–201. London: Free Association Books.

Heijden, F. van der. 1992. "Semi-closed Endarterectomy of the Superficial Femoral Artery." Unpublished thesis, University of Utrecht.

Heijden, F. van der, et al. 1992. "Endarterectomy of the Superficial Femoral Artery: A Procedure Worth Reconsidering." *European Journal of Vascular Surgery* 6: 651–58.

Hirschauer, S. 1991. "The Manufacture of Bodies in Surgery." *Social Studies of Science* 21: 217–319.

Latour, B. 1987. *Science in Action: How to Follow Scientists and Engineers through Society*. Milton Keynes: Open University Press.

Law, J., and A. Mol. 1998. "On Metrics and Fluids: Notes on Otherness." In R. Chia, ed., *Organized Worlds*, 20–38. London: Routledge.

Mannarino, E. 1989. "Effects of Physical Training on Peripheral Vascular Disease: A Controlled Study." *Angiology, The Journal of Vascular Diseases* (January): 5–10.

Mol, A. 1998. "Lived Reality and the Multiplicity of Norms: A Critical Tribute to Georges Canguilhem." *Economy and Society* 27: 274–84.

——. 2002. *The Body Multiple: Ontology in Medical Practice*. Durham: Duke University Press.

Mol, A., and B. Elsman. 1996. "Detecting Disease and Designing Treatment: Duplex and the Diagnosis of Diseased Leg Vessels." *Sociology of Health and Illness* 18: 609–31.

Mol, A., and J. Law. 1994. "Regions, Networks, and Fluids: Anaemia and Social Topology." *Social Studies of Science* 24: 641–71.

Mol, A., and J. Pols. 1996. "Ziekte Leven: Bouwstenen voor een Medische Sociologie zonder Disease/Illness Onderscheid." *Kennis en Methode* 20: 347–61.

Moreira, T. 2001. "Incisions: A Study of Surgical Trajectories." Ph.D. thesis, Lancaster University, UK.

Moser, I., and J. Law. 1999. "Good Passages, Bad Passages." In J. Law and J. Hassard, eds., *Actor Network Theory and After*, 196–219. Oxford and Keele: Blackwell/Sociological Review.

Nederlands Huisartgenootschap. 1990. "Perifeer Arterielle Vaatlijden." *Huisarts en Wetenschap* 33: 440–46.

Nettleton, S., and J. Watson, eds. 1998. *The Body in Everyday Life*. London: Routledge.

News Vessel. 1996. Organ of the Association of Vascular Patients. January.

Rabeharisoa, V., and M. Callon. 1998. "Reconfiguring Trajectories: Agencies, Bodies, and Political Articulations: The Case of Muscular Dystrophies." Paper presented to Theorizing Bodies: WTMC-CSI Workshop, Ecole des Mines de Paris, France, September.

Reiser, S., and M. Anabar. 1984. *The Machine at the Bedside: Strategies for Using Technology in Patient Care.* Cambridge: Cambridge University Press.

Strathern, M. 1991. *Partial Connections.* Savage, Md.: Rowman and Littlefield.

Strauss, A., S. Fagerhaugh, B. Suczek, and C. Wiener. 1985. *Social Organization of Medical Work.* Chicago: University of Chicago Press.

Willems, D. 1992. "Susan's Breathlessness: The Construction of Professionals and Laypersons." In J. Lachmund and G. Stollberg, eds., *The Social Construction of Illness: Illness and Medical Knowledge in Past and Present,* 105–14. Stuttgart: Franz Steiner Verlag.

NICK LEE AND STEVEN D. BROWN

The Disposal of Fear:
Childhood, Trauma, and Complexity

Every ugly thing told to the child, every shock, every fright given him, will remain like minute splinters in the flesh, to torture him all his life long.—Angelo Mosso

Although armed with his plastic sword and senior cousin Chloe . . . he started sobbing "Get me out, get me out!" within minutes of the curtain going up. —*Guardian*

Fear figures in a great many accounts of subjectivity and its development. Freud made fear the backdrop for the Oedipal drama, a locus classicus for all contemporary accounts of subjectivity. Fear, in the form of the Father's power over the family trinity, makes the cut that separates the child from the world, where previously, from the child's point of view, child and world had appeared indivisible. To create a subject, on this view, is to create a "residence," a site of property and belonging distinct from the world. Fear and the disposal[1] of fear are implicated in the making of subjects.

In the resolution of the Oedipal drama the disposal of fear within the subject serves to complete and to strengthen the division between world and subject, to establish the bounds and possibility of the subject's self-ownership. Fear becomes owned, contained, disposed of in the form of a possession—an experience that is owned. The subject becomes the home of the unheimlich. In this lies fear's power of unmaking. Psychoanalysis was established on the recognition that the traumas of hysteria and anxiety are the keys to understanding the fragmentation of identity. Trauma is the indelible mark of past hurt, of intense fear. It spread out across the subject like so many lines of fracture, dissolving coherent self-possession into a confetti of names and memories.

A powerful story. One that cries out to be challenged. So when Deleuze and Guattari (1984) eloquently announced their position as anti-Oedipus, this account of subjectivity emerging from the ownership and disposition of fear became their prime target. Similarly, when Foucault (1970) famously proclaimed the erasure of the figure of man from a central position in our thinking, he was announcing with it the collapse of the "grounds of possibility of all the sciences of man" (386) in the late nineteenth century, a cipher for ethnology and psychoanalysis. No more grand myths about the origins of the human subject. No more Totem and Taboo.

From these germinal works the contemporary social sciences inherit the now familiar conceptual operation of "decentering the subject." In recent years this operation has proved crucial in redefining the social study of science, technology, and medicine. Crudely put, the operation consists in breaching any, or ideally all, of the boundaries that separate the human subject from the media in which it subsists: language, discourse, materiality, technology, desire. What remains is very little: "A self does not amount to much, but no self is an island; each exists in a fabric of relations that is more complex and mobile than ever before. Young or old, man and woman, rich or poor, a person is always located at 'nodal points' of specific communication circuits, however tiny these may be. Or better: one is always located at a post through which various kinds of messages pass" (Lyotard 1984, 15).

Although it does not amount to very much, what remains of the subject is said to be "more complex." Lyotard makes a turn from the more or less stable possessive self to a complex and mobile relational self. Decentering the subject involves a turn from an ontology of the individual, bounded subject to a more complex relational ontology. As Lyotard envisages it, this relational self is spatially complex, distributed across "communication circuits." It is the result of the disposition of messages. Crucially, on this view, the self has no ability to possess and can provide no harbor. With no boundary the subject can own nothing, not even itself. The humanistic characterization of "experience" and "memory" as forms of property is put radically into question because what the subject seems to own, it is merely passing on. Fear shares the fate of all other properties in a relational ontology. Fear does not belong to the subject; it cannot be possessed. The subject can no longer be understood as the site of fear's disposal.

The various material semiotics and forms of ontological politics (Mol 1999) currently at work in science and technology studies urge us to expand the range of distributions we should consider beyond Lyotard's fascination with language. Selves are distributed through prosthetics and through technical devices (Latour 1999). They are elements of wider "actor networks" (see Ashmore, Wooffitt, and Harding 1994). Further, from the early stages of their development these approaches were concerned with temporal distributions alongside spatial ones. An early question for the actor-network approach, for example, was how relationships could persist over time (Bijker and Law 1992). They hinted at the temporal complexity of selves as forms of order.

Our interest in all this can be summed up quite simply. We want to know what happens to the experience of fear and to the persistence of fear (under the name of trauma) in a context where the subject is best understood as a "fabric of relations." If there is no bounded subject, then fear would seem to have no proper place. Is it then the case that without a place of possession, without a home, fear ceaselessly patrols the "communication circuits" that constitute us? In doing away with the bounded subject are we condemned to circle in ever more elliptical paths around our own complex traumas and anxieties? Or are there "timings" that allow for fear to be taken out of general circulation, to be "disposed of" or to take up residence with a subject?

The connection with "complexity" should be clear. Once, *complex* named specifiable arrangements of intrapsychic forces, a set of tensions that, even as they were resolved, left an abiding trace in the subject. Now, in an audacious reversal (founded on the suspicion that our accounts of insides and outsides were "inside out"), we give the name *complexity* to the fabrics and arrangements that constitute the subject in the moment that they escape possession by the subject (see Latour 1999). These fabrics, by implication, also escape exhaustive analysis and specification. This usage of *complexity* clearly bolsters contemporary social scientific emphases on the limits of analysis and adds to the current popularity of such terms as *undecideability* (Day 1998), *incommensurability* (Lyotard 1984), *unawareness* (Beck 1998), *ambivalence* (Smart 1999), and *modesty* (Haraway 1997). *Complexity* begins to look like a synonym for *poststructuralism*.

The contrast between possessive and complex relational views of the subject, then, forefronts the questions of persistence and possession. It also raises questions about whether a focus on complexity can be understood to achieve anything more than a confirmation of, by now, standard social scientific accounts of the limitations of social scientific analysis. Thus, as we examine fear's persistence, we will also attempt to make a clear and positive use of *complexity.*

In this essay, then, we will address the contrast between possessive and relational subjectivities, concepts that are crucial for how science studies understands the psychological subject. We will be led by the movement of a child's trauma through crosscutting psychological and legal discourses that are fixated on issues of good and bad timing. We will highlight the significance of the cultural performance of boundaries between the mature and the immature and between ontological realms of fantasy and reality in the production of persistent fear. We will pursue our interest in fear and its persistence by way of a single example, the case of the three-year-old boy, Morris, quoted in our second epigraph, who was traumatized by a theatrical performance.

PETER PAN AND THE LOST BOY

"Like a pirate from Never Never Land, the power of J. M. Barrie's original *Peter Pan* has reached out from a theatre stage to throttle recent, saccharine versions—unfortunately scaring a three-year-old witless in the process. The parents of Morris, who tried to hide under a seat and his Dad's coat as the tale of child kidnap, plank walking and the relentless croc unfolded, are taking legal action over his 'stress and trauma' " ("Peter Pan Producers" 1996, 1). *Peter Pan* is a popular family theatrical production in the U.K.[2] In the play a group of children are transported to "Never Never Land," where they have a series of adventures and pass through perilous situations. Peter Pan is their native guide. He is a peculiar figure—a boy who never grows up. He is a "lost boy," stuck in a state of perpetual childhood. This is a play, then, that thematizes fear, maturation, and failure to mature. The group's adventures in Never Never Land involve clashes with the pirate Captain Hook. This character does not have children's best interests at heart. He is a kidnapper of infants who enjoys drowning people. As you can imagine, this play could be a little scary.

In 1996 the three-year-old boy Morris, his grandmother, parents, and six-year-old cousin Chloe went to see a performance of the play. Grandma had booked the tickets early for her sixty-first birthday treat. We have seen how the play sounds scary. This production in particular capitalized on scariness. Peter Pan wore a dramatic cloak of black feathers. Wolves circled the stage. A crocodile character was huge and imposing. Morris was scared and, within minutes of the curtain going up, sobbed, "Get me out. . . . Get me out!" According to his mother, Morris was "absolutely petrified."

This was bad enough in itself. One would hope that once his parents had gotten Morris out, Morris would be able to leave his terror behind him. But the family's troubles continued. Morris did not leave his terror behind him. He had nightmares about the play. The events also distributed relationships within the family: "My own grandson now calls me 'Nasty Granny' for taking him to the theatre. . . . I'm distressed that I took him to see something so frightening" ("Peter Pan Producers" 1996, 1).

According to his parents, Morris had undergone "stress and trauma." In his dreams and in the way he conducted his relationships, Morris, it would seem, was still in that theater, still exposed to the terrors of Never Never Land. This little boy, like some of Peter Pan's fellow denizens of Never Never Land (characters called the "lost boys"), had gotten lost in time.

If we say, with his parents, that Morris was traumatized by the play, we are saying that fear had not loosened its grip on him and that he was unable to let a frightening experience go. Still marked by the traumatic incident, Morris is living his terror again and again. He has become stuck in the past, out of "synch" with the real world, lost in time. The danger is that Morris, with respect to his granny, will become like Peter Pan, the boy who never grew up. Stuck in the past, still fixated on one event, Morris will be unable to dispose of his feelings of fear. His parents decided to seek legal remedy for the stress and trauma occasioned by the performance.

CHILDHOOD AND TIMING

Understandings of childhood have long been informed by a division between ontological states of "being" and "becoming" (Qvortrup 1994). In terms of this division children are always becoming beings, passing through childhood toward a future in which their journey of development will end. In contrast, fully developed adults are taken to be beings already (Lee 1999). In this sense temporality is understood to be the substance of childhood, but it is merely the medium of adulthood. With childhood so closely linked to temporality it is hardly surprising that although we may be concerned about what happens to adults, we may also be concerned when certain things happen to children. Thus childhood is often conceived of as a period of special vulnerability to trauma, fear, and external influence. Childhood is a passing phase, and because of this it is also a phase in which the external world may mark the child permanently.

Childhood is also a period in which timing is of the essence. Because childhood is understood as a period of becoming, childhood vulnerabilities are understood to change in degree and in kind over time. Thus a good deal of psychological research and legislation concerning childhood has aimed at rendering childhood's vulnerability and its variation over time comprehensible and manageable. The complex timings of childhood needed to be charted in order to establish a basis of discrimination between good timings and bad timings for events in children's lives. The principal means by which these aims have been pursued are the detection of general laws of development and the attempt to show that these hold good for all children, and the determination of legal boundaries within childhood that are made to hold for all children within a given legislature. The regulation of the timings in particular children's lives by scientific, medical, and legal authority has long rested on the possibility of making general or, at least, generalizable statements about childhood.

There is evidence, however, of a drift away from the "becoming" view of children as the institutions that compose childhood change. Late modern processes of the individualization of risk (Beck 1998), for example, take place partly through the identification of "rights" for each and every particular individual regardless of age. Further, rather than seek out the general regularities of the process of becoming, recent students of childhood (Hutchby and Moran-Ellis 1998; James and Prout 1997) have focused on children as "beings," competent social participants who need to be studied "in particular." In this view, given the many variations in children's lives and circumstances across cultures, within societies and over historical time, the search for generalized natural laws of childhood and the attempt to regulate in general for childhood appears not only quixotic but also politically and ethically suspect. A refusal to recognize a person's "being" is, arguably, tantamount to refusing him or her full recognition as a human being. Generality and universality in knowledge nowadays carry the taint of imperialism or the command economy.

COMPLEXITY: BETWEEN THE GENERAL AND THE PARTICULAR

The changing image of the child is, for us, an instance of the relations between the "general" and the "particular." As we have suggested, the general and the particular have political resonances within the social sciences. In recent years the general and the particular have often been set against each other as competing epistemologies. The growth of the "politics of recognition" (Taylor 1992) as a sphere of cultural conflict has been reflected in social scientific conflicts over the relative merits of universalist and particularist theories, methods, and modes of explanation. As Geertz notes: "Many social scientists have turned away from a laws with instances ideal of explanation towards a cases and interpretations one" (Geertz 1983, 19).

Geertz's social scientists have changed their job descriptions. They are no longer in search of that moment of greatest explanatory power in which all particulars are aligned in commonality such that they might be taken to declare their shared indebtedness to the "general." It is now clear that the unification of particulars will result in a simplification that social scientists should no longer countenance. But this opposition to simplification does not necessarily add up to a recognition of social complexity. We would suggest that in the social sciences *complexity* best names the spaces and processes that lie between the poles of the general and the particular. It names the host of attempts made by social scientists, among others, to manage the relationship between the general and the particular in order to produce explanations of social phenomena. The general and the particular certainly can be played as competing epistemological viewpoints, but in this they most clearly exhibit their status as cultural resources of sense-making practices.

As we return to Morris's case, we will suggest, first, that he lies in this space between the general and the particular and, second, that it is his location here that allows for fear persistently to be disposed of onto him, generating his "trauma." Before we make these arguments, however, we need to see a little more of the cultural and theoretical context in which Morris's reaction to a scary play could become so significant as to require legal remedy.

THE GROWN-UP CAN DISPOSE OF FEAR

The day after Morris's story was reported, the *Guardian* (a U.K. national daily newspaper) published a commentary by the journalist Suzanne Moore. She argued that a recourse to legal remedy was inappropriate in this case: "A boy is scared in Peter Pan, and his parents are now suing the theatre. Is this right? We can't stop kids from having nightmares, nor should we. Growing up is all about coping with fear" (Moore 1996).

Morris's parents were seeking redress for his trauma, for his being "stuck in time." In their account Morris was traumatized, or had become stuck with a terrifying event, because the theater had gotten its timing wrong in two ways. First, the theater should have carefully considered the "age appropriateness" of the play, and, second, once it had considered this, the theater should have given parents fair warning of the play's content. As it happened, such a warning was given on handbills but only ten minutes before the curtain went up. Bad timing. Because the theater got its timing wrong, the timing, the benign intergenerational synchrony of grandchild and grandparent that should link Morris with his family, has been disrupted.

Moore tells us that we (including Morris's parents) should not be so "protective" of children. She tells us that children's exposure to frightening events, be they real, dramatic, or imaginary, is inevitable and under certain circumstances aids their maturation. After listing fictional characters such as "the Wicked Witch of the West," "Cybermen," and "Daleks" that terrified her as a child,[3] she writes: "When I think of these things now I still turn cold, but I'm a grown up and I've learnt to live with fears. These childish fears have been pushed aside by more adult ones and now it's the real world, not a fictional one, that terrifies me. Learning to live with fear is part of growing up. I am not suggesting that we deliberately expose our children to the stuff of nightmares but, even if we don't, they will continue to have bad dreams" (Moore 1996).

Here a premium is set on a process of learning to live with fear as a normal part of growing into an adult. Maturation involves learning how to dispose of fear, to push it to one side. If children encounter terrifying fictional characters, as long as adults are there to help them understand, these encounters will help them learn to cope with fear. Good timing in intergenerational relationships leads to good discrimination between the real and the imaginary. Such experiences of being assisted in discrimination will give children the impetus to overcome life's hurdles. For Moore, Morris's parents are overplaying their helplessness in the face of his terror. If he seems to be stuck in time, their job is not to protest about it and seek to blame somebody for it but to coax him back into synchrony. Through this encounter with terror Morris could be made stronger for the future.

But Morris's trauma is not only a matter of being "out of synch" with the rest of his family. Unless and until he can let go of the frightening incident, he will also be out of synch with his own appropriate development, which should take place through an ongoing accommodation to new experience.[4] This is the law of developmental health for Morris because it is the law of developmental health for children in general. Morris's ongoing accommodation has been stalled by trauma. As long as Morris is possessed by fear, his development will not be normal. The growing child should learn to tell the difference between "real" fear and "imaginary" fear, the real world and imaginary worlds, because to be in an adult state is to be able to dispose of one sort of fear (imaginary) and to manage one's response to another sort of fear (real). For Moore, the trauma event that holds Morris in its thrall involves a confusion on Morris's part between the real and the imaginary. Once marked by a trauma event, unless he is given the right sort of help, such a confusion may persist, threatening to stand in the way of Morris's making appropriate discriminations in the future.

HOW DO CHILDREN GET STUCK IN TIME?

Moore, Morris, and his family are not alone in this peculiar cultural space of good and bad timings, age-appropriate responses, and neatly categorizable fears. Throughout Morris's case, generalized forms of knowledge of what is good for children, which share an investment in the appropriate timings of normal development, were vying to be the best match for Morris's particular case. On the one hand, Morris's parents detected injury to him through the production company's bad timing. The company's timing was bad because the performance was too "old" for Morris. On the other hand, Moore tells us that if his parents were to intervene in his experience, this bad timing could have been converted into good timing, converting his trauma into a developmental hurdle successfully vaulted.

Bettleheim's psychoanalytic account of the developmental value of fairy tales (Bettleheim 1976) seems to provide one source for Moore's comments. If fairy tales, like the play *Peter Pan*, contain terrifying figures and events, for Bettleheim this is no reason to shield children from them. Children are involved in "the struggle for maturity" (Bettleheim 1976, 277) and can "transcend infancy with the help of fantasy" (123). In this struggle they will often find that they have powerful, ambivalent, and confusing feelings about the real world and, in particular, about their parents. Held in tension between dependency and growing autonomy, children may be overwhelmed with the fear that they are unable to manage such tension and may be pulled apart by it. Fairy tales, as forms of fantastic fiction, are sketchpads for the child's unconscious mind, materials on which to practice making appropriate discriminations, places to learn to disambiguate real from imaginary fears to gain mastery over themselves. By presenting children with manageable terrors fairy tales help them learn to dispose of those fears, which are rooted in the welter of ambiguous feelings that characterizes the childish mind. According to Bettleheim:

> Fairy tales, unlike any other form of literature, direct the child to discover his [sic] identity and calling. . . . Fairy tales intimate that a rewarding, good life is within one's reach despite adversity—but only if one does not shy away from the hazardous struggles without which one can never achieve true identity. . . . The stories also warn that those who are too timorous and narrow-minded to risk themselves in finding themselves must settle down to a humdrum existence if an even worse fate does not befall them. (24)

Development is a process of consolidating a "true identity" by confronting and disposing of fear. This struggle could not involve higher stakes. Not only might the child never learn to live with fear, or to dispose of it properly, and so be condemned to a humdrum adult life, but she or he might also never properly make it out of childhood itself. If childhood conflicts are not resolved, then no matter what the chronological age of the person, he or she, at some fundamental psychological level, will remain stuck in time. In such cases of faulty development "some people withdraw from the world and spend most of their days in the realm of their imaginings. . . . Such people are locked in" (Bettleheim 1976, 119). The best way to avoid this sort of bad fantasy life, with its eternal simplicity, its inertia resulting from the inability to have done with and dispose of particular fears and fascinations, is not to eliminate fantasy but to give it as much material to work with as possible. By living out a "rich and variegated fantasy life," the child allows her or his imagination full flight, which enables the child to move on from a "few narrow preoccupations" (ibid.). This then constitutes the royal road to a complete, integrated personality, one that is able to deal with the complexities of reality represented by the ambivalence between well-founded and fantastic fears.

A bounded "true self" is the goal of childhood "becoming." It is possible to tell when someone has become a fully fledged "being" when he or she is able to make appropriate discriminations between fantasy and reality. At every step along the journey of development, fantasy and reality threaten to become indiscriminable, but by the time we have reached maturity, if our development has been normal, we will be able to dispose of imaginary fears.

THE LINE OF NORMAL DEVELOPMENT

Our discussion of Morris's case has involved various articulations— by Morris's parents, by Moore, and by Bettleheim—of a shared sense-making resource. The propriety of timings, the conduct of Morris's parents, and Morris's likely degree of vulnerability have all been judged against a "line of normal development"—a line that leads from childish inability to categorize, and thus dispose of, fears to an adult integrity of self that is achieved by clear discrimination and successful management of fears. When Moore and Morris's parents seek to gain purchase on Morris and the trauma event, to make sense of what has occurred, this line of normal development proves very useful. As an article of generalized knowledge it would seem to help us understand the particular events involving Morris by giving us a general template with which to organize our judgments, a "skeleton key" with which to unlock understanding of any difficulties involving particular children.

The line of normal development gains its utility as an explanatory resource in this case by being potentially applicable to all children and therefore applicable to Morris. Note that its successful application requires a clear passage between the general and the particular. We could characterize such generalized knowledges as the line of normal development as "simple" and as "oversimplifying." But we are led to more than a condemnation of generalized knowledge and a championing of the specific and the particular. It is clear that generalized knowledge is valuable in making sense, in apportioning blame and responsibility, and in projecting futures for Morris. The question is whether the relationship between the general and the particular is like that of a skeleton key to a number of locks, whether general knowledge can successfully contain Morris as a particular instance and render him comprehensible.

Although the different views in the debate all mobilize this same general resource—the line of normal development—and although they match it to the same particular case, quite different effects are produced. Morris's parents use the matching process to detect an offense against Morris, whereas Moore uses it to reveal Morris's parents as mistaken. Although the general template promises to match up well to Morris's particular case in order to help us tell good timings from bad and well-founded fears from imaginary ones (our own fears for children as well as Morris's fears), in the movement from general to particular still more diversity of opinion is generated. In other words the more the generalized notion of the line of normal development is applied, the more complex the situation becomes. An iterative simplicity begets complexity.

The general and the particular are not related in the way that a skeleton key is related to a set of locks. There is no univocal match between the line of normal development and Morris's case. Indeed the generalized knowledge of the line of normal development can even be mobilized to prejudice claims based on the line of normal development, as when Moore criticizes Morris's parents. But it is the possibility of making that passage from general to particular that allows us to recognize Morris's trauma. Unless generalized knowledge of the developmental characteristics of children applies to Morris, we have no way of acknowledging his trauma. Or so it would seem. We will shortly offer an account of Morris's trauma as a "disposal" of fear onto him. We will suggest that this disposal took place through a play of the "general" and the "particular" and of the "real" and the "fantastic." First, however, we need to clarify our view of the general and the particular as cultural artifacts.

WHERE DID THE LINE OF NORMAL
DEVELOPMENT COME FROM?

The general and the particular are, as we have described, frequently understood as epistemological viewpoints. Essentialist approaches gamble on these viewpoints being integrable. Constructionist approaches tend to assert the impossibility of such integration between the general and the particular as epistemological viewpoints. What if both these views were mistaken about the nature of the general and the particular?

Foucault tells us that in the mid-eighteenth century, in a certain school of drawing, so as to produce skilled draughtsmen in the most efficient manner, the pupils were required to perform "individual tasks at regular intervals; each of these exercises, signed with the name of its author and date of execution, was handed in to the teacher, the best were rewarded; assembled together at the end of the year and compared, they made it possible to establish the progress, the present ability and the relative place of each pupil" (Foucault 1977, 157).

Within these practices judgments about pupils' work were not limited to whether the work was good or bad but whether the work was good or bad relative to the accumulated time that the pupils had spent at their studies. The specific journey a pupil took through her or his education became tied to the general passage of time marked out by the regular intervals between tasks and by the passage of years. By comparing different students, according to these timings, standard expectations could be derived. Such expectations could govern judgments about the relationship between a specific pupil's progress through the curriculum and the general progress of time. Steps could be taken to synchronize a specific pupil's changing levels of attainment with a standard.

This was a pedagogy that aimed at keeping different timings in synchrony with one another. This pedagogy worked on a mass of different timings, defined by pupils' differing degrees of skill and diligence to spin

270   Nick Lee and Steven D. Brown

a single thread—a line of normal progress. With respect to this line, constructed by comparisons between individual performances, a given pupil could be a slow or a rapid learner. With such practices of comparative judgment and record keeping, a truth regime emerged in which it made good sense to describe each pupil as slow or fast in their passage along the line of normal progress.

It seems here that "discipline," the formation of the student body into a set of individual subjects, involves a number of simplifications. A collection of bodies in interaction with one another is boiled down into a number of individuals who can, to all intents and purposes, be treated as independent of one another. Minute variations in performance, which approximate the random and the incalculable—slips of the pen, illness, inability to attend—the myriad backward and forward steps to be expected of persons can be safely offset against the record composed of regular measurements, ignored, that is, until they themselves become a regularity. A single governing chronology emerges, spun from a bundle of times hitherto at odds with one another, and along with this chronology emerges a picture of each pupil as being in possession of a specifiable degree of competence, the increase of which can be measured over time.

Foucault, then, tells us how the practices of testing and record keeping, the technologies of pedagogy, allowed for the production of a line of normal development. These practices produced this line by ensuring first that each pupil could be treated as an individual case. Once each pupil is individualized in this manner, the individual cases could be compared to produce a general norm. This suggests that the general and the particular are not just different kinds of knowledge to be set in mutual complicity or antagonism but are fundamentally linked products of attempts to set pupils in order.

The task of disciplining is not finished with the establishment of such an ordering scheme, however. To render these pupil's and children's lives knowable requires continual efforts to integrate the general and the particular. In Foucault's school of calligraphy these efforts took the form of yearly assessments of each pupil. In Morris's case, as we have seen, the general and the particular appear integrable, the line of normal development applicable, in different ways. Different commentators choose different passages between the general and the particular. It is when the bid for understanding becomes distanced from the technologies that ground the line of normal development that we see that a truth regime is also a regime of controversy. It turns those who would "know," and be able securely to apportion responsibilities for Morris's trauma, into disputants.

So how, at once, can we register the inadequacy of the line of normal development for understanding childhood yet avoid disposing of specific fears as belonging to a particular child like Morris? Perhaps by describing how a fear that originally belongs to no one comes to be made the property of a child. Perhaps by charting the disposal of a fear, that itself has no proper place, onto a child. Let's go back to the theater with Morris and take with us the intuitions that the operation of fear is complex because fear "belongs" nowhere and that the "competence" to discriminate between real and imaginary fears is complex because no one, not even an adult, has full possession of it.

It would seem from all that has been written about his case that Morris has a problem with distinguishing between fantasy and reality. Because he is such a very young child, he cannot tell that the events on the stage are only pretend. If he were further along the line of development, the producers of the play would not have been at fault. The material they were presenting would have been age-appropriate. As it stands, Morris is not competent to tell the vital difference, and that is why he is afraid. When he feels fear, then, it is a fear that belongs to him and is simply and logically attached to him by his pregiven age-determined incompetence. On this reading the events in the theater could not have turned out any other way. The play's producers are at fault for making Morris afraid, and for disturbing his passage along the line of proper development, because they were inattentive to his incompetence and got the timing of their warnings wrong.

But is an incompetence over the disposal of fear age-determined? Is fearfulness or a susceptibility to fear proper to childhood? Is Morris's fear originally his own?

Let's look at the play again and ask what sort of performance it is. We can quickly and easily say that the events staged were "pretend" and thus that Morris's fear was inappropriate, a reaction only an incompetent would have. However, Captain Hook, his crew, and those snapping crocodiles were all given physical substance. If they were really there, with what certainty can we characterize Morris's reaction as that of an incompetent? To make a parallel example, we adults "know" that a ride on a roller coaster, an experience reserved for those understood to be old enough, exposes us to imaginary danger; but we are, nevertheless, propelled through space. The roller coaster is a machine for generating fear effects that we can then manage, perhaps with the help of others. The roller coaster is a test of our fear-disposal competences. It takes us, as adults, in and out of the competence proper to an adult. If we cannot do the disposal work ourselves, our companions at the fair will help us, either by scorning us for being afraid of something that is "pretend," saying, "Don't be a baby," or by nurturing us with the reassuring "Don't worry, it'll be over soon." To be frightened on a roller coaster, then, can be a "becoming child" that is procured for us by a real, twisting journey through space. There is a sense in which we are never fully competent disposers of fear. The roller coaster does not reveal a fearfulness that already lies within us, determined by our age, waiting for exposure; rather, it provides an opportunity for the dramatization of the difference between competent and incompetent, adult and child, reality and fantasy.

The family play *Peter Pan* is no different in this respect from the roller coaster. Real things happen on the roller coaster so that fear effects are generated, competences and incompetences are distributed, and fear is given a disposition in the sense that it is laid on certain people. The difference between the roller coaster and *Peter Pan* is that the play is about producing a "becoming child" in those who are already understood to be children. In the case of the roller coaster the settlement of the question of who is to comfort or scorn whom will depend on the various adults' reactions to the experience. But in the case of the play, those attending already know that they are of different generations. It is a peculiar feature of the play, among other fear generators, that it aligns competences and incompetences in the disposal of fear with ready-made generational differences. As we have argued through the example of the roller coaster, incompetence in the business of disposing of fear is proper, in general, to no one. But the play brings this incompetence into alignment with a scale of maturation.

With respect to the susceptibility to fear, we have by now left the line of proper development behind us as an instrument for rendering events comprehensible. However, there are some assemblages, and the play is among them, where the "intergenerational effect" we have called "becoming child" is played out between those who are already "adult" and those who are already "children." Although we have left the line behind us, we have not found ourselves in unaccountable space. Although we have left the line behind us, we have not abolished the specificity of childhood fear.

The performance of the play in the theater does not end at the footlights. The separation between players and audience is not a simple fact. It is itself an actor in a larger play that involves all the adults and children in the theater. It is an actor in a play in which specifically intergenerational differences in competence can be generated. The division between stage and audience, fantasy and reality can be called upon by adults to help children dispose of fear. Fear, then, is generated by the complex tension between the fantastic and the real, and the theater is the engine of its generation. A very specific collective fear haunts the theater. Costumes, actors, adults, stage effects, children, and lighting all participate in its generation. But it is not yet proper to Morris. We have yet to come to the question of how this collectively generated fear is marked out as "his" and how, subsequently, he comes to be marked, traumatized, by it.

What marks Morris as the fearful one? Although other children may have been startled by the play's events, and may have covered their eyes at certain moments, only Morris sobbed the words "Get me out. Get me out." It would certainly make sense to "read backward" from his words to impute a specifically childish incompetence in Morris, the sort of incompetence we expect from one so young, an inability to tell pretend from reality, which results in an inability to dispose of fear. To do this would be to reconfirm the pertinence of the line of normal development. But we can also "read forward" from his words. As soon as Morris made his speech, the fantasy/reality or stage/audience split became untenable. As we have suggested, this division was a vital actor in the theater-wide play of maturity and competence, and once it was unable to perform, the characteristics of that play were bound to change. As his caregivers became stirred by his words and became concerned for him, the physical reality of the events and characters on the stage became apparent. And as this reality revealed itself, so the events and characters on the stage left their fantastic zone of freedom from accountability and responsibility. Prior to Morris's speech, for example, Captain Hook had been able to menace and abduct children without police officers storming the stage. After Morris's speech however, with the deactivation of the reality/fantasy actor, the events on stage entered a legal and psychiatric regime of accountability. It was Morris's speech that led his parents to take the play's producers to court. It was through Morris's speech that a fear, deliberately generated and, up until that moment, belonging to no one, found Morris, rather than any of the other children, and claimed him for its own. It was Morris's speech that made that homeless fear Morris's own.

Although Morris's fear is "constructed," through complex contingent and culturally specific circumstances, rather than predetermined, it is still real and still his. Although his age does not determine that he will experience fear, as the line of normal development would lead us to think, fear has found him in circumstances partly composed of intergenerational relations. To this extent, and in this manner, Morris is fearful because he is a child. In the midst of the conflict between the line of normal development, the becoming view, that would have Morris's fear be originally his property, and the being view that would dispose of the idea of specifically childish fears, we have tried to show how childhood vulnerability can be recognized without recourse to the line of normal development and its simplification and generalization of the states of childhood and adulthood. With Morris's inadvertent assistance we have teased the question of competence in the disposal of fear away from chronological age. Rather than just failing to recognize a real distinction between fantasy and reality, Morris stalled that distinction's ability to act within the theater. With his speech he broke the stage/audience boundary, opening the events onstage to a regime of accountability. This gave grounds for his parents to take the play's producers to court.

What have we to say, then, of Morris's continuing trauma? Now that fear has marked him for its own and made itself belong to him, now that fear occupies the same space as Morris, now that an originally homeless fear has been disposed of onto Morris, any comment Morris himself makes on the events in the theater can be read as emerging from that fear rather than from Morris. After the visit to the theater Morris should continue to do the work of a grandchild, to secure the bond between his parents and their parents as an intergenerationally shared repository of love.

He should do this work by being particularly well behaved in his grand-mother's presence. But he, or something else, spoils it all. Among the evidence of his trauma we find that he now calls his grandmother "Nasty Granny." Could this be Morris talking, expressing his own judgment of the events? Perhaps he has found grounds to dislike his grandmother. How could this statement be revealed as a sign of trauma? Only under circumstances where Morris and the fear disposed onto him have become fully identified with one another. Morris is "traumatized" because he and an originally homeless fear have become each other's property.

CONCLUSION

Fear was generated in a theater. It was "set up" to be disposed of. If we take the view that this fear was imaginary, we can reach a position in which Morris's experiences are to be accounted for as a specific instance of general phenomena: because of his position on the line of normal development, Morris was unable to discriminate between the real and the imaginary, unable to dispose of fear by accounting for it as imaginary, and thus was bound to be traumatized. Once this position has been reached, commentators and participants could "discipline," assigning the blame for Morris's trauma either, like his parents, to the theatrical pro-duction company or, like Moore, to his parents.

To reach this disciplinary position, it is necessary to view the events onstage in the theater as imaginary. As we have argued, however, these events were both real and imaginary. They were simultaneously to be taken seriously enough to be engaging and fear provoking and lightly enough that such fear could be disposed of. Morris's cries effectively put the reality of the real/imaginary distinction into question. Morris's cries rendered the space of the theater, its division into stage and audience, so ambivalent that fear, for Morris's well-being, leaped from the stage to claim Morris's parents and to set them in search of the locus of blame. From this point on the business of integrating the particular with the general could proceed, and attempts could be made to characterize Mor-ris as a particular exemplar of general phenomena in terms of his compe-tence and his position on the line of normal development. Once the play of the real and the imaginary was spoiled, blame had to be assigned, and Morris's experience and reactions could be understood as "trauma," producing him as possessor of a persistent memory of fear by virtue of his peculiarity as a child. Through this disposal of fear, traced through timings good and bad, Morris, a "nodal point" in a "specific communication circuit" (Lyotard 1984, 15), became a "harbor," capable of possession.

So here is the key point we want to make. Science studies, and social science more generally, cannot choose between the possessive and the relational views of self in the way that Latour (1999), among others, suggests. Yes, we are doubtless relational selves, defined in complex webs of discourse, technology, and practice. But circulating through these same webs are forces set in play by the assemblages of law, science, and medicine—forces that are also played out in settings as mundane as the theater. Fear is one of these forces. It is less an "emotion" than an affective movement of connection that traverses relationships, a movement that is at once real and produced. Subjects become possessive selves (or should that be selves possessed?) when they are positioned as owners of this circulating fear, when through their actions—maybe just the simple act of crying out—the job of disposing of fear falls onto them alone, a job for which we may all, at times, be singularly ill equipped.

NOTES

1. We owe this usage of *disposal* to Munro (1995).

2. The play is derived from James Matthew Barrie's novel, which also forms the basis of the Spielberg film *Hook*.

3. These characters are from *The Wizard of Oz* and the long-running U.K. television program *Dr. Who*, respectively.

4. The Swiss psychologist Jean Piaget is widely regarded as founding the contemporary discourse of developmentalism (e.g., Piaget 1952). In brief, Piaget argues for a linear process of development, marked by distinct stages, in the course of which the child's cognitive powers become more complex and accurate in the task of processing reality. Key terms are *assimilation* and *accommodation*. The child develops by assimilating new information, which then becomes accommodated into new cognitive configurations as the child revises the structure of their mental representations. For antidevelopmental accounts of childhood see Burman (1994); Stainton Rogers and Stainton Rogers (1992).

REFERENCES

Ashmore, M., R. Wooffitt, and S. Harding 1994. "Humans and Others: The Concept of 'Agency' and its Attribution." *American Behavioural Scientist* 37, no. 6: 772–91.

Beck, U. 1998. *Democracy without Enemies.* Cambridge: Polity Press.

Bettelheim, B. 1976. *The Uses of Enchantment: The Meaning and Importance of Fairy Tales.* London: Penguin.

Bijker, W. E., and J. Law, eds. 1992. *Shaping Technology/Building Society.* Cambridge Mass: MIT Press.

Burman, E. 1994. *Deconstructing Developmental Psychology.* London: Routledge.

Day, R. 1998. "Diagrammatic Bodies." In R. Chia, ed., *Organized Worlds: Explorations in Technology and Organization with Robert Cooper,* 95–107. London: Routledge.

Deleuze, G., and F. Guattari. 1984. *A Thousand Plateaus: Capitalism and Schizophrenia.* Trans. B. Massumi. London: Athlone Press.

Foucault, M. 1970. *The Order of Things: An Archaeology of the Human Sciences.* Trans. A. Sheridan. London: Routledge.

———. 1977. *Discipline and Punish: The Birth of the Prison.* Trans. A. Sheridan. Harmondsworth: Penguin.

Geertz, C. 1983. *Local Knowledge: Further Essays in Interpretative Anthropology.* New York: Basic Books.

Haraway, D. 1997. *Modest Witness@Second Millennium.* London: Routledge.

Hutchby, I., and J. Moran-Ellis, eds. 1998. *Children and Social Competence: Arenas of Action.* London: Falmer.

James, A., and A. Prout, eds. 1990. *Constructing and Reconstructing Childhood: Contemporary Issues in the Sociological Study of Childhood.* London: Falmer.

Latour, B. 1999. *Pandora's Hope: Essays on the Reality of Science Studies.* Cambridge, Mass.: Harvard University Press.

Lee, N. M. 1999. "The Challenge of Childhood: Distributions of Childhood's Ambiguity in Adult Institutions." *Childhood* 6, no. 4: 455–73.

Lyotard, J. F. 1984. *The Postmodern Condition: A Report on Knowledge.* Manchester: Manchester University Press.

Mol, A. 1999. "Ontological Politics: A Word and Some Questions." In J. Law and J. Hassard, eds., *Actor Network Theory and After,* 74–89. Oxford: Blackwell/Sociological Review.

Moore, S. 1996. "Scary Monsters, Super Creeps." *Guardian,* March 5, 10.

Mosso, A. 1896. *Fear.* Trans. E. Logh and F. Kiesow. 5th ed. London: Longmans, Green.

Munro, R. 1995. "The Disposal of the Meal." In D. W. Marshall, ed., *Food Choice.* London: Blackie.

"Peter Pan Producers Sued over the Boy Who Wouldn't Look Up." 1996. *Guardian,* March 4, 1.

Piaget, J. 1952. *The Origins of Intelligence in the Child.* New York: International Universities Press.

Qvortrup, J. 1994. "Childhood Matters: An Introduction." In J. Qvortrup, M. Bardy, G. Sgritta, and H. Wintersberger, eds., *Childhood Matters: Social Theory, Practice, and Politics.* Aldershot: Avebury.

Smart, B. 1999. *Facing Modernity: Ambivalence, Reflexivity, and Morality.* London: Sage.

Stainton Rogers, R., and W. Stainton Rogers. 1992. *Stories of Childhood: Shifting Agendas of Child Concern.* Hemel Hempstead: Harvester Wheatsheaf.

Taylor, C. 1992. "The Politics of Recognition." In C. Taylor, ed., *Multiculturalism and the Politics of Recognition.* Princeton: Princeton University Press.

Andrew Barry is Senior Lecturer in Sociology at Goldsmiths College, University of London.

Steven D. Brown is Lecturer in Psychology in the Department of Human Sciences, Loughborough University, United Kingdom.

Michel Callon is Professor of Sociology at the Ecole des Mines de Paris and a member of the Centre for the Sociology of Innovation.

Chunglin Kwa is Lecturer in Science Dynamics at the University of Amsterdam, the Netherlands.

John Law is Professor of Sociology and Science Studies at Lancaster University. He is the author of *Organizing Modernity* (1994) and *Aircraft Stories* (2002).

Nick Lee is Lecturer in Sociology at Keele University, United Kingdom.

Annemarie Mol is Professor of Political Philosophy at Twente University, the Netherlands. She is the author of *The Body Multiple* (2002) and the editor, with Marc Berg, of *Differences in Medicine: Unraveling Practices, Techniques, and Bodies* (1998).

Marilyn Strathern is Professor of Social Anthropology at Cambridge University.

Laurent Thévenot is Professor in the Groupe de Sociologie Politique et Moral in the Ecole des Hautes Etudes et Sciences Sociales, CNRS, Paris.

Charis Thompson is a Visiting Assistant Professor of the History of Science and Women's Studies at Harvard University.

Attribution. *See* Writing devices: authorship

Audit, 82 n.16, 156–58

Authorship. *See* Agency; Subjectivity; Writing devices

Autism, 74

Background, 103. *See also* Figure-ground reversal

Baroque, the, 20; and allegory, 26; communication in, 46–47; complexity, 21–47; and German drama, 29; as looking down, 25–26; materiality, 26–27; music, 26; nonholistic, 46–47; painting, 26; theater, 26; uncertainty as ontological, 47. *See also* Turbulence

Barrie, J. M., 261, 277 n.2

Barry, Andrew, 19

Bauman, Zygmunt, 2

Beck, Ulrich, 263

Being and becoming. *See* Childhood

Belousov-Zhabotinskii reaction, 41–43

Benjamin, Walter, 29–30

Bennington, Geoffrey, 161 n.12

Berg, Marc, 251 n.7, 252 n.11

Berlin Wall, 149

Bettelheim, Bruno, 267–68

Bible. *See* Service: handbook

Bifurcation, 40, 42–44

Big science, 152

Bilum, 95–98, 103–6, 112 n.20

Binarisms, 149–50. *See also* Oscillation

Biodiversity. *See* Nature

Birke, L., 100

Bjerkenes, Vilhelm, 30–31

Body, 10, 250 n.4; knowledge of, 252 n.9. *See also* Atherosclerosis; Corporeality

Boltanski, Luc, 8, 9, 55, 60–61, 78, 80

Borges, Jorge Luis, 14

Boundary object, 82 n.11

Bounded rationality, 214 n.2

Bourdieu, Pierre, 55–56, 149

Braun-Blanquet, Josias, 25–26

Bréviglieri, M., 72

Brouillon, L., 34

Brown, Steve, 18, 20

Brusselator. *See* Belousov-Zhabotinskii reaction

BSE ("mad cow disease"), 145

Bureaucracy, 148

Calculation. *See* Agency: economic; Subjectivities

Callon, Michel, 18, 19, 150, 160 n.6

Canberra aircraft, 125–26, 134

Capitalism: global, 12

Caravaggio, Michaelangelo da, 27

Cases, 13, 14, 16

Casey, E. S., 90–92, 111 n.11

Catachresis, 47 n.1

Catastrophe theory, 39–40, 42–44

Cellule de Prospective. *See* European Commission

Centering, 137–38

Cervical screening program, 139 n.25

Chance, theories of, 3

Charney, Jules, 31

Chemical equilibrium. *See* Equilibrium, chemical

Chemistry, physical, 33–34

Childhood, 18, 258–77; being and becoming and, 262–64; vulnerability and, 263

Choreography. *See* Time

Civic regime. *See* Regimes of coordination

Classification, 14, 243–44

Claudication, intermittent, 219–20, 222, 224, 247; and lifestyle limitation, 222–24. *See also* Atherosclerosis

Clements, Frederic, 25–26, 28, 36

Clinamen, 45–46

Clinical: improvement, 225–26; practice, 221–22, 225, 239–41; trials, 3. *See also* Atherosclerosis

Coexistence. *See* Multiplicity

Collective, 193, 199, 204, 207, 214; configuration of, 59. *See also* Agency

Common, the. *See* Sociology, political and moral

Comparison. *See* Similarity and difference; Simplification

Complexification, 192; recomplexification, 13. *See also* Simplification

Complexity: and the baroque, 21–47; difficulty and complicatedness, 183–87; in economic calculation, 191; general versus particular, 264; in health care, 222–24, 229–33; interference, 11, 20; material heterogeneity, 20; mediation, 20; moral, 53, 74–79; as more than one and less than many, 17, 227, 247; multiplicity, 20; and networks, 147; oscillation, 20; performativity, 20; poststructuralism and, 260; reduction, 142–43, 159; and romanticism: 21–47; of science and technology, 20, 144, 155, 159–60; and simplification, 6, 20, 143–44, 192, 222–23; and systems, 23, 34; theory, 21 n.7, 111 n.13. *See also* Agency: economic; Atherosclerosis; Disease, images of; Interference; Irreducibility; Materiality; Mediation; Multiplicity; Oscillation; Performativity; Simplification

Complicatedness. *See* Complexity

"Compossibility," 29

Compression. *See* Elephants

Compromise, 61, 64–65

Conditions of possibility, 138

Conflict, social, 55, 60, 175

Conservation biology, 169, 175, 178–80, 181–82, 185–86, 189 n.18

Conservation of nature. *See* Nature

Consumers. *See* Agency; Demand, economic supply and

Context, 92, 97, 108

Contracts. *See* Demand, economic supply and

Controversy, 129–30, 175–87. *See also* Science, natural

Convenience. *See* Regimes of pragmatic engagement

Conventions, 83 n.18

Cooper, Robert, 110 n.4

Coordination, 10, 58–60, 83 n.18. *See also* Regimes of coordination; Sociology, political and moral

Corporeality: in pilots, 122–24

Crozier, Michel, 55

Cruise company. *See* Service

Culling. *See* Elephants

Cussins, Charis, 13, 251 n.8. *See also* Thompson, Charis

Customers. *See* Agency; Demand, economic supply and; Writing devices

Cuvier, Georges, 25

Cybernetics, 39–40, 42, 47 n.1

Darwin, Charles, 30, 32–33; as romantic, 32–33

Davis, J., 110 n.6, 111 n.16

Decentering the subject. *See* Subjectivities

de Certeau, Michel, 16

Decisions, 214 n.2. *See also* Agency;
  Subjectivities
Deferral. *See Différance;* Heterogeneity
Deleuze, Gilles, 27, 29, 131 n.13, 144, 259
Deligny, Fernand, 74
Delors, Jacques, 149, 155, 163 n.48
Demand, economic supply and, 192–93,
  195, 199–206, 209–11; contractual, 204;
  segmentation, 209–10. *See also* Writing
  devices
Denunciation, 61
Depth. *See* Space: scaling
de Ruiter, Liesbeth, 49 n.40
Derrida, Jacques, 13, 134
Design: as heterogeneous, 135–36
Design, aircraft, 116–38; aspect ratio, 117,
  131–32; planform, 131–34
Detail, 15. *See also* Cases
Development, childhood. *See* Childhood
DG-XIII, 148–55, 162 n.36; Forecasting
  and Assessment of Science and Tech-
  nology in, 148–49, 154
Diabetes, 252 n.14
Différance, 13, 134, 137. *See also*
  Heterogeneity
Difference. See *Différance;* Similarity and
  difference
Difficulty. *See* Complexity
Directorate General for Science, Re-
  search, and Development. *See* DG-XII
Disciplining, 271
Discontinuous transition. *See* Bifurcation
Discours, 21 n.4
Disease, images of, 226; chronic, 253 n.21;
  as complex, 227, 246–49
Disposal. *See* Fear, disposal of
Distinction, 149
Diversity, unity in, 152–53
Domain of attraction. *See* Attractor

Domestic regime. *See* Regimes of
  coordination
Durkheim, Emile, 54, 56

Ecological succession, 35–36, 44
Ecology, 20, 23–24, 28, 33–34, 37–40
Economic anthropology, 191
Economics, evolutionary, 152. *See also*
  Agency
Ecosystems, 28, 37
Efficiency, technical, 64
Elephants, 19, 166–87; compression, 169,
  170–71, 176–77, 186; culling of, 170,
  172–73; migration, 171, 174. *See also*
  Animal rights
Embryo, 101–2
Endarectomy. *See* Atherosclerosis
Engagement, 81 n.1. *See also* Regimes of
  pragmatic engagement; Sociology,
  moral and political
Engines, aircraft, 128–30
English Electric Company, 116–17, 122,
  127–28, 131–32, 134, 137
Enlightenment, 1
Entities. *See* Objects
Entropy. *See* Thermodynamics, laws of
Environment, 67, 111 n.11. *See also* Nature
Epidemiology. *See* Atherosclerosis
Epistème, 8, 56
Epistemic practices, 82 n.15
Epistemology. *See also* Ontology;
  Reductionism
Equilibrium, 37, 39; chemical, 33–34; eco-
  system, 34; multiple, 39–40
Equivalences. *See* Sociology, moral and
  political
Estimation: in natural law theory, 58
Ethnomethodology, 56, 148
EU. *See* European Union

European Commission, 19, 144, 148–49, 153, 155, 158, 162 nn.25 and 36; Cellule de Prospective, 149; gender and, 163 n.46; intellectuals in, 149, 155. *See also* DG-XII

European Community. *See* European Union

European Parliament, 158; STOA in, 160 n.7

European Union, 19, 63, 142–60; as government-in-the-making, 143; harmonization in, 145, 151; subsidiarity in, 153–54, 163 nn.47 and 48. *See also* European Commission

Evaluation. *See* Atherosclerosis; Audit; Sociology, political and moral

Event, singular, 42–43

Evolutionary economics. *See* Economics, evolutionary

Evolutionary theory, 30, 32–33, 35, 38, 40, 43

Faces, masked in Mt. Hagen, 105–8

Familiarity, regime of. *See* Regimes of familiar engagement

Fantasy and reality, 261, 267–68, 270, 272, 274–76

FAST. *See* DG-XII

Fear, disposal of, 18, 258–61, 264–68, 272–77

Field, in physics, 27

Figurative. *See* Literal versus figurative

Figure, 21 n.4

Figure-ground reversal, 88–90, 92–94, 96–97, 105–9; and modernism, 89. *See also* Oscillation

Files. *See* Writing devices

Fluctuation, 40–41, 44–46

Fluidity. *See* Space

Fold: in catastrophe theory, 40

Forecasting and Assessment of Science and Technology. *See* DG-XII

Fossey, Dian, 187 n.7

Foucault, Michel, 4, 14, 56, 151, 159, 161 nn.11 and 20, 206–7, 253 n.19, 259, 270–72

Fox, N., 253 n.17

Fragments: as independent things, 29–30

Framing, 200–201; and overflowing, 200–201, 213, 215 n.5

Franklin, Sarah, 112 n.19

Freeman, Christopher, 152

Freud, Sigmund, 258

Friedberg, Erhard, 55

Functionality, 62

Galdikas, Birute, 187 n.7

Gangrene, 219

Geertz, Clifford, 264

Gehry, Frank, 12

Gell, A., 110 n.9

Gender, 187 n.7. *See also* European Commission; Maasai

General and particular. *See* Oscillation

General practice. *See* Atherosclerosis

Go, game of, 12

Good, the, 8, 17; common, 54, 61; complexity and, 76–78; the real and, 54, 76

Goodall, Jane, 187 n.7

GOR 339. *See* OR 339

Governing, 142–60; and metrics, 142

Gramsci, Antonio, 148

Greenhouse, C. J., 91

Green regime. *See* Regimes of coordination

Gryphius, Andreas, 29

Mestiza, 11

Meterology, 20, 30–32; as romantic, 32

Methodology: symmetry, 184

Metrication, 251 n.5; in health, versus clinical practice, 221. *See* Governing; Standardization

Metrology. *See* Metrication

Mimesis. *See* Oscillation

Missiles. *See* Surface-to-air guided missiles

Mode of convenience. *See* Regimes of pragmatic engagement

Mode of ordering, 9, 10, 11, 14. *See also* Multiplicity

Modernism, 89–91, 94, 107–8, 110 n.7, 137, 184; and difficulty, 184. *See also* Figure-ground reversal

Modernity, 21 n.14, 180

Moi, Daniel, 173, 188 n.14

Moisdon, J. C., 214 n.2

Mol, Annemarie, 10, 19, 78

Monadology, 26–30

Morality: as complex, 53, 74–79, 186; objects in, 53, 74–79. *See also* Agency: moral; Sociology, political and moral

Moreira, Tiago, 255 n.30

More than one and less than many. *See* Complexity

Morgan, Gareth, 9

Morphogenetics, 39

Morris (child), 261–62, 264–77

Moss, Cynthia, 170–72, 174, 176–77, 187 n.7

Mosso, Angelo, 258

Mouffe, Chantal, 162 n.24

Mountain Ok peoples, 95–98, 104

Multiplicity, 7, 227, 232–33, 235–37; as co-existences, 8; market and professional, 245–46; and modes of ordering, 7; of

timings, 271. *See also* Atherosclerosis; Heterogeneity; Oscillation; Regimes of coordination

Munro, Rolland, 277 n.1

Museums, 14

Namelok, Kenya, 177

Narrative. *See* Agency

Natural law theory, 57–61

Nature, 29, 67, 75–76; conservation, 166–87; philosophies of, 166–87; politics and, 167

Neo-Lamarckianism, 33, 38

Netherlands, health care in. *See* Health care

Networks: in Europe, 147, 150, 153–54, 156, 158–60; regional industrial, 156; and scale, 163 n.49. *See also* Complexity

New World Order, 150

Nietzsche, Friedrich, 159

Nilsson, Lennart, 94, 99–103

Nonhumans. *See* Humans

Nonlinearity, 38–39, 41, 45–46

Normal versus pathological, 221–22, 247, 253 n.21

Normativities, 17

Nuclear power, 150–51, 155, 162 n.36

Numerical standardization. *See* Standardization

Objectification. *See* Writing devices

Objects: in Alfred North Whitehead, 28; in evaluation, 58, 70; as mediators, 56–57, 74; in a moral world, 53–80; qualified, 60; and subjects, 248

Odum, Eugene, 33, 36–38, 43

Odum, Howard T. (Tom), 36–38, 43

Oedipal drama, 258–59

Office of Scientific and Technological Options Assessment (STOA). *See* European parliament

Ok, Mountain. *See* Mountain Ok peoples

Olindo, Perez, 169–70

Olodare, Kenya, 177

Oloitiptip, Koikai, 172, 175, 177, 189 n.15

Oloitiptip, Stanley, 189 n.15

Ontology, 47, 48 n.16, 136; relational, 259. *See also* Politics

Operation, surgical. *See* Surgery

Operational requirements. *See* OR 339

Opinion, regime of. *See* Regimes of coordination

OR 339, 125–26, 128, 131, 134

Ordering, political and moral. *See* Sociology, political and moral

Order of Things, 14, 56

Orders, 7, 11, 185

Orders of worth. *See* Regimes of coordination

Organicism. *See* Holism: and organism

Organism. *See* Holism: and organism

Organizations, 9, 83 n.21, 191, 215 n.10; instruments in, 192, 199–200. See also *Actigramme*

Organization studies, 9

Orientalism, 126

Ørsted, Hans Christian, 25

Oscillation, 109, 111 n.13, 116, 134; between absence and presence, 18, 117–18, 134–35; between general and particular, 18, 264–65, 269–70; between interpretation and direct perception, 89, 93–94; between mimesis and alterity, 116; between order and messiness, 255 n.32. *See also* Interpretation

Otherness, 137. *See also* Heterogeneity

Overflowing. *See* Framing

Overviews, 14, 16

P1B, 128

P17A, 116–17, 123, 127–29, 134

Pain, 250 n.4; walking distance and, 219–22

Papua New Guinea, 94–98, 105–8, 112 n.24

Paradigm, scientific, 4

Partial connections, 10, 17

Particular. *See* Oscillation

Path dependency, 72

Pathological. *See* Normal versus pathological

Paths, 71–73

Patients, 251 n.8, 252 n.13, 253 n.18. *See also* Atherosclerosis

Pattern, Bernard, 33, 38, 40

Peer review. *See* Science, natural

Percutaneous transluminal angioplasty, 250 n.2

Performativity, 19, 144, 147–60. *See also* Science and technology: performativity of accounts of; Writing devices

Peter Pan, 18, 261–62, 267, 273

Peters, Peter, 48 n.21

Phase space. *See* Equilibrium

Philosophy. *See* Political philosophy; Science, natural: models of

Photographs. *See also* Visual materials

Physical chemistry. *See* Chemistry, physical

Physical therapy. *See* Atherosclerosis

Piaget, Jean, 277 n.4

Pictures, 18. *See also* Visual materials

Pilots, aircraft, 122–23, 128–29

Pintupi, 90

Place. *See* Space

Planform. *See* Design, aircraft

Planned action. *See* Regimes of planned action

Poaching. *See* Ivory

Political philosophy, 8, 81 n.7, 146

Politics: of objects, 74–75; ontological, 260. *See also* Nature; Science, natural; Sociology, political and moral

Pols, Jeannette, 250 n.1

Poole, Joyce, 174, 177

Population dynamics, 39–40

Poststructuralism, 4, 260

Power, 74

Power, Michael, 156

Pragmatic engagement. *See* Regimes of pragmatic engagement

Pragmatic regimes. *See* Regimes of pragmatic engagement

Presence. *See* Absence and presence

Price, F. V., 99–100

Prigogine, Ilya, 35–37, 40–44, 111 n.13, 149, 157

Probability. *See* Chance, theories of

Prout, Alan, 263

Psychoanalysis, 4, 258, 267–68

Pufendorf, Samuel von, 57–60

Punctualization, 120

Purification. *See* Purity

Purity, 4, 21 n.14, 78, 255 n.32

Qualification. *See* Regimes of coordination

"Quality Charter," 203–5

Quantification. *See* Metrology

Queneau, Raymond, 53

Rabinow, Paul, 111 n.14

Rameau, Jean-Philippe, 48 n.21

Rapp, Rayna, 101

Rationality, 2, 4; bounded, 214 n.2. *See also* Agency: economic

Rawls, John, 8

Reader, 206

Real, the, 54, 57, 109, 122. *See also* Fantasy and reality; Good, the

Realism, 57, 62, 70, 72. *See also* Real, the

Reality. *See* Fantasy and reality

Recomplexification. *See* Complexification

Reductionism, 184, 186, 247; epistemological, 48; as simplification, 4; as violence, 4. *See also* Complexity; Oscillation

Reflexivity, 20, 144, 152, 154, 156, 183–84

Regimes of coordination (justification): civic, 67, 69; domestic, 65–66, 69; green, 67–68, 80, 83 n.20; industrial, 64–65, 68–69; inspiration, 67; market, 60, 63–66, 68–69; as multiple, 62; renown (opinion), 66–67; responsibility, 78–79

Regimes of familiar engagement, 69, 71–73

Regimes of planned action, 69, 73–74, 79

Regimes of pragmatic engagement, 54, 57, 68–69, 76, 83 n.17

Regional industrial networks. *See* Networks

Rembrandt, 27

Renown, regime of. *See* Regimes of coordination

Representation. *See* Cases; Interpretation; Lists; Mapping; Writing devices

Repression, 4

Responsibility. *See* Regimes of coordination

Revolution, scientific, 4

Risk, 3, 263. *See also* Chance, theories of

Roads, 17, 53–80

Romanticism, 20; and abstraction, 26; complexity and, 23–47; conceptual unity in, 23, 46; and holism and organicism, 24–26, 27–28, 38, 184, 189 n.20

Rousseau, Jean-Jacques, 24–25, 82 n.12

Royal Air Force, 125, 130

Royal Navy, 129

Ruberti, Antonio, 153

Ruins, 29

Russia, 125–26

SACEUR, 125

Said, Edward, 126

Sartre, Jean-Paul, 72

Scale. *See* Space

Scan, ultrasound. *See* Ultrasound scan

Schaffer, Simon, 189 n.16

Scholem, Gershom, 29

Schrödinger, Erwin, 34–36

Schrovers, Pieter, 48 n.11

Science, natural, 20, 176–82; controversy, 173–87; and its constituencies, 176–82; law and, 180–81; models of, 178–82; and peer review, 176–77; and politics, 177–78, 180, 186; and values, 181; and witnessing, 177–78, 189 n.16. *See also* Reflexivity

Science and technology: performativity of accounts of, 144, 147–60. *See also* Complexity

Science and technology policy, 150–52, 155. *See also* Innovation: linear model of

Scribe. *See* Writing devices: authorship

Segmentation. *See* Demand, economic supply and

Self. *See* Agency; Subjectivities

Self-evidence, 18

Semiotics, 118, 127, 206

Series, convergent and divergent, 29

Serres, Michel, 45

Service: companies, 18–19; cruise company, 193–203, 206, 210–11; economy, 192–214; handbooks, 198–99, 201–206; marketing, 18, 19; meal vouchers, 193, 195, 197–98, 202, 211. *See also* Demand, economic supply and; Writing devices

Shapin, Steven, 189 n.16

Shore, C., 160 n.4

Similarity and difference, 218, 233–46, 252 n.11. *See also* Atherosclerosis

Simmel, Georg, 82 n.13

Simon, Herbert, 214 n.2

Simplicity and complexity, 192, 246–49; coexisting, 16

Simplification, 4, 11; and complexity, 16, 192, 218, 264. *See also* Complexity; Simplicity and complexity

Sindiyo, Daniel, 169

"Single European market," 146

Singleton, Vicky, 139 n.16

Singularity. *See* Interpretation; Multiplicity

Slobodkin, Lawrence, 40, 49 n.53

Smuts, Jan, 24, 36

Social studies of science and technology, 12, 55, 251 n.5, 259

Sociology, political and moral, 53–80; and collective coordination, 55, 57–60; and the common, 55–56, 61, 78; compromises in, 64–66, 78; engagement, 57; equivalences, 56; evaluation and qualification, 55, 57, 60–61, 63–64; justification, 78. *See also* Regimes of coordination

Sociology of scientific knowledge. *See* Social studies of Science and technology

Soete, Luc, 152

Somport tunnel, 62–68

Soret effect, 37

Sovereignty, 156

Space, 1, 7, 20, 107, 110 n.10, 144; Cartesian, 64–65; domestic, 66; fluidity and, 251 n.5; linearity and, 20, 107, 221; mapping, 1, 20; measurement, 142; place in relation to, 18, 90–92, 96–97, 110 n.10; scaling, 2, 15, 88, 92, 98–99, 103–4, 109, 153–54, 163 n.49, 185; and state in natural law theory, 58; time and, 91–92

Spatiality. *See* Lists; Space

SPEAR, 157

Specificity. *See* Detail

Spencer, Herbert, 33, 38, 48 n.34

Spheres, social, 8

Standardization, 65; in the European Union, 145, 151; numerical, in health comparisons, 221, 248

State: as heterogeneous, 160 n.6; in natural law theory, 58

Stengers, Isabelle, 42

Strathern, Marilyn, 10, 18, 20, 163 n.49

Strauss, Anselm, 253 n.18

Striation, 144, 161 n.13

Strum, Shirley, 176

Subjectivities, 253 n.17; decentering, 259; and fear, 258; relational, 260. *See also* Agency; Atherosclerosis; Humans; Objects

Subsidiarity. *See* European Union

Sullivan, W. M., 111 n.14

Superorganisms, 36

Supply. *See* Demand, economic supply and

Support Programme for Evaluation Activities of Research. *See* SPEAR

Surface-to-air guided missiles, 126

Surgery, 218–19, 223–25, 227–32, 234–36, 241–42, 244, 253 n.17

Symbols, 113 n.26

Symmetry. *See* Methodology

Systems: closed, 37; large technical, 136–37; open, 37–38; stability and instability, 42–44; theory, 148, 154; weapons, 135–38. *See also* Complexity

Tansley, Alfred, 28, 30, 34, 36

Taussig, Michael, 116

Technical standards. *See* Standardization

Technology policy. *See* Science and technology policy

Teleology, 42, 62

Temporality. *See* Time

Tensions, 20, 192

Texts: academic, 3. *See also* Writing devices

Theater. *See* Peter Pan

Thermodynamics, laws of, 31, 40–42; Second Law, 34–35, 36–37, 161 n.17; Third Law, 161 n.17

Thévenot, Laurent, 8, 9, 17

Thom, René, 39, 42, 49 n.51

Thomas, J., 111 n.15

Thompson, Charis, 19. *See also* Cussins, Charis

Threat, 126–27

Time, 11, 64, 91–92, 109: as choreography, 13; linear, 1, 11, 13, 20, 91–92; and modernism, 91; and orders, 11, 64; tidal, 13; and timing, 261–63, 266–67, 269–71. *See also* Space

Timing. *See* Time

Todorov, Tzvetan, 10

Library of Congress Cataloging-in-Publication Data

Complexities : social studies of knowledge practices /
John Law and Annemarie Mol, editors.

p. cm. — (Science and cultural theory)

Includes bibliographical references and index.

ISBN 0-8223-2831-3 (cloth : alk. paper)

ISBN 0-8223-2846-1 (pbk. : alk. paper)

1. Complexity (Philosophy) 2. Knowledge, Sociology of.

I. Law, John. II. Mol, Annemarie. III. Series.

B105.C473 C65 2002   001—dc21   2001007279